OFFICIAL

Myth®

The Fallen Lords

Strategies & Secrets™

by Bart Farkas

SAN FRANCISCO PARIS DÜSSELDORF SOEST

Associate Publisher	ROGER STEWART
Acquisitions Manager	KRISTINE PLACHY
Acquisitions Editor	DAN BRODNITZ
Developmental Editor	MAUREEN ADAMS
Production Coordination	LABRECQUE PUBLISHING SERVICES
Copy Editor	LISA AUER
Project Editor	JONATHAN LOUCKS
Proofreaders	RACHEL FUDGE AND TORY McLEARN
Project Coordinator	THERESA GONZALEZ
Book Design and Production	WILLIAM SALIT DESIGN
Production Associate	LISA LUSK
Cover Designer	ARCHER DESIGN

Library of Congress Card Number: 97-80632

ISBN: 0-7821-2140-3

Manufactured in the United States of America

10 9 8 7 6 5 4 3 2 1

DEDICATION

For Cori, without whom the replacement ceramic mug industry would struggle to survive.

ACKNOWLEDGMENTS

I'd like to thank all the folks at Bungie who helped me to understand and conquer the great game of *Myth*. Matt, Doug, Tuncer, Jay, Ryan, Rob, Mark, Diane, Alex, and Jonas, thanks for all the help you gave when it was your turn. I'd also like to especially thank the two Jasons, Jason Regier and Jason Jones, who made room in their incredibly busy schedule programming *Myth* to help me out when the time was short. I owe you both a frosty mug of "Surly Dwarf" Ale!

Special thanks also go to Dan Brodnitz, Roger Stewart, and Hartley Lesser for their support, and for just being such great guys. Maureen Adams deserves a round of applause for holding me together during the dark hours, and her superb editorial touch is evident throughout the book. Thanks also go out to the production folks: Labrecque Publishing, Theresa Gonzalez, and Jonathan Loucks. Last, I'd like to thank my cats for not sleeping on my keyboard (very much).

TABLE OF CONTENTS

CHAPTER 3

Cutting Your Teeth 45

CHAPTER 4

The Plot Thickens 73

CHAPTER 5

Into the Cold 89

CHAPTER 6

We Are the Champions 113

INTRODUCTION

As a computer strategy guide author, games come and go through my consciousness like the pages of a calendar turning over from day to day. So it's a very pleasant surprise for me when I get to write about a game that's as truly special, truly groundbreaking as *Myth: The Fallen Lords*.

Ever since *Warcraft* burst onto the gaming scene in 1994, real-time strategy games have been flowing steadily onto the market. As you might expect, the games are becoming less inspired with each new release. This genre has needed something new and exciting to rekindle the love affair between gamers and their games, and *Myth* has clearly stepped forward into that role.

Bungie took parts of the 3D engine from their award-winning, first-person perspective game, *Marathon*, and added a dash of inspiration from their twisted yet brilliant minds to come up with the best new game of 1997. Although you can classify *Myth* as a real-time strategy game, it falls outside the normal boundaries of what we've come to expect from this gaming category. *Myth*'s true 3D engine, panoramic camera angles, and lack of resource management have swung the focus of the game much more toward the tactical aspects of combat than any game we've seen yet.

The lack of resource management might make you think that *Myth* will lose its appeal after a few hours of play. Instead of having a game with fewer compelling components, Bungie has actually created a game that's considerably more interesting than any of its competitors. Indeed, it's a game that'll have you wondering why the sun is coming up at 10:00 PM, only to discover that you've been playing right through the night.

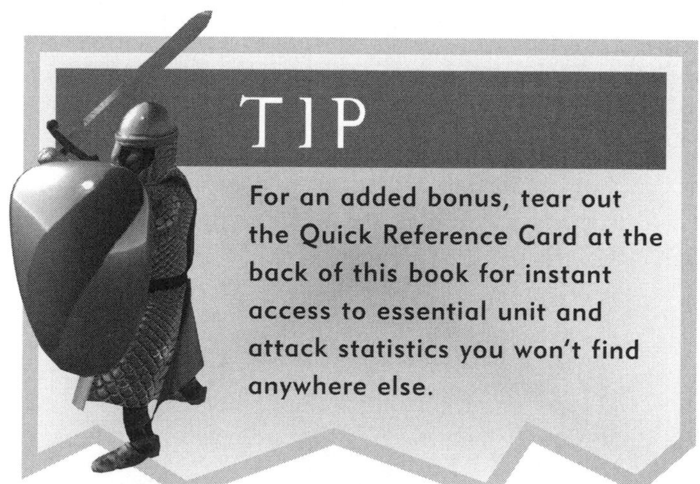

TIP

For an added bonus, tear out the Quick Reference Card at the back of this book for instant access to essential unit and attack statistics you won't find anywhere else.

This book will help you maximize your experience with *Myth* so that you don't miss any of the hundreds of tiny details that come together to make this a grade-A gaming experience.

I'm here to give you a hand when you get into a pickle and just can't figure out how to emerge victorious. With that said, I encourage you to explore *Myth* in its entirety—look into every corner of every map and hunt down and kill the Undead with extreme prejudice. I know I did.

1

General Overview

M*yth: The Fallen Lords* is an extension of the timeless and epic battle of good vs. evil, and as usual you are fighting for the good guys. You will lead the forces of Light against the Undead minions in an attempt to get Balor's head thrown into the Great Devoid, thus ending the Undead's reign of terror. But you're just starting out, so you'll need a little help to get your feet firmly planted on the soil of *Myth*.

This chapter is intended to give you a good feel for what *Myth* is about, and in conjunction with Chapter 2, *Combat Tactics,* provides you with enough inside information to quickly become successful in gameplay. *Myth* is a deceptively complex game, and even though Bungie has done an admirable job of covering the basics in their manual, there's just too much to cram into a single document. It should be noted that whenever relevant I've included information about both the multiplayer and single-player aspects of *Myth.* Some of the information is duplicated in Chapter 11, *Moshing with Myth (Network Play),* but for the most part you'll find every section of the book very informative. And best of all, I went straight to the source (Bungie) for much of this information, so I hope this book helps you to understand the basics of *Myth: The Fallen Lords* and gives you the power to kick *Myth*'s butt.

GAME STRUCTURE

Myth is divided into roughly 10 segments based on story components and geography. You'll notice trends towards a snowy landscape, or a desert landscape, or even several scenarios that deal with a particular item or character. I've taken the liberty of using these natural separations to divide this strategy guide into distinct chapters

in the interests of providing a usable structure for the reader. You will also notice that I do not go into any detail regarding *Myth*'s storyline. I did this purposely to avoid taking any of the enjoyment you'll get from watching the animated cutscenes and reading the scenario openers. It wasn't necessary for me to delve into the story to help you though the game—I've left that up to you.

THE SCENARIOS

There are 25 scenarios in *Myth,* as you can see in Figure 1.1, and you'll have to finish each scenario in order to proceed to the next one. This is where I come in. If you're having trouble with any one mission, I can help you to find your way to victory and the enjoyment of seeing the next scenario.

THE FORCES

Myth is a battle between the forces of good and evil. And believe me, it will get seriously ugly before the game is through. Knowing yourself (your units) is critically important to your victory. Not only because you'll need to exploit every advantage your units afford, but also because your enemy knows the capabilities of your troops as well as you do. Which brings up the next point: as much as it may frighten you, it's always wise to know your enemy, indeed, even fear them. In fact, I can guarantee that you'll be worrying extensively about each new hideous evil creature that comes at you with nothing more than total carnage burned on its malignant brain.

This section is specifically designed to introduce you to each creature and briefly touch on some of the capabilities of each. Although you can't control the evil units (in a single-player game anyway), it's a very good idea to understand exactly what the bad guys can do. There are two sides in single-player *Myth*, each of which has its own groups of units, and the line of division is that of life and death. As you work your way through *Myth,* you control the Light or Living forces, while the computer controls the Dark or Undead minions. Read this section carefully, then refer to Chapter 2, *Combat Tactics,* to get the lowdown on the specialties of some of the more powerful characters.

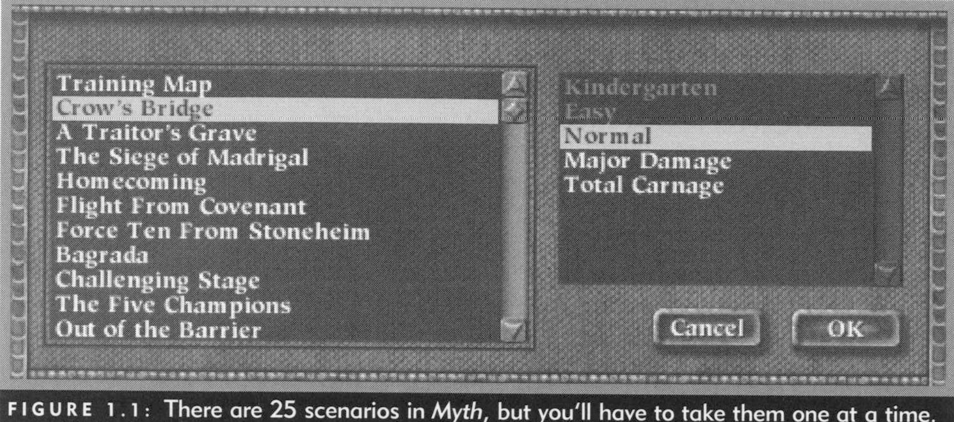

FIGURE 1.1: There are 25 scenarios in *Myth*, but you'll have to take them one at a time.

LIGHT (LIVING)

These are the guys you'll be leading into battle in the single-player version of the game and for many of the multiplayer games as well. Get used to them, because if you can learn how to use them properly, they'll save your skin many times over, and you'll have a heck of a lot of fun along the way.

Avatara

The Avatara is probably the most powerful creature in the Living side's arsenal. In this version of *Myth*, you only see one Avatara, and that's Alric, who is an important part of the story. Avatara are capable of using their great intelligence to summon powerful Dreams, which can be used to inflict considerable damage on the enemy units. Alric has but one Dream in *Myth*: the Dispersal Dream. This dream causes the enemy units to explode in a chain reaction, and will come in very handy for you late in the game.

You won't have access to Avataras before the Pools of Iron scenario, but when you do you'll find that it comes as a welcome addition to your troops. Avataras and their Dispersal Dream give you what no other unit can in the single-player game can: an alternative to physical combat. The Avatara are also very tough when fighting one-on-one with an enemy, but as soon as they are facing two or more units in close combat, they fall quickly.

Berserk

In a way Berserks go right to the root of *Myth*. The Mel Gibson movie *Braveheart* contributed to the inspiration for *Myth*, and the Berserks bear a striking resemblance to the Scottish warriors in that movie. The Berserk units are human, have long hair, carry huge claymores (two-edged swords), and have imposing patterns of war paint.

Berserks are a special unit, and are your best weapons for hand-to-hand fighting. They literally go nuts when they are engaged in combat, and in force they can wipe out large numbers of Thrall or Myrmidons. When you send them to attack the enemy, they charge recklessly with their claymores held high. If you can take a hoard of Soulless by surprise, your Berserks will turn them into piles of purple powder in no time. To give you an idea of how the folks at Bungie feel about Berserks, this is how they refer to them: "These fearless, shieldless humans wield giant claymores and live only to return the Undead to the uneasy slumber that comes from being hacked into a hundred wiggling pieces."

Dwarf

Dwarves are arguably the most potent day-to-day weapons in *Myth*. They are small, swarthy fellows with thick, gray beards and surly attitudes, and, unfortunately, are small in numbers. Dwarves are critically important because they have unlimited supplies of Explosive Bottles. They inflict their rain of fire on the Undead minions by lobbing these bottles at groups of the scum. When a bottle goes off right in the middle of a pack of Thrall, you'd better duck because body parts will be flying everywhere. If managed properly, a solitary Dwarf can single-handedly decimate an evil force.

But wait! That's not all! Dwarves can also carry little packets called Satchel Charges. They (usually) start each scenario with four charges in their pouch and can place them anywhere they are able to go themselves (you can do this by pressing the T key when the Dwarf is selected). These charges can then be ignited by an Explosive Bottle lobbed in from a distance, thus causing a much larger explosion than the bottle alone would have caused.

If Satchel Charges are laid in the path of oncoming enemy forces and then detonated when those forces are near the charge, the enemy can be dealt a devastating (and gruesome) blow. The drawback? Dwarves are not very fast and can be easily

run down by the Undead Ghols. They are also popular targets for the spears of Soulless and, in fact, are usually the *primary* target of Soulless. Dwarves are fairly scarce and are usually not available more than two at a time. See Chapter 2, *Combat Tactics,* to learn more about Dwarves and Satchel Charges.

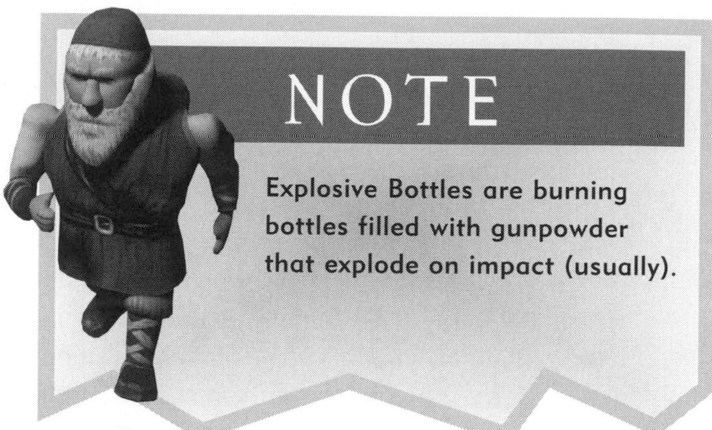

NOTE

Explosive Bottles are burning bottles filled with gunpowder that explode on impact (usually).

Forest Giant

Forest Giants are huge wooden creatures that are the Light side's equivalent of the Trow and equally difficult to destroy. They can kick the stuffing out of enemy troops that happen to get too close. A group of Forest Giants let loose on a horde of Thrall will produce a gigantic pile of Thrall kibble. Forest Giants kill the enemy in spectacular fashion: they punch and kick with their massive frames until the enemy is dust. It's really quite satisfying to watch a Forest Giant pulverize a large group of Thrall. As with all units, the Forest Giants are much more powerful when attacking in force. If you can, try to get a 3:1 advantage on the enemy.

Archer (Fir'Bolg)

Fir'Bolg is a rather cumbersome name, so in this book I'll refer to them as Archers. Archers are another absolutely critical component of the Light's forces and, if used properly, they can tilt the battle in your favor.

Unfortunately, Archers come with a price: they require a little more skill to use safely and effectively during battle, and they cannot fight effectively in hand-to-hand combat. Archers fire a traditional bow and arrow and can hit the enemy from a considerable range. If you have enough Archers, they can even pick off advancing troops before they get close enough to do you damage, but this is generally a risky proposition, and it's always smart to have some Warriors handy just in case.

Journeyman

The Journeyman is the spiritual backbone of your force. They're slow moving and generally not a great attack weapon, but they can sustain a ton of damage and carry a long axe to defend themselves when necessary. Journeymen use their magical powers in conjunction with Mandrake Root (they carry six of them) to perform a variety of special functions for your forces.

Journeymen have power over the Undead because the Mandrake Root has a reverse effect on Undead creatures. For example, if a Journeyman "heals" a Thrall, the Thrall dies right then and there.

This is also true in multi-player games in which you may have a Wight (described below) and a Journeyman on the same team. If the Journeyman's power is used on the Wight, the Wight disintegrates and leaves behind a pair of special pouches called Puss Packets. These packets can then be picked up by Ghols for other uses, but you'll learn more about that in Chapter 2, *Combat Tactics*.

NOTE

Mandrake Root is an herb from the Nightshade family used by the Journeymen to heal injured warriors. Without this root, the Journeyman's ability to heal is gone.

Journeymen can also be used to heal Living troops. This is why it's often a good idea to keep one near a group of Archers, because as your Archers take damage, your Journeyman can heal them and keep everyone fresh and ready to kill again. Journeymen are so versatile that they can even heal themselves, provided they are not under active attack. The only limitation to the Journeymen is the number of Mandrake Roots they carry, but remember, if any Journeymen die on the field of battle, they'll give up any roots that they haven't used. This leaves the roots free to be picked up by another Journeyman and put to use for his side.

Warrior

Warriors are the bread and butter of your armies. They are strong fighters and are equipped with armor, a helmet, and a short sword. For close-in combat these guys are surprisingly solid fighters, and when you consider that they're usually matched up against the weaker Thrall on the Dark side, they definitely have an advantage.

Keep that in mind when you're going into battle—if you can attack with a force of even 65 or 70 percent of your enemy's (Thrall) force, you should emerge victorious. In the single-player game, Warriors often represent the bulk of your forces, so use them wisely and take advantage of formations that benefit them. You can learn more about this in Chapter 2, *Combat Tactics*.

Special Units

Throughout the game there are special instances where you'll get units that are "super" units. That is to say that they will look like a Dwarf, or an Archer, but they'll be special in some way, like they can fire their weapon faster or they can take more hits before dying. For the purposes of this book, I'll call these units *Special Units*. You'll have access to Special Units in Sons of Myrgard (Pathfinder Dwarf) and in The Five Champions/Out of the Barrier scenarios. When you get a unit that's been "enhanced," be sure to use it to its maximum ability, and protect it at all costs.

DARK (UNDEAD)

The Undead are the trash that you'll be facing in battle (in the single-player version anyway), and although you won't get the chance to actually use any of these units until you play a multiplayer game, it's always to your advantage to know as much about your enemy as possible. So cover your nose and put on some latex gloves, we're going into the scum-filled world of the Dark side.

Fetch

Fetches are highly dangerous Undead weapons. By clasping their hands together firmly in front of them, they can create high-voltage lightning bolts that pass out of their bodies. This weapon can take out entire blocks of Light forces in a few

seconds. Fetches can be defeated by regular weapons, but it can be very difficult to get near them. You can usually take a Fetch out with the slightly longer range Archer; however, you must work quickly and accurately, or you'll be popcorn. The Fetch can also be killed with a mad rush of Berserks (or other fast units), because the Fetch cannot attack if an enemy unit is within a certain distance (fairly close). So if you can get a Berserk past the Fetches' attack perimeter, you'll be able to hunt him down without worrying about getting electrocuted.

TIP

If a Fetch is standing near a Satchel Charge when it throws its lightning, the Satchel Charge will explode from the electrical pressure. This is a great way to kill Fetches if you can lure them over near your explosives.

You'll notice that when a Fetch dies, they sort of deflate. This is because the Fetch is (in the words of Jason Jones, *Myth*'s lead programmer) an "other worldly being that has taken the flesh from an earthly creature and wrapped it around itself." For this reason, a Fetch is not truly Undead, but it still sides with the Undead forces. Too bad—that lightning is cool.

Ghol

For some reason, Ghols are the natural enemy of Dwarves, and according to the *Myth* legend, they have a long and bloody history. Ghols are the fastest units in the game and are often used to run down Dwarves and take them out. Often Dwarves can't get an Explosive Bottle launched quickly enough before the Ghols are on top of them hacking and slashing them to pieces.

Ghols are strange creatures, and they have a few quirks that can benefit the Dark side (or you, if you're playing multiplayer). Ghols can pick up and throw the Puss Packets left behind by disassembled Wights. They can only carry one packet at a time (Wights contain two packets), but a single packet can paralyze or destroy fairly large numbers of enemy forces. Actually, Ghols can pick up many different items that are scattered about the map, and then throw them at you. Blades, heads, arms, Puss Packets; you name it, Ghols can throw it.

Ghols are creepy, too; they carry giant cleavers into battle and lope around the field collecting the hands and heads of their enemies because, as the Ghols say, "If I've got your severed head and both your hands in a sack hanging around my neck, then you're dead!" Make sure to keep your Dwarves well protected from these scoundrels.

Myrmidon

Myrmidons are best described as the equivalent of the Light side's Berserks. They look like walking skeletons and carry a wicked double-edged blade. They are very fast, and they can approach their enemies very quickly (much like Berserks). You must be very careful of these creatures when they get near Dwarves and Archers because they'll quickly run in and lay waste to your troops before you even have time to notice. Always keep defensive forces near your most precious units (Archers and Dwarves).

Shade

Shades are essentially the reanimated corpses of dead Avataras and are very tough customers to deal with. As you might expect, the Shade has the ability to use a Dream against your forces, and believe me, this is not something to take lightly. Fortunately you won't see your first Shade until you play the Out of the Barrier scenario.

Soulless

Soulless are the Undead equivalent of Archers, save for a couple of choice differences. Because Soulless don't have legs, they have the ability to pass over terrain that Archers find impassable (deep rivers, hills, etc.). Unlike Archers, Soulless can use their spears in close combat, although they will usually choose to run rather than engage in any hand-to-hand combat. The Soulless' weapon of choice is a barbed spear anointed with a venom that causes excruciating pain but is not itself fatal. Regardless, getting hit with enough of the spears certainly *is* fatal, so try

to stay out of their range whenever possible. Soulless carry bundles of spears, and much to the Light side's chagrin, they never run out of them.

Spider

Spiders are of more importance in the multiplayer version of *Myth* than they are in the single-player game. However, they still deserve mention. In the single-player game the Spiders are merely a natural life-form that gets in your way, they aren't actually part of the Undead forces. In the multiplayer game, Spiders can be part of any player's forces and should be used in large numbers to be effective. Spiders are not particularly strong, and they can be killed easily, but they can make up for that in numbers, so be careful if they're coming at you.

Large Spider

As you might expect from the name, the Large Spider is just a bigger, meaner version of the regular Spider. You'll get to face off against the Large Spider in the Smiths of Muirtheme.

Thrall

These walking dead are the least intelligent but most numerous minions of the Dark side. They are too slow and clumsy to wield a large sword effectively, so the Fallen Lords have equipped the Thrall with axes. As mentioned earlier, even though Thrall are roughly equal to Warriors (both are essentially the "base" unit), one-on-one the Warrior can kick the Thrall's butt all the way back to its sorry little grave.

However, Thrall usually mill around in fairly large bunches, which can be a very real threat to your forces. One huge advantage for the Light side is that Dwarves can move a little bit faster than Thrall, thus enabling them to stay at a safe distance while blasting the Thrall into hundreds of individual chunks.

Trow

Trow are incredibly strong, massive creatures that will literally kick the stuffing out of anything nearby. They can plow through enemy troops by killing several of them

at a time with one kick, so be very, very cautious around them. Trow are rumored to be very tough, and it's said that near the Poles where it's extremely cold at night, the Trow will freeze and recover without incident the next morning. Now *that's* tough.

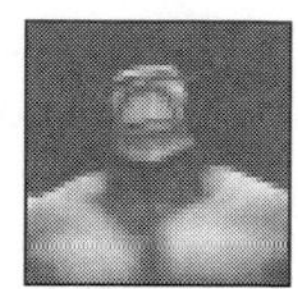

However, fear not, there is an effective way to deal with Trow, but you need to have a fair chunk of your forces to do it properly. Simply throw everything you've got at them all at once. Although you may lose some troops, if you can get the Trow surrounded with Berserks and Warriors on all sides, you should be able to take them out. To kill a Trow with small units (like Berserks and Warriors) you need to come at the Trow from all sides and attack in a large bunch. Once surrounded, the Trow falls fairly easily.

> **TIP**
>
> Jason Jones Tip: The best way to kill a Trow is to use the "anvil and hammer" method. This means that you divide your forces into two groups and hit the Trow simultaneously from the front and back. Then hack away as fast as possible and you should kill the Trow without having your force wiped out.

Wight

This is the foulest of the Undead creatures. The Wight is nothing more than a walking bomb, waiting until it's close enough to the enemy to explode. It has a large explosive capability, and when it blows it not only kills with the concussion of the explosion, but also releases clouds of foul disease on its enemy as its body is

> **TIP**
>
> When you're playing multiplayer, whatever you do, don't keep your Wight with the rest of your forces. If the enemy can blow it up with Soulless or Archers, the Wight will take out everything nearby.

ripped open (killing itself in the process). The noxious fumes then paralyze the units that didn't get destroyed in the explosion. Wights are slow and your Archers can easily pick them off from afar, but they'll try to sneak close to a group of your troops when you are not paying attention. Always keep a close eye on the enemy's Wights.

In the network game, Wights can be dismantled by Journeymen, leaving their two Puss Packets lying on the ground. Ghols can then pick up the packets and use them individually as explosive disease-carrying pouches. Used in this way with the very fast Ghols, the packets are often more effective than being stuck in a slow-moving Wight.

THE ELEMENTS

Myth is a fantastically unique game, and it contains some very special features that help to make it so. One of these features is the incorporation of natural elements like wind, rain, and snow into gameplay. Rather than acting as nothing more than a cosmetic or artistic touch, the elements actually change the way you play the game, depending on what Mother Nature has thrown your way. Although you could play the game without ever realizing some of this information, knowing how the elements affect the game can give you that little bit of an edge you may need to beat your fiercest rival.

WATER

Water in *Myth* behaves much like water in the real world, putting out fire and making some areas impassable because of its depth, but there's more to water in *Myth* than these truths. For example, when a unit walks through water, its normal progress will be noticeably slowed and, depending on the depth of the water, the unit may not be able to pass at all. If a unit cannot breathe as it passes through the water (i.e., the water is too deep), then the unit will go around—it won't kill itself trying to cross the body of water. There are five levels of water, some of which are too deep for many of your troops.

On the Undead side, they don't have to worry about breathing because they're already dead! As a result many Undead units can cross any body of water and indeed even hide beneath it. You'll find this out in the first scenario, Crow's Bridge,

as a whole mess of Thrall emerge from hiding in the river to attack two of your Warriors.

The Undead can also use water as a defense. If you are chasing down some Undead units with a Dwarf, all the enemy has to do is hop into the old river or pond to foil your plans to disintegrate them. The Explosive Bottles your Dwarves throw must always hit the ground before they can explode, and when they land in water, they are put out. This can be very frustrating, but if you're the one getting chased by the Dwarf, it can be a real boon.

SNOW

Snow doesn't have a particularly profound effect on gameplay, but it *can* affect the Dwarves' Explosive Bottles by extinguishing them before they hit the ground (see Figure 1.2). Which brings us to the next point. If snow is falling, there's probably snow on the ground, too, and therefore the bottle is even more likely to go out when it hits the snowy ground. The main point to be wary of in a snow-covered landscape

FIGURE 1.2: Explosive Bottles are often snuffed out by snow.

is this: don't set yourself up in a situation where you depend on Dwarves to blow things up with precise timing, or you'll be six feet under.

RAIN

Rain is much like falling snow, except that it will just about always extinguish a Dwarf's bottle. However, rain often comes and goes, so you will be able to use explosives from time to time in some scenarios. The interesting thing about the rain and snow in *Myth* is that each drop is actually a real 3D entity. Every drop or flake is affected by the physics of gravity and wind, and every drop is factored into the gameplay. It may not seem like much, but when you're saved from an enemy Dwarf by some newly falling rain, you'll be thanking the *Myth* programmers plenty.

WIND

Wind in *Myth* is completely out of your control. You cannot influence it, predict it, or reliably see where it is blowing. However, wind only plays a minor role in the game. Basically, it affects the elements like rain and snow, but it does not have any effect on Dwarves' bottles or Archers' arrows. In short, it makes the game prettier to look at, but not much more.

TERRAIN

Although there isn't a great deal of difference among the various terrain types you will see throughout *Myth*, it's still important to mention some of the subtleties and how they affect gameplay.

DESERT

The desert is actually nothing more than a waterless environment in which to play *Myth*, as you can see in Figure 1.3. It often doesn't have as many height differentials (high places for Archers and Dwarves to shoot from), so it levels the playing field a little bit. However, a hot, dry environment greatly benefits your Dwarves, and you can expect that the bottles will blow up with a very high degree of certainty. After you've spent some time in the rain or snow, this can be a real treat, especially if you love to blow things up.

FIGURE 1.3: The desert is dry looking, but that's about it.

MARSHES

Again, marshes don't actually have any significant effect on movement or on any other portion of the game, other than the fact that there tends to be a fair bit of water lying around. That said, water slows units down and provides hiding places for some Undead units, so when in the marshes you should be slightly more aware of these factors.

FROZEN TUNDRA

You might expect that your units would be weaker or not function as well under the cold and snowy condition of some maps. This, however, is not the case. The main factor in a snow-covered land is that snow puts out fire, thus making it hard for your Dwarves to be the factor you would like them to be in a major battle. In fact, they are so ineffective in these conditions that in a tight battle it's not worth taking the time to micromanage them when you have other units to take care of.

The other factor with a snow-covered land, and indeed, in a desert as well, is that there isn't a whole lot of definition in the landscape. Let's face it, there just aren't always a lot of landmarks available to tell you where you are or where you're going. If you run into this problem, be sure to keep your map on at all times (by pressing the Tab key) to keep your orientation. After all, a disorganized army is an army that's ready to get its butt kicked.

CAVES

The caves are for effect only, and since you will not actually be fighting any major battles inside the caves, there's not much to mention about them. But they *are* there, and there's nothing about them that should worry you. Besides, you'll only see the caves in a couple of scenarios.

MUDPIT

The mudpit is a multiplayer map; however, for the purposes of this book mudpit also refers to any map with rain that comes and goes. The mudpit deserves mention because of its unique impact on both the single-player and multiplayer games of *Myth*. If you have a situation where the rain is coming and going, it's best to set everything up the way you want it while it's raining, then be darn good and ready to unleash the power of your Dwarves when the rain stops. The rain is random, but it generally will break for at least a minute in between downpours (and sometimes longer), so try to take full advantage of these letups. If you're aware of the rain and your opponent(s) aren't, then you can really make them pay with their lives.

OTHER COOL STUFF

Myth is not just a battleground game bound together by an interesting story, but rather it's an engrossing, all-encompassing experience that includes many tiny nuances that help make the game awesome. One of these little extras is the presence of a Magic Bow. The Stone Bow (found in the Silvermines) enables an Archer to turn certain creatures into stone with one arrow. The only downside is that not all the enemy units are affected by this, and there is a finite number of charges, so be careful not to run out at the wrong time.

ITEMS

Most of the Items and Relics in *Myth* are there for the purposes of plot development. Therefore there's usually not anything that many of the objects can do for you; you just have to find them (or rescue them) in order to satisfy an objective.

2

Combat Tactics

Despite some similarities to other games of the same genre, *Myth* is a very complex game that requires careful planning and superb tactical execution to win on a regular basis. There are many subtle aspects of gameplay in *Myth* that will make the difference between a glorious victory and a deeply disappointing defeat. That's why I'm here, not only to help you squeeze every last bit of power and health out of each one of your units, but also to give you an awesome understanding of all the little things that can make you a *Myth* God.

EXPLOSIVES

Explosive devices and units are the most decisive factors in *Myth*, and players who fail to use them will quickly find themselves on the losing end of the battle. That explosives are important to winning is only a part of what makes them great. The fact is, explosives are (excuse the pun) a blast! They're what makes *Myth* one of the most entertaining games ever, and if you don't believe me, just watch the ground ripple and the body parts fly after a Dwarf throws a bottle into a crowd of Thrall. Boom…splatter. This section will teach you everything you need to know about explosives, and even a few things you didn't want to know.

WIGHTS

Wights are lumbering Undead creatures that carry foul satchels called Puss Packets. These are disease-filled explosive bags that (when detonated) throw a pink cloud

over the enemy, paralyzing many units (for several seconds) while damage is inflicted.

The Wight has two main functions. First, it's a walking bomb that lumbers across the landscape toward enemy units, ripping itself open in a huge suicidal explosion of Puss Packets when it gets close enough to do damage. These explosions are the most spectacular in *Myth* and, as you will see, they rock the landscape with a very cool ripple effect. Frankly, it's worth detonating the Wight just to see this. Second, the Wight serves as a reservoir for Puss Packets (in the multiplayer game), as shown in Figure 2.1.

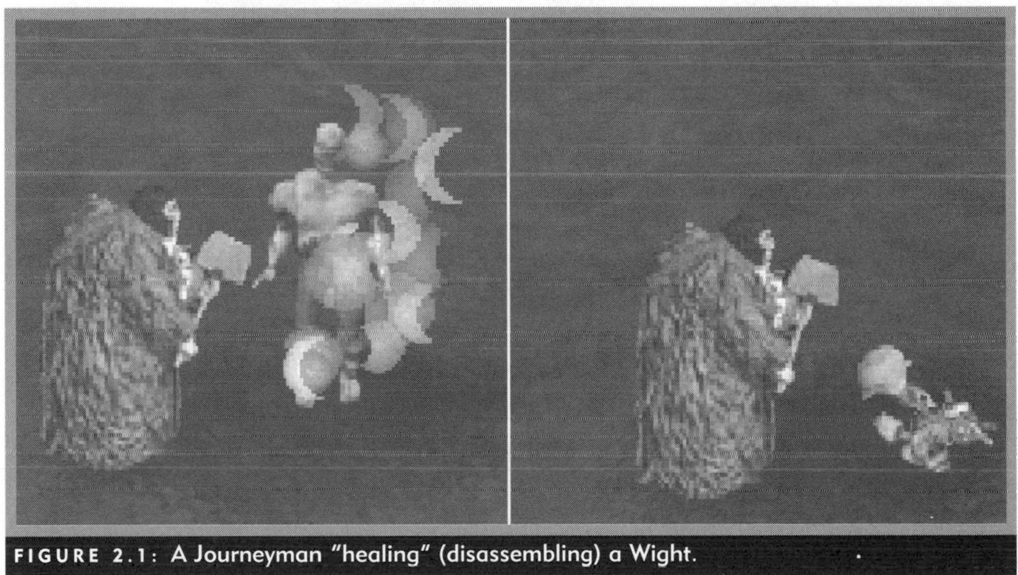

FIGURE 2.1: A Journeyman "healing" (disassembling) a Wight.

Puss Packets

Because the Wight is Undead, it can be killed by having the Journeyman heal it. (Journeymen and Wights appear together only in multiplayer action.) Why would you want to do this? Well, the Wight disintegrates, but it leaves two Puss Packets behind. These Puss Packets (see Figure 2.2) can then be picked up, but only by Ghols (so if you don't have any Ghols, don't bother trying this).

Many gamers never use their Wights for anything except to disintegrate them for their Puss Packets. This is primarily because the slow-moving Wights are very

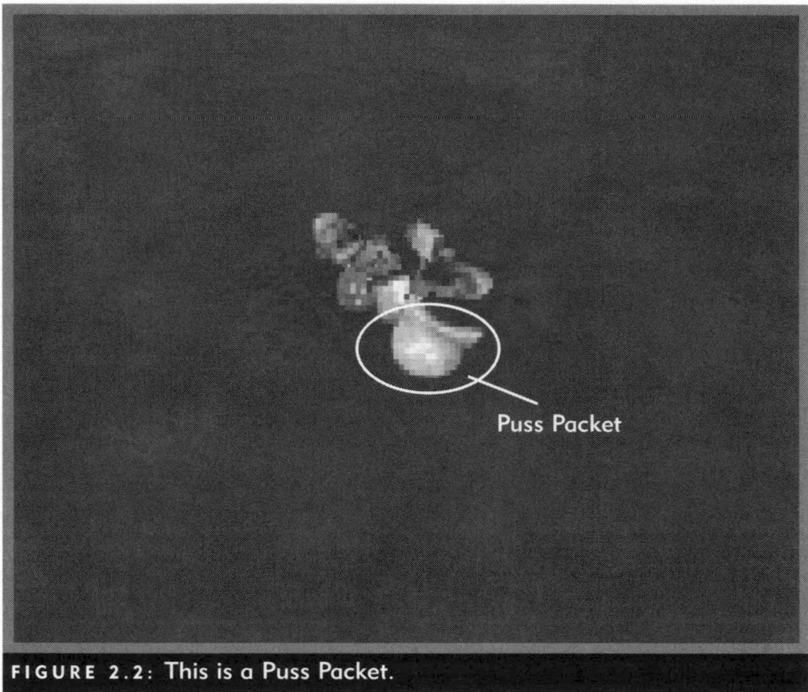

FIGURE 2.2: This is a Puss Packet.

vulnerable to ranged attack from Archers or Dwarves. If you try to get your Wights close to enemy forces, they'll almost certainly get pulverized by enemy arrows before they can do their putrid damage.

The Wight as a Weapon

As I mentioned before, the Wight doesn't make a very good weapon because it's so slow and can be picked off at long range. However, there are certain situations in which the Wight can be used as a devastating weapon. In short, the Wight has to be snuck into the battle without your opponent noticing. In this case, diversion is the key, and the best time to pull the old sneak-a-roo is in the middle of hot-and-heavy hand-to-hand combat. When there's a very evenly matched hack 'n slash battle going on, the winner is often whoever manages their troops better in the battle, and that takes a lot of attention. This is where you sneak the Wight in; while the enemy is concentrating on thwarting your attack, you drift in and hit his troops with your Wight, as shown in Figure 2.3. A single Wight explosion can effectively turn an entire formidable force into chicken soup without the chicken.

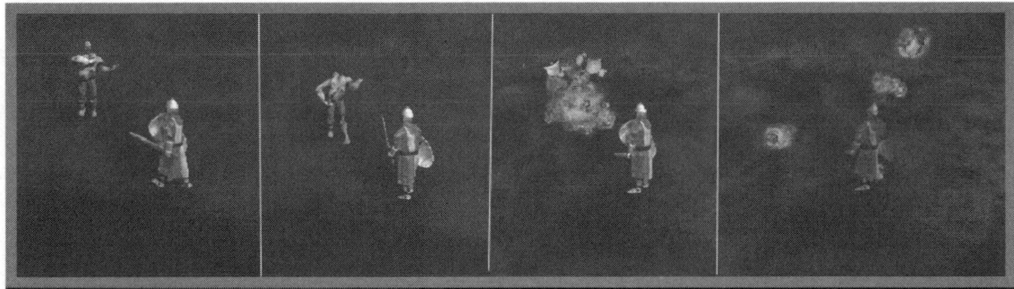

FIGURE 2.3: The Wight can inflict serious damage when it self-destructs.

Here's what I do. I use about half the force I would normally bring to an all-out attack on the enemy's forces, and at the same time I start my Wight walking slowly toward the enemy position. Although my force is smaller than the enemy's, they are going to take my attack very seriously, and most likely will respond with most of their units. My forces will begin to lose the battle, but I keep them close together in their defeat, and just as it looks like all's lost, the Wight comes in and blows the tar out of everything, destroying the bulk of the enemy's units in one fell swoop. In the meantime, I still have half my forces, while what is left of the enemy is badly damaged from the Wight explosion. Of course, this doesn't always work, and you're taking a terrible risk doing it; but if it does work, you'll be laughing all the way to the bone yard.

DWARVES

These little guys are your bread-and-butter explosive experts. They carry not only an unlimited supply of Explosive Bottles but also four Satchel Charges (sometimes more) each. When used properly, the combined firepower of these two weapons can easily turn the tide in a battle, either for or against you. Many a time have clumsy players accidentally had their Dwarves lob a bottle into a group of friendly troops, only to destroy any chance of victory.

Explosive Bottles

These are glass bottles filled with gunpowder that have a bit of cloth stuffed into the necks. When tossed, the bottles arc gracefully through the air, trailing smoke as they fly (see Figure 2.4). The bottles may or may not explode when they hit the ground depending on a number of factors, including rain, snow, and water. The more rain

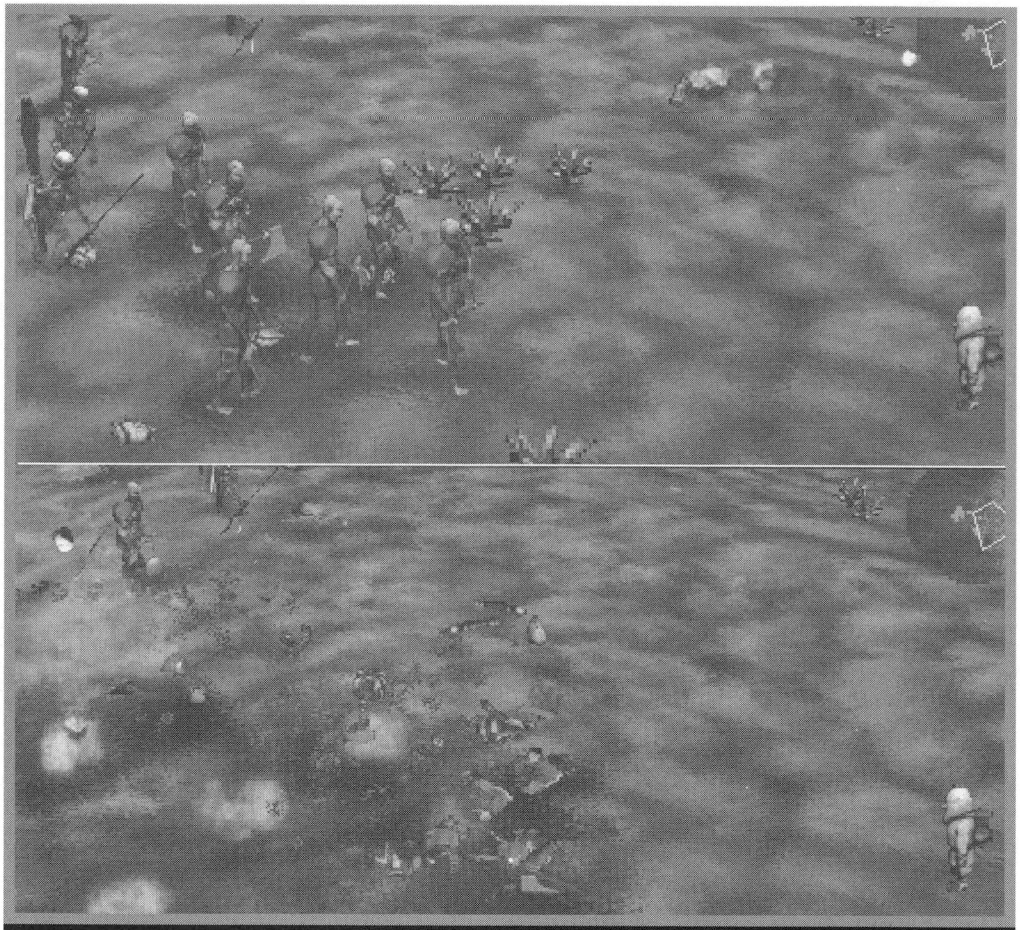

FIGURE 2.4: Explosive Bottle en route to a bang of a good time.

or snow that is falling the less likely the bottle will explode when it reaches its target. As you can imagine, a little rain can go a long way toward ruining your plans.

These bottles are actually designed to bounce when they hit the ground. You'll notice that a Dwarf may attempt to hit a target that's out of throwing range by aiming short and counting on one bounce of the bottle to cover the extra distance to the target. The bottle may bounce, explode before it gets a chance to bounce, or bounce but fail to explode. This uncertainty regarding the Explosive Bottles is one of the things that make *Myth* so much fun: you just can't ever be sure what the bottles will do.

Rain: Dampening the Bottles

Believe it or not there's one big advantage to having lots of precipitation fall from the sky. Although the rain or snow extinguishes your Dwarves' Explosive Bottles, as you throw them they just continue to pile up on the ground. Even though they won't explode it the rain, once the drops stop falling, they're good to go. In a landscape where the rain comes and goes, you can pile up a bunch of unexploded bottles in one spot, much more than you ever could when the weather is clear.

Once it stops raining, lure the enemy close and toss a bottle over near the others. Kaboom! This is especially effective when you're playing the multiplayer mission Last Man on the Hill, and you load up a pile of explosives near the flag. When the crunch is on at the end of the game, you can blow everyone else off the hill and take it for yourself.

Satchel Charges

The Satchel Charge is one of the most powerful (and versatile) weapons in *Myth*, and one charge can turn the tide of a battle. However, the Satchel Charge is not without its downside. Satchel Charges can only be carried by Dwarves (who carry up to eight charges each), who can detonate them by throwing an Exploding Bottle at them.They can also be ignited by other means. Satchel Charges are essentially burlap sacks full of explosive powder with a force roughly equal to one Explosive Bottle (according to Bungie), but in the game they appear to be have a greater punch.

Satchel Charges are typically laid down (by a Dwarf) along a path you think the enemy will follow, as shown in Figure 2.5. Then, when the enemy hordes come chugging toward you, you can blow them to teeny, tiny, little bits by lobbing an Explosive Bottle at the charges just before they get in striking distance. The cool thing is that successive charges will go off one by one if they're laid close enough together, thus destroying large chains of your enemy's forces. Successfully using Satchel Charges can be fantastically satisfying, especially if you manage to catch

FIGURE 2.5: These Satchel Charges pose a serious danger if they get ignited.

one of your friends (when playing multiplayer *Myth*).

The downside to Satchel Charges is that they can blow the heck out of your troops just as easily as the enemy. If any of your Dwarves are killed by Soulless (or any other creature), any extra Satchels they were carrying end up in a pile on the ground. If, during multiplay, an enemy lobs an Explosive Bottle nearby, or a Fetch uses the Lightning Dream, you go BOOM. If you're unlucky enough to have this happen, at least take the time to enjoy watching all the body

TIP

The Satchel Trick: If you are playing a game where one location is critical (like King of the Hill), you can protect your interests by laying down all your Satchel Charges around the flag on the hill. At the end of the game when everyone rushes the hill (there's often two or three players fighting for the flag on the crowded hill), all you have to do is throw an Explosive Bottle and all of the enemy troops will magically turn into blood-spewing projectiles. Victory: you.

parts fly across the map. If it happens often, you can make a game of it by trying to predict where the parts will land!

In certain scenarios, Satchel Charges must be used to blow up objects on the map. For example, in River of Blood you must use your charges to blow up the gate to the city to gain entrance, and this will take most of your charges! Satchel Charges are powerful tools that can help you beat seemingly insurmountable odds, but they can also kick your own butt all the way back to the Stone Age, so be careful.

GHOLS

The Ghols can carry one Puss Packet each, which they use as an explosive, paralyzing agent against enemy troops, as shown in Figure 2.6. They can throw it at either

FIGURE 2.6: This Ghol is throwing a Puss Packet at a group of unsuspecting Archers.

an enemy or the ground.The Puss Packet will most likely explode; however, there's a chance that it may not ignite. The one advantage of Puss Packets is that they are not affected by rain or snow, and their explosive properties are enough to ignite an unspent bottle or Satchel Charge. If there's plenty of moisture, the best thing to use to start an explosion is a Puss Packet, so it's always handy to keep one around just in case.

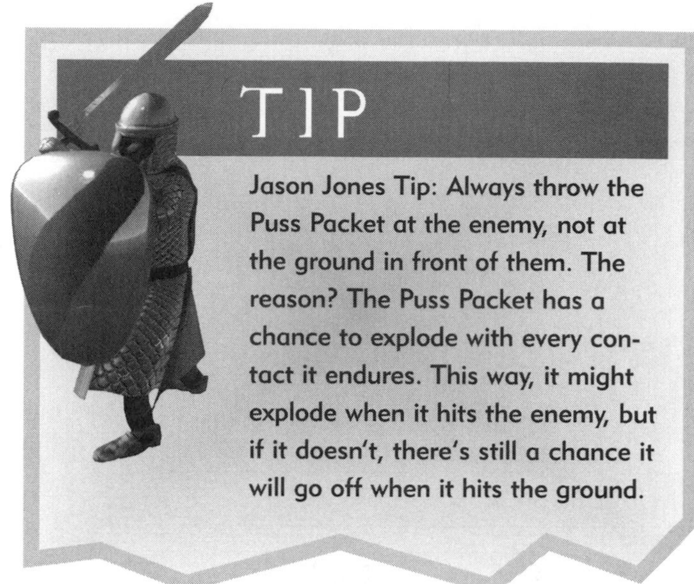

TIP

Jason Jones Tip: Always throw the Puss Packet at the enemy, not at the ground in front of them. The reason? The Puss Packet has a chance to explode with every contact it endures. This way, it might explode when it hits the enemy, but if it doesn't, there's still a chance it will go off when it hits the ground.

RANGED WEAPONS

A ranged weapon is any weapon that doesn't require the attacker to be directly beside the enemy in order to inflict damage. In *Myth*, Archers, Soulless, Dwarves, and Ghols all have some form of ranged weaponry, but since we've already covered Dwarves and Ghols in the Explosives section, I'll limit the discussion here to Soulless and Archers.

ARCHERS

Archers fire a traditional bow and arrow and are great for long-range attack, but they are very vulnerable in hand-to-hand combat. Fortunately, Archers are of above average speed, can keep their distance from most units, and can even outrun Thrall. In fact, if it comes down to Thrall vs. Archers, the Archers should be able to win hands down. They can just keep walking away from the Thrall, and when they get to a safe distance, they can turn and fire, then run again. Unfortunately, it's not always that easy.

Archers, like all other units, are affected by experience. The more kills they have, the more accurately they shoot, and the quicker they release their arrows. If

Archers ever get cornered, you can have them punch the enemy by double-clicking on the Archer. Experienced Archers are much, much better than newbies, so for this reason it's always important to try to get them each a couple of kills early in a scenario. A pack of eight Archers with three or four kills each is a force to be reckoned with; they can even take out Ghols before they can get close enough to hack the Archers to pieces.

TIP

Ah, ah, ah, ah, stayin' up high, stayin' up high. Whether you have Soulless or Archers, make sure that you are at least on level ground when fighting opposing ranged weapons. If five Archers at the bottom of a hill are matched against five Soulless at the top of the hill, the Archers will get smoked. It's simple physics—it's just harder to shoot up hill. That darned gravity!

SOULLESS

Soulless are the equivalent of Archers in every respect except their movement. No, it's not their speed that's the factor—it's that Soulless are *dead*. Because Soulless float above the ground, they can cross deep water or otherwise impassable areas that Archers or other terrestrial units could never negotiate. They can also climb lofty buttes that are inaccessible to other units (see Figure 2.7). The height lets them take out enemy units easily. Be sure to take advantage of this ability when you have a chance in certain multiplayer games.

MAGIC

There are two categories of "magic" in *Myth*: natural abilities and Dreams. Natural ability is what your Journeyman uses (along with Mandrake Root) to heal an injured Warrior, or unheal an Undead fleabag. The Fetch's use of lightning is also a natural ability. Some weapons in the game are "magical" (for example, the Bow of Stoning).

FIGURE 2.7: This hill gives the Soulless a height advantage that Archers, because of their legs, can't enjoy.

The bulk of cool magical events and spells that occur in *Myth* are what the game's creators call Dreams. These are used by only a few of the characters. Lucky for you that you get to actually use some of them.

DISPERSAL DREAM (AVATARA)

This is the Dream that's used by Alric, the Avatara that you have access to in Pools of Iron. The Dispersal Dream packs the power of a Satchel Charge for each enemy it hits, and it can be extremely effective against large groups of enemies. This Dream acts like an explosive on the unit you cast the "spell" on, but it doesn't necessarily stop there. If another unit is within a certain distance of the unit you blew up, it will also blow up, scarring the landscape with the explosion (see Figure 2.8).

FIGURE 2.8: The Avatara's Dispersal Dream in action.

Likewise, any units that were unlucky enough to be close to the second unit that blew will also blow up, and so on. If the enemy is fairly tightly grouped, you can blow them *all* up with ease. Watching this Dream work on a large group of Myrmidons is reminiscent of popcorn popping. The only drawback occurs when you cast the Dream when the enemy is too close to your own troops. When this happens, you become part of the "fuse" and blow up yourself, or at least take heavy damage.

SHADE'S DREAM

The Shade's Dream is basically the same as the Avatara's Dispersal Dream. If you get close to a Shade, he'll take out a group of your units in a few seconds. The key to dealing with the Shade is to keep your units spread out so that the Dream cannot spread from one unit to another. When a Shade dies, you can see glowing green orbs left behind. These orbs are unspent Dream charges, and if you accidentally ignite one, you won't be around to see the aftermath.

TROOP MOVEMENT

Unlike *Warcraft* or *Command & Conquer*, *Myth* is a true tactical game. That means that there's no resource management going on; you are simply trying to win the game with what you've got (in terms of units), and the only way to win is to beat the enemy tactically. For this reason, troop movement is a critical part of the game. After all, if you cannot manage how your troops are moving around the battlefield, you're probably going to be pureed by your foe before you even know what happened.

Moving your units around successfully is the *first* thing you should learn, because in challenging scenarios (in both single- and multiplayer games) you'll need to be able to manage your troops without consciously thinking about it. Although that may seem like a tall order now, it's kind of like riding a bike: once you've learned it, you never forget.

GROUPING UNITS

This is perhaps the single most important command for managing your troops in *Myth*. Select the troops you want to group, and then press (and hold) Alt + 1 to 0 (Command + 1 to 0 on the Mac) to set that group as a preset. You can have up to 10 preset groups in the game, thus giving you the ability to quickly grab command of just the units you want, as shown in Figure 2.9.

At the beginning of a scenario, many players like to group their like units together before they set out. Archers, Warriors, and Berserks can all be in separate groups that can be accessed quickly by pressing Alt plus the assigned number key (Command plus the assigned number key on the Mac). This means that no matter how dispersed your troops are, you can still grab command of them and send them to perform a task. Managing your units this way is critical to victory, so get a handle on this quickly. The manual covers the process in detail, so feel free to do some back reading if you need help.

FORMATIONS

Now that you've gotten a handle on grouping your units, you'll need to take it a step further and make sure that your groups are in some sort of formation. Why is this important? Well, when large groups of troops are being moved around without formations, they tend to just jumble together in a mishmash of bodies.

FIGURE 2.9: Grouping units is critical to managing your troops.

In the case of Archers, the lack of a formation can result in many of the Archers at the front of the pack getting hit from behind by those in the back. Believe me, you don't need this grief. The way to make sure that your troops will always be safe is to set them into a formation. To do this, press the 0–9 keys after you've selected a group. When you click on a destination for that group, they'll line up in the formation you've requested.

Specifying formations as a part of movement is important for concentrating or dispersing a force and allows you to attack with precision instead of as a wild mob (which can occasionally also be helpful). Pressing numbers 0–9 will choose alternate formations, and you can flip through formations as many times as you want before you click a destination, so take the time to get the right formation. Here's a breakdown of what the formations are and a little about what they're used for. Keep in mind that the use of formations is personal, and every player will have their own opinions on how to utilize each formation.

Short Line

The Short Line formation (1 key) is a good choice when you have small groups of four or less units and you want them all standing side by side facing a certain direction. This is often used with Archers and Warriors.

Long Line

The Long Line formation (2 key) is best used for covering a large area defensively. If you are worried that a unit might sneak past you, or want to spread your Archers very wide to keep them from all being destroyed by one explosive, the Long Line is a good formation. The Long Line will put eight units abreast and then start a second line.

Loose Line

The Loose Line formation (3 key) is similar to the Long Line—the only difference is that the Loose Line is, well, loose. The units are slightly staggered along an axis. This is also used largely as a defensive position and is meant to keep enemy Ghols or other units from getting behind your troops.

Staggered Line

The Staggered Line formation (4 key) is an excellent formation for Archers. It enables a large group of Archers to have excellent lines of sight in a reasonably tight formation without any risk of them hitting one another. For most players, the Staggered Line is the formation of choice for large groups of Archers (or Soulless).

Box

The Box formation (5 key) has some inherent limitations that are glaringly obvious when the enemy has a Dwarf or Fetch handy. If your troops are rumbling forward in a tight box and a Dwarf puts an Explosive Bottle in the middle of the pack, you're going to lose all of those troops in a hurry. Another drawback is that the Box prevents the units on the inside of the formation from getting at the enemy. If you go up against a Trow with your troops in a Box formation, you might as well turn off your machine because that battle is lost. Boxes are good for grouping units into tight areas early on in the game (heck, I use them all the time), but once a battle breaks out nearby, change the formation.

Rabble

The Rabble formation (6 key) is a loose and widely spaced (more or less random) formation. This is generally how your units will arrange themselves naturally, so choosing a Rabble isn't always necessary. Sometimes a Rabble is as good an alternative as any when rushing an enemy position, and its wide unit dispersal will ensure that every unit meets an enemy.

Shallow Encirclement

The Shallow Encirclement formation (7 key) is essentially a shallow U with the units facing inward. This is a handy formation for protecting a certain object when you know the direction the enemy is coming from.

Deep Encirclement

To be totally honest, I never use the Deep Encirclement formation (8 key). However, it could come in handy if you want to move across a map and protect a unit from flank attacks. The Deep Encirclement is a deep U shape with all the units facing inward and can be used to house a unit in the middle of the formation.

Vanguard

The Vanguard is an age-old formation (9 key) that is excellent for head-on attacks. It may provide you with some flanking if the enemy moves to fight the units at the tip of the Vanguard first. This formation is occasionally used with Archers because it provides a good dispersal of arrows from the front to the back of the Vanguard.

Circle

The Circle formation (0 key) is pretty much used for one thing, and one thing only. It's designed specifically to set up your troops to protect an object, unit, or flag. It sets a group of units in a perfect circle, all facing outward. You'll see this used over and over again in multiplayer action, and occasionally in the single-player game. It's a solid defensive formation that provides a somewhat better measure of defense than most others.

HEIGHT DIFFERENTIALS

As I mentioned before, height is a very important factor in *Myth.* In real battle, troops that are fighting downhill perform better, but that's not the case in *Myth.* Instead, only the ranged weapons such as those of Soulless, Archers, and Dwarves are affected by height, but since they're such a critical part of the game, height advantages become very important if you want to win consistently.

Archers and Soulless that are fighting from a lofty perch will almost always prevail in an otherwise evenly matched fight, so try to keep at least on level ground with your opponents. The Dwarves also have an advantage if they are up high, and when they are at the bottom of the hill, tossing upward, they have a severe disadvantage. Because of their size and shape, Dwarves' bottles are affected by gravity much more than are the sleek arrows of an Archer. A bottle that doesn't make it to the top of a hill will have a tendency to come right back down and blow up the thrower. You must always watch your Dwarves to make sure they aren't making any suicidal throws without your knowledge. If a Dwarf gets close enough to an enemy, it'll toss an Explosive Bottle without your approval and, in their desire to take out the enemy, they'll often end up killing themselves.

HANDLING UNITS

To select all units of a certain type, double-click one of them and all nearby ones will be selected. This is probably the most common way to select a group and is a good way to help group units at the beginning of a scenario.

You can select any group with the mouse by clicking and dragging a box around the units you want highlighted; then shift-click on additional units to add them to the existing group. There's one other aspect to handling units that's very important in *Myth*, and that's the gesture + click. This is done by right-clicking (option + click on a Mac) on a point nearby where you want to move the group. As you release the button, move the mouse in the direction you want the units to face. When the group gets there, they'll turn to face the direction you specified with mouse. If they were given a formation, it will be oriented in that direction as well. The gesture-click can take a while to get used to, but it's important that your troops face the right direction when the enemy is near.

PERSPECTIVE

One of the great things about *Myth* is that it's a fully 3D game. Objects in the game, like arrows or bits of flesh that have been blown up are actually independent parts of the game and behave as individual objects. This very cool 3D environment means that the perspective may take some getting used to. You can only see a portion of the terrain at any given time, so you need to adjust your view frequently to know where you are and where you're going. There are a few ways you can do this, but probably the best way to gain perspective in *Myth* is just to play with the game and get used to the point of view. Once you've got it down, it won't present any problems for you.

ORBITING

Keeping your orientation in *Myth* is critical, so you need to be sure you have a grasp of the controls necessary to do so. The Q and E keys will orbit you around a fixed point, giving you a much better idea of what's around you. Sometimes the orbit won't work if you're too close to the side of the map, and you'll have to move away from the sides if you want to orbit.

ZOOMING

Press the V and C keys to zoom in and out of the battlefield. This is usually not critical to do, but it looks cool, and every once in a while there's something small like a Mandrake Root or a Puss Packet that you'll need to zoom in on to pick up.

MOVING

Moving forward and backward and turning left and right is accomplished by using the W, S, A, and D keys, Panning (moving left and right) is activated with the Z and X keys.

SPECIAL ABILITIES

Many units in *Myth* have special abilities, which are activated by pressing the T key. For instance, the Journeyman heals the selected unit when T is pressed (provided the Journeyman has Mandrake Root), while the Dwarf drops a Satchel Charge.

These special abilities are important, so experiment with the various units to be sure you know how to use them. Here's a list of the units and their special abilities:

- Archers: Use special bow (T key)
- Dwarves: Drop Satchel Charge (T key)
- Avatara: Dispersal Dream (T key)
- Wights: Blow themselves up (T key)
- Journeyman: Heals (T key)

RULES OF COMBAT

Although every person has their own style when playing *Myth*, there are a few truths that everyone should try to follow to be successful. I'll just briefly touch on a few key areas, but be sure to read the notes scattered throughout the book to get more detailed tips on how to succeed in *Myth*.

FLANKING

Flanking is something that's as old as warfare, and in scenarios like the Traitor's Grave, you'll be flanked (annoyingly so) by Ghols. When the enemy senses you are close enough, the Ghols will rush in from all sides and rip your Archers to shreds. You can learn something from this example. Whenever possible, try to get to the side of, or better yet, behind the enemy without letting them notice. Once you begin your attack, the enemy will feel confident in their defenses until you bring a small but deadly force up from behind and sandwich them! The moral of the story is this: always try to attack from multiple locations at the same time.

NUMERICAL SUPERIORITY

Always, always attack with more units than the enemy has unless you have special units like Dwarves. You can greatly lessen your losses by attacking with a 2:1 or 3:1 ratio rather than just a 1.5:1 ratio. The more units you can send in on the enemy, the less damage each of your units will suffer, and the quicker the enemy will buy the farm.

SPECIAL UNITS

Use your Journeymen, Dwarves, and Avataras to their full potential. Lay down some Satchel Charges, and then bait the enemy into an explosive trap. Be sure to use your Journeyman to heal any ailing units. In short, use every last bit of power at your fingertips in each situation, because in the single-player game there's many times where the next set of enemies you'll face will be overwhelming.

3

Cutting Your Teeth

These first few scenarios are the proving grounds where you'll have to get a firm handle on the game controls and combat tactics. To move forward later on, you need to learn to use the units at your disposal with skill and cunning, or you'll soon be dog meat. Not to worry, because Crow's Bridge is an excellent welcome mat to the world of *Myth*, and although Traitor's Grave can be challenging, I'll help you through it step by step. The last of these initial scenarios, the Siege of Madrigal, will test you right to your limits, but at the same time you'll get to see some very cool stuff. So sit back, prop this book up next to your monitor, and let's run headfirst into the realm of *Myth*.

CROW'S BRIDGE

As you might expect from the name of this first scenario, the bridge on this map is where the heavy action will take place. You begin the scenario in control of the bridge, but your two sentry guards quickly realize that they're going to be sautéed by the 14 Thrall who are lurking in the water under the bridge. To win this baby you'll need to find a way to retake the bridge even though the Undead have more soldiers. At the beginning of this scenario the core of your forces are kicking back in the town near the southeastern corner of the map; you'll have to use them carefully in order to overcome the odds.

MISSION OBJECTIVE

Protect the bridge and town, then force the enemy back across the bridge.

YOUR GUYS

In Crow's Bridge you will always start with the same units. This early in the game, their veteran units haven't had a chance to develop, so you'll always have four Archers, one Dwarf, and a handful of Warriors. Here's what you get:

- Archers
- Warriors
- Dwarf

THE EVIL HORDE

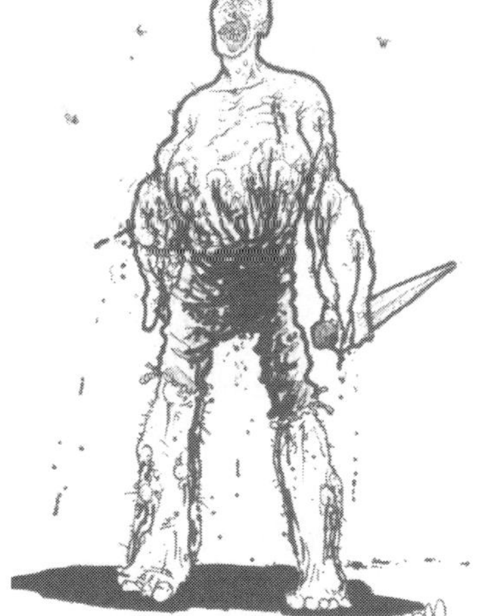

The Thrall that climb out of the river will be a big surprise. They may seem numerous, but they're not alone. Two pairs of Ghols and another entire army of Soulless and Thrall will show up when the Thrall guarding the bridge begin to falter. Here's what they get:

- Thrall
- Soulless
- Ghols

LAY OF THE LAND

There's only one way for your troops to cross the river that divides the upper and lower portions of the map, and that's the Crow's Bridge. Having your hands on this bridge when the dust settles is your main objective, but there are more than a few Undead slimebags that want to squash your dreams of victory. Believe it or not, there are

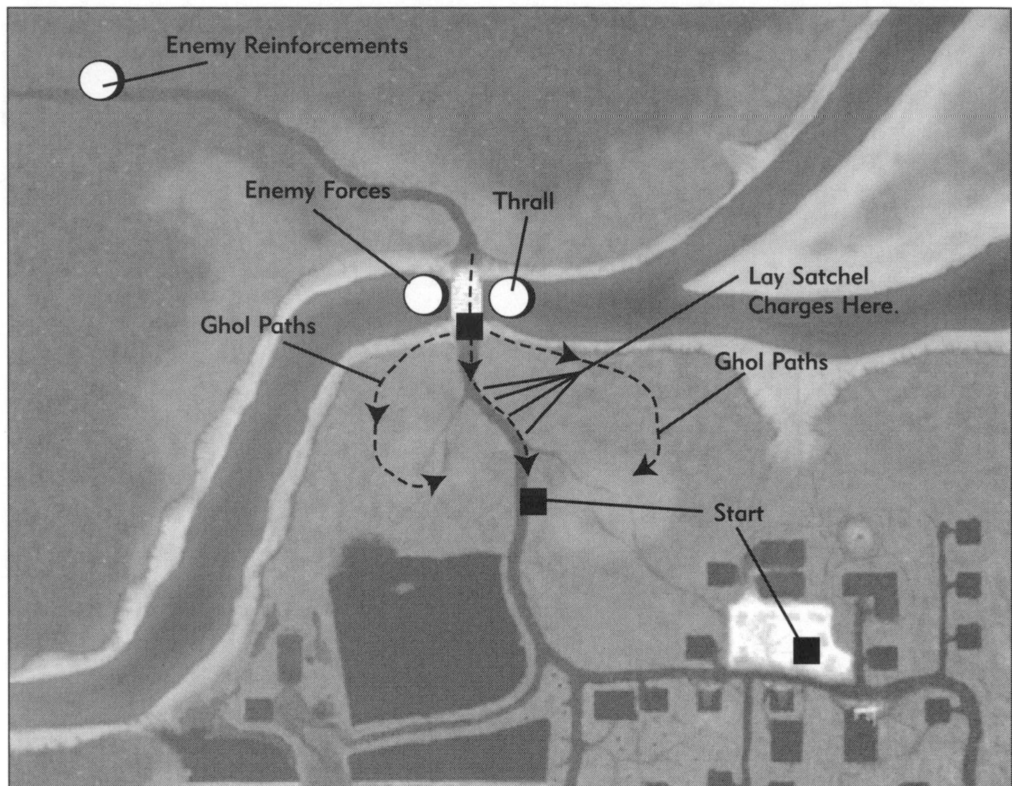

around 14 Thrall waiting patiently just below the surface of the water (under the bridge). The rest of the enemy troops are waiting patiently in the upper-hand corner of the map.

The town site isn't really important other than the fact that the majority of your troops start out there (Archers, a Dwarf, and four Warriors). However, if you are losing the battle to the Undead, the town can provide some much needed cover for your men. Let's hope

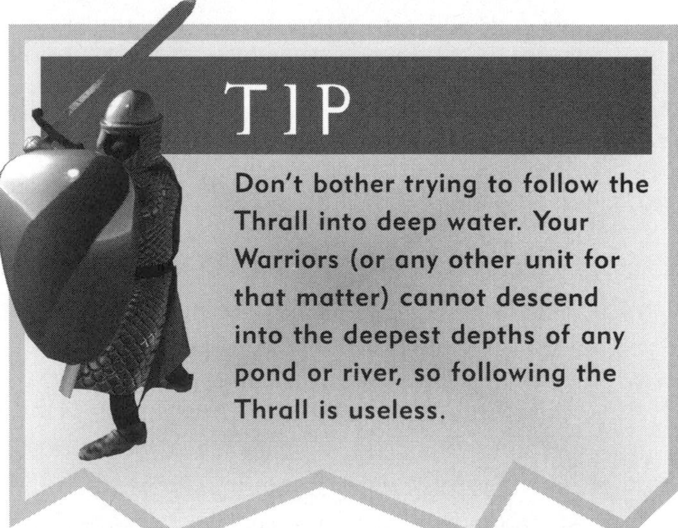

TIP

Don't bother trying to follow the Thrall into deep water. Your Warriors (or any other unit for that matter) cannot descend into the deepest depths of any pond or river, so following the Thrall is useless.

you won't need to take advantage of it. The rest of the terrain is not of great significance in this scenario.

BATTLE PLANS

Crow's Bridge begins with two of your Warriors being ambushed on the bridge, as shown in Figure 3.1. If you are fast you can either send the Warriors over the bridge to the north side (where they will most likely be hung out to dry), or you can pull them back down the road (to the south). Either way, you've got to move quickly, or the Thrall emerging from the river will hack them to pieces. Fortunately, the Thrall won't follow your men once they get a short distance away, so just keep them moving. Now that this is taken care of, you can begin to plot your counterattack to retake the bridge.

Group your Archers, Dwarf, and Warriors that are in town into two separate groups: the Archers and Warriors as one group, and the Dwarf as another. Run your

FIGURE 3.1: Get these guys off the bridge and away to a safe location before the Thrall make mincemeat of them.

Warriors and Archers group to the area southeast of the bridge, and move the Dwarf up the road and close to the bridge, but not close enough to get the Thrall's attention. If they start chasing the Dwarf, run away until they break off their attack (the Thrall won't attack unless you get fairly close).

TIP

Instead of having one large group, you may choose to group two Archers and two Warriors together to better manage your flanks. This way you can attack from a distance on both sides of the road.

In the meantime, the enemy will be routing two sets of Ghols (two in each set) around the left and right side of the Warriors on the road. Get your Archers that are in the east to resin up their bows and start laying a licking on the Ghols headed their way. Send the pair of Warriors out to attack the Ghols on your left flank. Remember, though Ghols are in serious need of dental work, they're fast and can outrun all of your units. The goal (pun intended) here is to keep a persistent attack on the Ghols (to keep them away from the main action), while your Dwarf turns the Thrall into a pile of charred body parts.

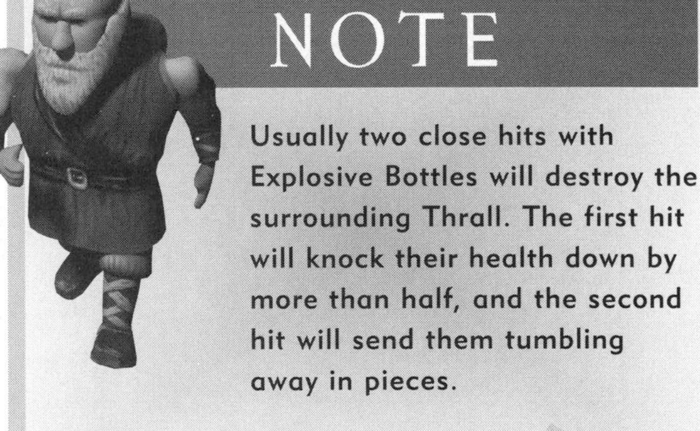

Once your Dwarf gets fairly close to the bridge and to the Thrall, drop your Satchel Charges in a line leading away from the Thrall, as shown in Figure 3.2. The Satchel Charges will come in very handy when the enemy rushes at you en masse. A detonated Satchel Charge packs an impressive Thrall-crunching

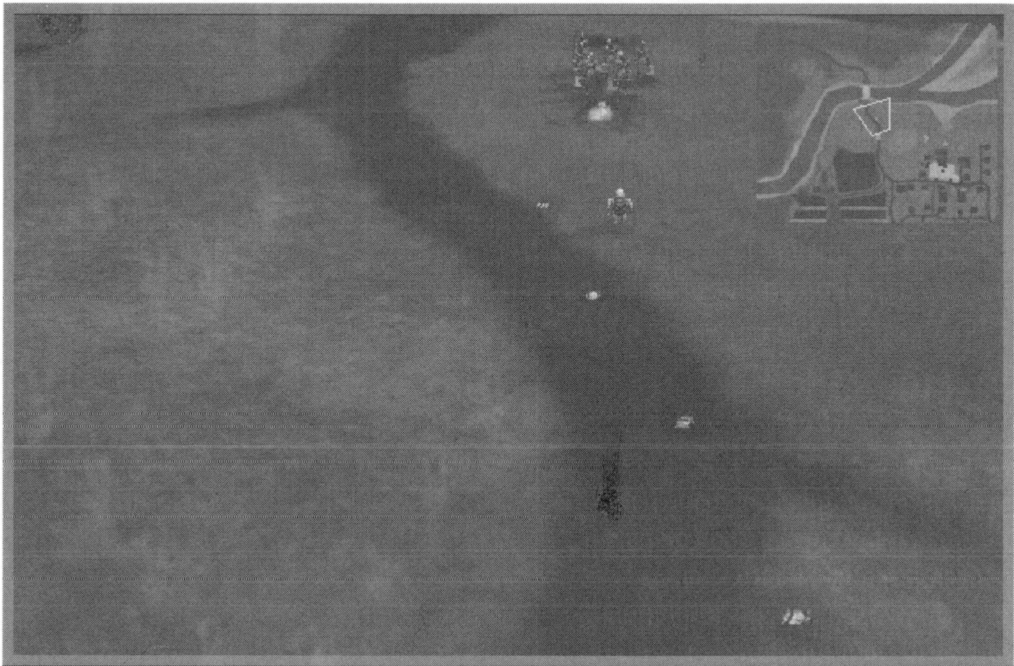

FIGURE 3.2: Taking the time to lay your Satchel Charges out before the battle begins can make your life much easier.

punch, which is always a blast to watch. Once all your units are in place, have your Dwarf start throwing Explosive Bottles at the Thrall. The Thrall will be somewhat less than impressed, and will start after you with a vengeance; keep lobbing bottles at them as you back away.

Keep firing and backing away until all the Thrall are nothing more than dog chow. The Dwarf is more than capable of taking out all the Thrall, as seen in Figure 3.3, but if the Thrall are closing on your

TIP

Use this first scenario to become proficient with the Dwarf's Satchel Charges. They can be laid on the ground and used as extra explosive packs. If you can throw an Explosive Bottle near a Satchel Charge when the enemy is near, the resulting blast will take out anything nearby. It's like having a double Explosive Bottle.

FIGURE 3.3: If managed properly, the Dwarf can single-handedly take out the Thrall as they come off the bridge.

Dwarf, just pull some of the Warriors (the ones waiting on the road) up to finish off any advancing Undead.

Don't get too comfortable after you've taken care of the first group of Thrall (the ones that came out of the river), because the fun is just beginning. You'll now be faced with an onslaught of reinforcements that will include a group of Soulless. The Soulless will quickly target your Dwarf with their spears. If you're not careful they can have you calling for the MASH unit in a hurry. This is where those Satchel Charges can come in extra handy.

You're gonna have to make every shot count, so try to explode a Satchel Charge when there's a crowd of enemies nearby. One shot can often take out five or six bits of Undead trash. By the time the Soulless move within range of your Warriors, you've probably already taken out the bulk of the Undead forces, so you can send the Warriors forth to teach them a lesson. Don't worry if some of the Warriors tangle with the remaining Thrall before they move forward; they can handle themselves well against the Thrall. It's also a good idea at this point to bring in your Archers to pick off any stragglers.

As soon as the second throng of Thrall are wasted, the Soulless will begin to retreat, and you will soon hear the announcement that you've won the scenario. Congratulations, enjoy the moment because it only gets harder.

TIP

The general strategy outlined in the paragraphs above requires the proper use of the Dwarf to take out the majority of the enemy Thrall. In fact, the Dwarf will often end up killing nearly all of the Thrall if he is well managed. If you have trouble operating your Dwarf, the next best alternative is to fight the Thrall from a distance with your Archers, occasionally using your Warriors whenever the Thrall get close. This, however, is a much more costly (and risky) method.

Blow by Blow

- Get the two Warriors that are on the bridge off the bridge and move them quickly to the other group of Warriors are waiting on the road to the south.
- Group your units into two main clusters. One bunch of Warriors (the ones on the road), and one bunch of Archers and Warriors. You can then make the Dwarf a single group, and the Warriors from the bridge another group.
- Move the Archers/Warriors group into position in the open area on the right side of the road, and move the two Warriors from the bridge to the left of the road.

Continued on next page

Continued from previous page

- Move your Dwarf close to the bridge and lay Satchel Charges in a line leading away from the bridge. (This is optional but provides a much bigger bang for your buck and makes your job easier.)
- Set the Archer/Warrior group to attack the eastern set of Ghols, and engage the two Warriors in the west to attack the leftmost Ghols.
- Use the Dwarf to lob Explosive Bottles at the Thrall guarding the bridge. As the Thrall advance, be sure to pull the Dwarf back while still firing bottles. You should be able to blow up all the Thrall with this technique without taking any damage. After the Thrall are toast, get ready for the next wave.
- When the second onslaught of Thrall cross the bridge (with the Soulless backing them up), you can again use the Dwarf to lob explosives at them. Lure them over the Satchel Charges, and then let it rip! You should be able to take out multiple Thrall with just one shot.
- When you've thinned out two-thirds of the Thrall, move the Warriors that have been waiting on the road up to take out the Soulless. The Soulless will scatter as soon as they see the whites of your Warriors' eyes. In the game they may be purple, but when it comes to hand-to-hand combat, the Soulless are yellow.
- Continue to thin out the enemy ranks, and bring in the Archer/Warrior group from the right side of the map. You'll win eventually. Congratulations on your first victory!

A TRAITOR'S GRAVE

The ratfink Mayor of Otter Ferry is the scumbag you seek in this scenario. Mr. Mayor is about to betray 60,000 of your fellow troops, so it's critical that you deal with the situation before your troops are stabbed in the back. This time around it won't be a war of attrition; instead you'll have to use your wits more than your brawn. You begin with only a group of Archers, a Dwarf, and a Journeyman sitting directly in the middle of the map and surrounded on all sides. You'll have to slip through the enemy positions in order to find and assassinate the Mayor, who'll be heavily protected as he marches off the map. Timing and careful resource management are very important if you want to win this scenario.

MISSION OBJECTIVE

Get past the extensive Undead forces and personal guards and assassinate the Mayor before he escapes off the map.

YOUR GUYS

This is one of those scenarios where the units you have are very limited, thus forcing you to use your wits more than your might. Your Archers and Dwarf are your weapons. Your Journeyman will be used primarily to heal damaged units and also serves as a decoy. Here's what you get:

-  Archers
-  Journeyman
-  Dwarf

THE EVIL HORDE

There are plenty of nasty Undead villains running around this map, but the biggest threat to your troops are the roving bands of Ghols that circle the map. Ghols can strike quickly and take out your Archers before you know it. The Soulless are the second most deadly units to worry about, and the Thrall are merely a lumbering menace. A circle of Thrall guards the Mayor, making it hard to hit the Mayor with arrows from afar. Here's what they get:

-  Thrall
-  Ghols
- Soulless
- Mayor

LAY OF THE LAND

You must get close to the stone in this scenario.This is where the Mayor waits until you get close and force him to run. The Mayor will often attempt to escape on the path that runs from the stone up to the north (through the forest). The surrounding forest hides many a Thrall, and it also makes it very difficult to hit the Mayor from afar as he travels up the path. The desert area that lies to the south is not of any particular importance except that if you approach the Stone from the north, the Mayor will flee across the desert rather than up north.

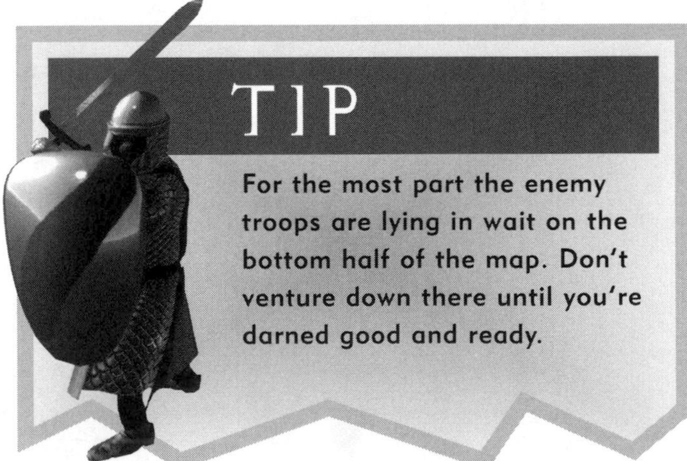

TIP

For the most part the enemy troops are lying in wait on the bottom half of the map. Don't venture down there until you're darned good and ready.

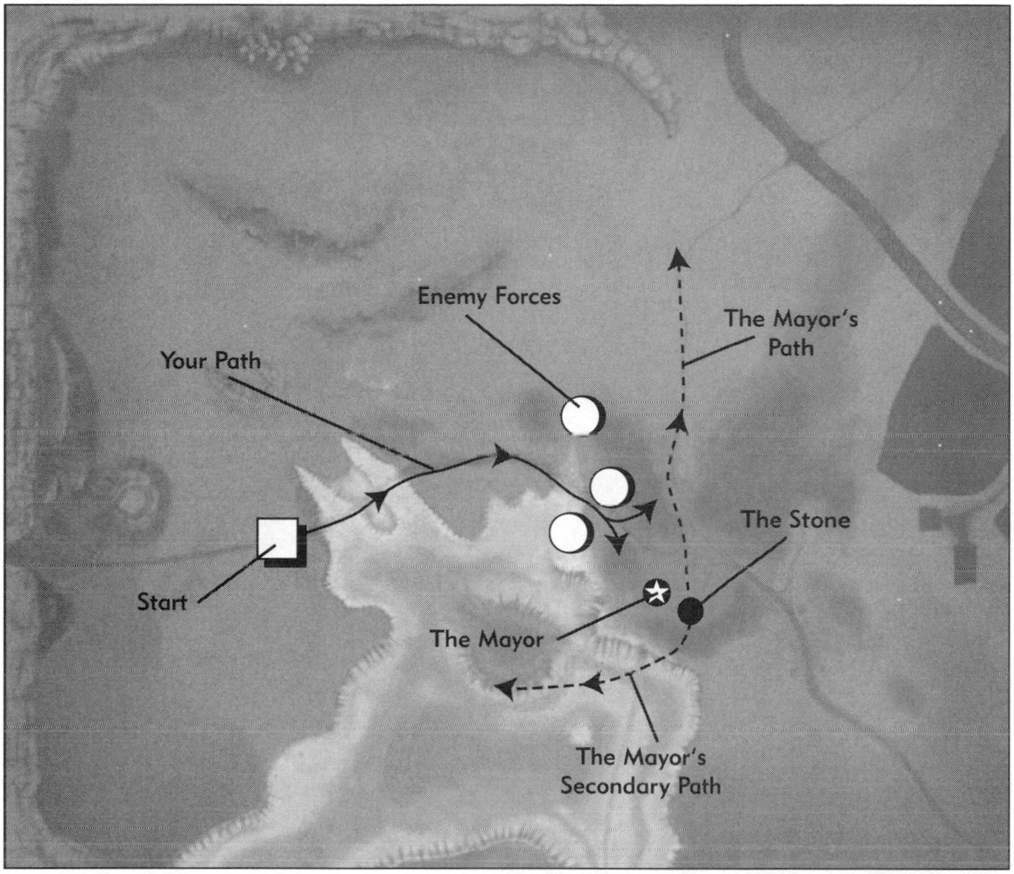

Enemy Forces
The Mayor's Path
Your Path
The Stone
Start
The Mayor
The Mayor's Secondary Path

BATTLE PLANS

You start with all your forces together in the middle of the map. Take your troops and follow the Villager, but proceed very slowly. If you advance too quickly, you'll end up with all the enemies attacking you at once. You want to move your troops forward just fast enough to have the enemy notice you a few units at a time. This way

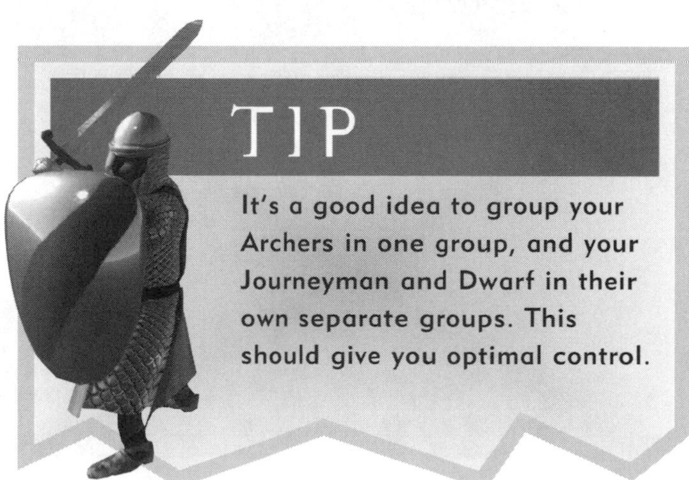

you can thin out the Undead ranks without having your Archers hacked to death by Ghols all at once.

The stone lies just southeast of your location, but don't be tempted to head in that direction. Instead, continue inching east (right) until you come face-to-face with the main group of Thrall and Soulless. This is the tricky part: advance your Dwarf and park him behind a tree that's between him and the enemy Soulless. If you play your cards right, the Soulless will see the Dwarf as the main threat, and throw everything they've got at the tree, as shown in Figure 3.4.

While the Soulless are occupied, you can use your Archers to take them out one at a time. As soon as the Thrall get close to the Dwarf, make a run for it. Mop up the Thrall with your Archers and Dwarf. If any Thrall get close to your troops, you can

FIGURE 3.4: Hiding your Dwarf can trick the Soulless into firing at the tree. Cheap, but handy.

use your Journeyman to heal the Thrall to death. This battle is tough, but it can be won, even on the higher skill levels.

Once you've smoked those Undead losers, you'll need to follow the Villager until he spots the Mayor (near the stone shown in Figure 3.5). You will immediately have several Ghols come in from the left flank, so use a combination of your Dwarf and Archers to take them out before they can do damage.

After you've taken out the Ghols, move northeast toward the path to intercept the Mayor (who's surrounded by Thrall, as shown in Figure 3.6). At this point the Thrall will start coming out of the woods hoping to rip you to pieces. Unfortunately there's really no easy way to deal with the Thrall, and it's impossible to kill them all. The best thing to do is just gun for the Mayor and kick his butt all the way back to Otter Ferry. Once you've killed the Mayor, you need to get away from the enemy (a short distance) to win the scenario. All of your units are faster than the Thrall, so it should be easy to get away.

TIP

Jason Regier Tip: This is a little cheat that Jason pointed out that can make this scenario cheaper. Since the Dwarf is fairly maneuverable, and the Soulless will try to lead their targets with spears, you can do what I call the Dwarf Juke. To do this, wait for the Soulless to get ready to throw, then have your Dwarf turn around and run the other way. Weave your Dwarf back and forth as you approach (or run from) the Soulless, and they will usually overthrow and miss.

FIGURE 3.5: This is where the Mayor is hiding out.

FIGURE 3.6: The Thrall who surround the Mayor can make it difficult to sink an arrow in the traitor's heart.

TIP

Jason Regier Tip: After winning the initial battle and killing the Ghols that charge at you from the left side of the map, run your Dwarf to the path where the Mayor will try to make his escape. Then move your remaining troops forward so that the Mayor begins his escape. The Dwarf can then kill the Mayor with one or two carefully lobbed Explosive Bottles. This method eliminates the difficult chase through the forest.

Blow by Blow

- Group your Archers into a bunch of six. Then group your Dwarf and Journeyman separately as individual groups. This will afford you easy control when time is tight.
- Move all your troops slowly toward the east (follow the Villager), being careful not to attract all of the enemy at once.

Continued on next page

Continued from previous page

- Ghols will begin to surround you. Move your Archers to take them out one at a time. If the Ghols get too close to your Archers, use your Dwarf to introduce them to thermodynamics.
- Move a little closer and waste the Soulless with your Archers while you blow the crud out of the advancing Thrall.
- After you've made it through this tough battle, use your Journeyman to heal any wounded units before you move on.
- Continue to move toward the location north of the stone. You will soon see the Mayor guarded by six Thrall, as well as a pack of three Ghols heading down from the left side of the map. Deal with the Ghols first.
- You will also likely see many new Undead units heading straight for you. Use your Archers to take out the Mayor. As soon as the Mayor is dead and you've moved away from the enemy, you win.

THE SIEGE OF MADRIGAL

The name of the game in this scenario is diversion. Your job is to annihilate the Undead force on the other side of the bridge, and then take control of the town of Comfort. If you survive this, you must get the attention of the large Undead force on the edge of the map and make them follow you back to the bridge. If you think the previous scenarios were rough, you ain't seen nothing yet baby! This will be your toughest test yet, so save often, and follow these instructions.

MISSION OBJECTIVE

Defeat the forces on the other side of the bridge, and then move into the town of Comfort. Grab the attention of the main enemy force, and lead them back to the bridge without losing all of your units.

YOUR GUYS

This time around you have a pretty decent force at your fingertips; however, you're going up against a couple of very large Undead armies. You have two sizeable groups of Warriors and a decent bunch of Archers to give you a long-range threat. There's no Journeyman to heal your wounds, so you'll have to fight carefully. Here's what you get:

- Warriors (two groups)
- Archers

THE EVIL HORDE

You name it, they've got it. You'll see every Undead unit you've encountered so far plus a new unit, the Wight, and he's a real blast. Perhaps the most annoying feature of the Undead forces in the Siege of Madrigal is that there are lots of them. You'll need to use very solid tactics to grab a W in the win/loss column on this one. Here's what they get:

- Soulless
- Thrall
- Ghols
- Wights

LAY OF THE LAND

This map is similar to Crow's Bridge in that there is only one way for you to cross the river dividing the territory. Unfortunately, Undead units, like Thrall, Soulless, and Wights, can all cross the river without using the bridge. This can be frustrating, but for the most part you don't have to worry about it until late in the scenario. Just past the bridge lies the sleepy town of Comfort, where you'll be heading after you knock off the army defending the bridge. In Comfort, you'll have to keep your sanity while one Wight after another tries to pump you full of disease or blow you to pieces. The key to this scenario is the bridge. You must use it to your advantage when fighting the first army; if you can do so, the rest is in the bag.

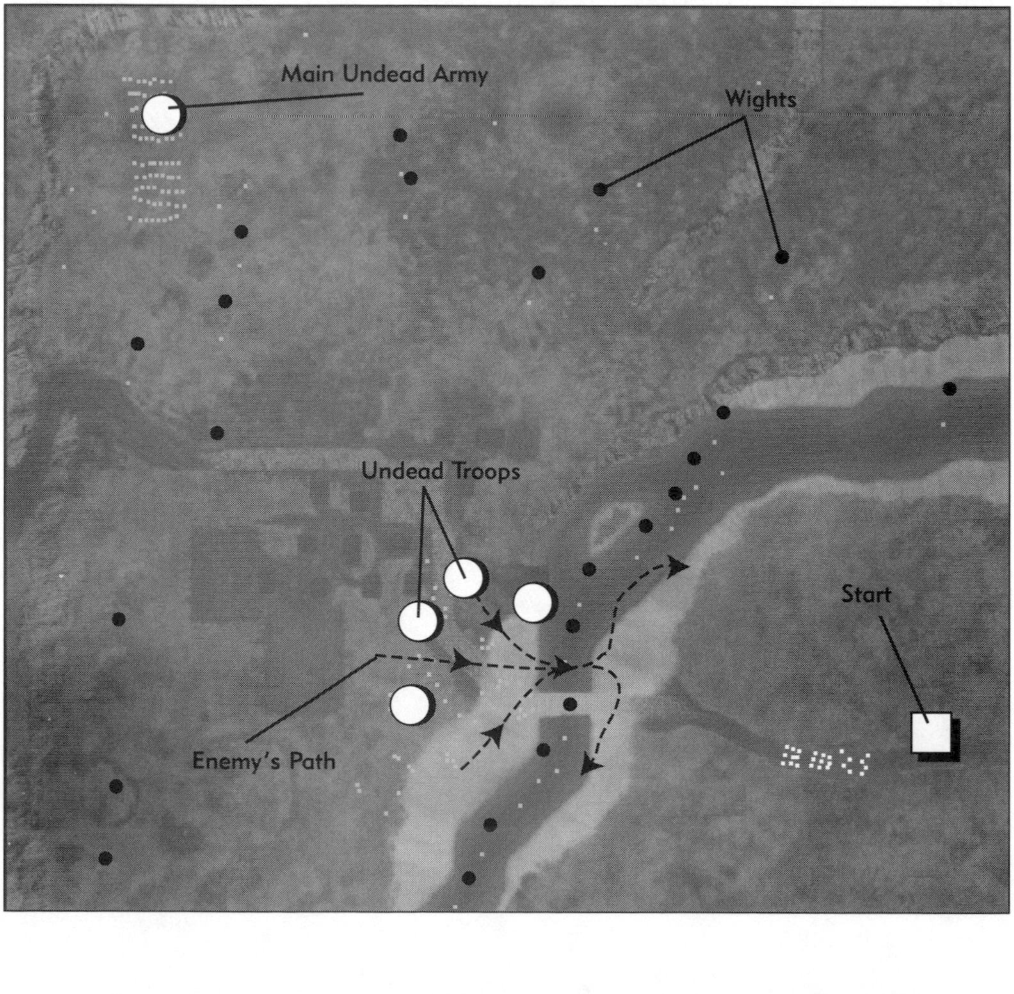

BATTLE PLANS

You begin the Siege of Madrigal with your troops approaching the bridge that spans the river near Comfort. Before you're able to get to the bridge and close the door on enemy troops filing over the river, approximately a dozen Ghols will spill across the bridge. This force will divide into three groups: one on either side of your force and a small group that guards the bridge. At first none of the Ghols will have the guts to come out and fight, so you don't have to worry about them if you don't want to (for now). A few arrow shots will send the Ghols on the bridge running back home to mommy.

> **WARNING**
>
> Dealing with Ghols: Those nasty (and, in my opinion, gutless) Ghols will not actually try to rush you unless they sense a weakness. A few Archers left exposed or maybe a lone Dwarf walking through the woods are the usual targets for Ghols. However, Ghols are famous for looping behind you in groups, and then attacking when the main Undead force hits you from the front. To prevent this, use your Archers (backed up by a few Warriors) to hunt down errant Ghols.

After sending the Ghols on the bridge packing, the best thing to do is put a small force of Warriors on either side of the bridge to protect your flank. Then, just to be safe, move a couple of Warriors to guard your backside as well. As you're setting this up, you'll notice a small group of Soulless have come up the bridge and are firing spears at you. You can send a couple of Warriors up the bridge to distract the Soulless while your Archers turn the Undead spear-throwers into pink dust.

Now that you've finished with the Soulless on the bridge, move four Archers to the area to the left of the bridge (on the riverbank) and four Archers to the right of the bridge (see Figure 3.7). These two groups will provide your air support once the enemy

FIGURE 3.7: Setting up your Archers like this is a good way to lay a little hurt on the Undead when they rush the bridge.

rushes the bridge. Remember, keep some Warriors nearby to support the Archers in case the Ghols decide to rush (and they will).

Now move up a group of five or six Warriors onto the bridge, and keep inching them forward until they get close enough to provoke the Undead attack. Once the Undead rushes your position, fall back a little. Let them try to cross the bridge while your Archers take out their Soulless from across the water. Because they see the Warriors on the bridge as the greatest threat, the Soulless will generally concentrate on them and leave your Archers to escape relatively untouched. Expect the Ghols behind you to attack now, but don't worry, because you've got some Warriors waiting for just such an attack.

As the battle rages, and your Warriors hack the Thrall to death on the bridge, a few Thrall will try to be sneaky and walk through the water to cross the river. You may not realize they're coming until you see their heads popping out of the water (see Figure 3.8) as they approach your Archers. Again, this is a good time to use those Warriors near your Archers. Once the main enemy force has been waxed, you can cross the bridge with the remainder of your troops and take out any straggling Undead. If all has gone well, you should still have four or five Archers and at least

FIGURE 3.8: The Undead commanders will try to sneak some Thrall across the river to take out your Archers, so be ready for them.

as many Warriors left over for the next stage.

Now move your troops over to the town of Comfort. You'll now see a series of enemy units approaching you, one unit from each direction. Meet the Wights. The Wights are walking bombs that want nothing more than to get close to you and blow the stuffing out of your troops. Use your Archers to take out the Wights while you keep your other units at a safe distance, as shown in Figure 3.9. The Puss Packets

TIP

Dealing with Wights in the Siege of Madrigal: First, you can send a unit on a suicide mission to protect the rest of your troops. However, if you do this you'll run out of units very quickly. Second, you can use your Archers to take out the Wights from a distance. This is the preferred method, and just so you know, it takes three arrows to blow up a Wight.

FIGURE 3.9: Use your Archers to hit the Wights from a distance, or the resulting explosion will damage (or kill) your units.

the Wights throw outward (and upward) when they explode can do a great deal of damage to your units, including paralyzing them, so stay clear.

After you've taken care of most of the Wights, take three or four Warriors and head to the top of the map. As soon as you see a *major* enemy force moving toward you, turn and run for the bridge. At the same time, keep your Archers near the bridge as backup in case your Warriors get killed. The Undead like to hide Wights in the river, so always keep an eye out for them there. Once you get your Warriors (or Archers, if that's all you have left) back to the bridge with the Undead army chasing you, you win! Now, was that so hard? Well, OK, I guess it was.

Blow by Blow

- Set your units into three groups: two equal Warrior groups and one Archer group. Although you won't be using them very much, later on in the scenario they can come in handy to regroup your units.
- Move your Warriors into defensive positions around the mouth of the bridge so that the Ghols that made it across can't attack you from the sides or from behind.
- Take out the Ghols and Soulless that come up to defend the bridge (initially).
- Move your Archers into two equal groups on either side of the bridge (along the riverbank). This will enable you to pick off the Soulless when the Undead rush the bridge.
- Move a group of five or six Warriors over the bridge to trigger the Undead attack. Then fall back to your side of the bridge and get your Archers ready.
- Use your Archers to take out the Soulless across the river, while your Warriors deal with the Thrall on the bridge and the Ghols behind you.
- Cross the bridge and finish off the Undead army.
- Move into Comfort (the town), and prepare for a new kind of assault.
- When the Wights come at you, use your Archers to blow them up before they can get close. A Wight will blow up if hit with an arrow three times.

Continued on next page

Continued from previous page

- Move your Archers back toward the bridge and keep them looking for Wights. Then move your Warriors up toward the top of the map. When they get close enough to see the enemy army, get them running back toward the bridge. Beware of Ghols chasing you. However, a few Warriors can easily handle two or three Ghols.
- Get back to the bridge and cross it. You win. Whew!

NOTE

If you don't have any Archers left, you're in trouble. You have to try to keep away from the Wights while still running up to get the main Undead army's attention. You then have to again avoid the Wights, and the Undead army chasing you, as you head back to the bridge.

4

The Plot Thickens

OK, you've cut your teeth and taken your licks in the previous three scenarios, so you're ready for some more challenging scenarios, right? You'd better be, because the next couple of levels are going to test you even more than you've already been pushed. Homecoming is the most difficult scenario so far. It calls for tactical ability and a little strategy. Flight from Covenant is a test of wits and patience. It can also be one of the more difficult scenarios you'll face if you don't know what to do. However, if you follow my directions you'll do just fine. In both these levels you are outnumbered, so again you'll have to use your Archers and Dwarves to their maximum ability to squeak by.

HOMECOMING

You must now travel through a World Knot (a teleport between two worldly locations) to an area near Covenant. You have been instructed by one of Balor's old enemies to fight your way to the ruined city of Covenant where you will find and retrieve the Total Codex (a large book with special powers). Sadly, there are plenty of Undead standing guard in the ruins of Covenant, so you'll have to use your tactical savvy and iron will to emerge victorious. Follow me and you'll be able to scrape the Undead off your boots and send them back into the sludge holes they came from.

MISSION OBJECTIVE

Find the Total Codex, and then escape with it off the southeast edge of the map.

YOUR GUYS

Your units in Homecoming will beam onto the map through the World Knot. You will have Warriors, Archers, and even a couple of Dwarves at your disposal. Best of all, you'll have a Journeyman there to heal your most critical wounds. Here's what you get:

 Warriors

 Archers

 Dwarves

 Journeyman

THE EVIL HORDE

The Undead forces are similar to those you've seen before, but there's one new development in Homecoming. There are plenty of Ghols on this map, and they're very active in picking up the many unexploded Puss Packets that lie about the old battlefield in and around Covenant. Ghols toting Puss Packets should be dealt with carefully. Here's what they get:

 Soulless

 Ghols

 Thrall

LAY OF THE LAND

Your scenario begins with all of your units arriving through a World Knot located behind a very impressive amphitheater. This theater looks cool, but it can be deadly. Don't let your units get trapped inside with Soulless picking them off from around the high edges of the theater.

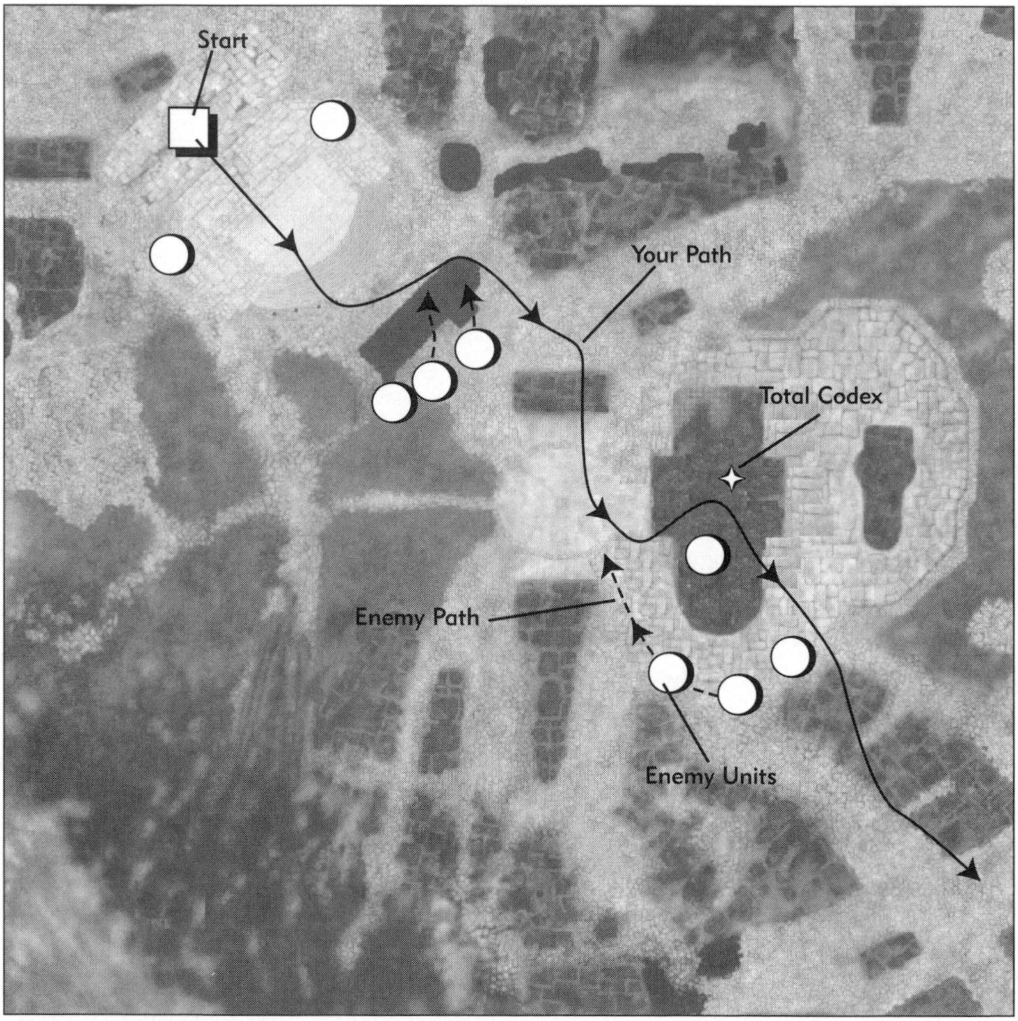

There are several pools of brown goop on this map. Despite their appearance, they have the same properties as water. So when a bunch of Thrall come at you

from across a sludge hole, be aware that your Explosive Bottles may not find their mark. The rest of the map is flat and dry (great for bottles), and the ruins of Covenant provide excellent cover for your troops once you advance on the city. One last warning though: this map is covered with unspent Puss Packets and Satchel Charges. Be careful where you're standing before you drop an Exploding Bottle nearby.

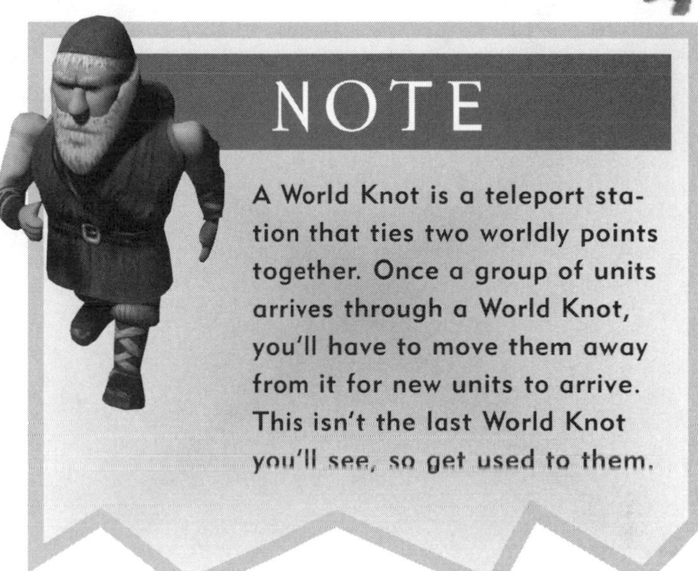

NOTE

A World Knot is a teleport station that ties two worldly points together. Once a group of units arrives through a World Knot, you'll have to move them away from it for new units to arrive. This isn't the last World Knot you'll see, so get used to them.

BATTLE PLANS

The Codex is relatively close; it lies near the bloodied bodies from a recent battle in the ruined city of Covenant. You can only pick up the Codex with a Dwarf or a Journeyman, so protect those units. It'll take patience and cunning to complete this scenario, but you have a decent force of good guys to help return the Undead to the ground. Your forces arrive in the scenario in bunches through the World Knot, as shown in Figure 4.1.

The first through the Knot will be your Warriors. I suggest you move these away from the Knot as soon as possible because Soulless scouts will be picking at them. The next group through will be your Archers and Dwarves. As soon as they come through, get them to start firing back at the Soulless. This will provide you the cushion you need to get set up. The last unit through the knot will be your Journeyman, and he is of double importance in this mission, so take good care of him.

Group your units together in any manner you like. My preference is to put the Archers together, the Dwarves together, and the Warriors in two separate groups. At this point you can move through the theater to the upper lip on the far side. You'll see a brown pond of sludge and some Ghols circling around.

Move your Archers forward a little, and soon you'll see a small Undead force of Soulless and Thrall approaching. The best thing to do is to move a few sacrificial Warriors out of the theater and toward the enemy troops. Then move your Archers just outside the theater on the slope leading down to the sludge pond. When the

FIGURE 4.1: Your units will arrive via this World Knot. Be sure to move units away from the knot after they arrive.

enemy begins its approach, use your Archers to take out the Soulless. Bring your Dwarves up to bomb the Thrall back into the Stone Age. Once this enemy force is eliminated, you're halfway there.

Ghols are a big problem in this scenario. They run around and pick up the Puss Packets that are strewn about from an earlier battle that was fought near Covenant. They'll then approach your troops (often your Archers) and throw their Puss Packets at them. This can cause you a lot of damage, so keep your Archers on the alert

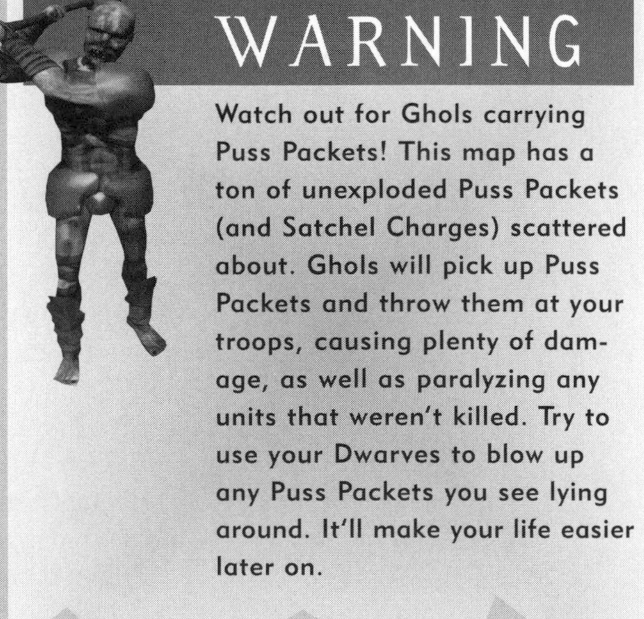

WARNING

Watch out for Ghols carrying Puss Packets! This map has a ton of unexploded Puss Packets (and Satchel Charges) scattered about. Ghols will pick up Puss Packets and throw them at your troops, causing plenty of damage, as well as paralyzing any units that weren't killed. Try to use your Dwarves to blow up any Puss Packets you see lying around. It'll make your life easier later on.

to take out any marauding Ghols. You can also use your Dwarves to blow up any Puss Packets you see lying around; if enemy troops are nearby, you can even use them to your advantage.

Now move your troops carefully toward the plaza (the circular brick area with the large statue in the middle). Group your remaining Warriors into one group, and bring them up along with your Archers and at least one Dwarf. As you approach Covenant you will see plenty of bodies in the area, as well as some Thrall that will not take notice of you until you get close or fire some arrows at them. As soon as you get close enough, a large group of Thrall and Soulless will approach from the south. You should be able to deal with them easily with just your Archers and Dwarves. Do the Dwarf Juke (described in detail in Chapter 3) to avoid getting stung by the Soulless' spears. If the Thrall get too close to your Archers or Dwarves, use your Warriors to clean up the area.

Now that the Undead have been cleansed from Covenant, you must find the Total Codex. It's usually lying amidst the body parts surrounding the ruins (see Figure 4.2). You may have to zoom in your view a little to see it clearly. You must now secure the Codex. Remember, only a Dwarf or Journeyman can pick it up; if

FIGURE 4.2: The Total Codex might be amongst other debris and therefore hard to spot, so be sure to check out the piles of dead bodies if you are having trouble.

you've lost those units, you cannot win this scenario. Pick up the Codex and head for the southeast corner of the map. You will meet a few guards, but they shouldn't pose any difficulties. Just beware of Ghols as you make your way off the map.

Blow by Blow

- Move your units off the World Knot to let more units arrive. Move your Warriors away from the theater to avoid getting sliced to ribbons by the Soulless scouts.
- Once your Archers arrive, get them firing on the Soulless (who will then scatter).
- Group your units into two groups of Warriors, one Archer group, and one Dwarf group (optional).
- Move through the theater taking out any Soulless and Ghols you come across.
- Sit on the upper lip of the theater (above the brown sludge pond). Then send a couple of Warriors down to draw in the Undead forces.
- Move to the plaza (the area with the big statue) and heal any units that need to be repaired.
- Move slowly toward Covenant, and have your Dwarves blow up any unexploded Puss Packets.
- Move far enough south to trigger the main Undead force to attack. Then take them out with your Dwarves and Archers, using your Warriors to finish off any Undead that get close.
- Grab the Total Codex (with a Dwarf or Journeyman) out of the rubble and head Southeast.
- Kill the guards in the southeast and exit the map. You win.

FLIGHT FROM COVENANT

Now you've done it. You've grabbed the Total Codex, but you still have to survive this scenario. In Flight from Covenant you have to make it past hordes of Undead soldiers en route to a secret tunnel that will get you safely away. You will probably lose more than 50 percent of your troops before you make it to the tunnel. (If you're like me, you'll lose 80 percent of your troops.)

MISSION OBJECTIVE

Flee from Covenant through the ruined city wall. Once outside the city, locate the hidden tunnel and escape through it with the Total Codex (which you retrieved in the last scenario). This means that you must get your Journeyman to the tunnel.

YOUR GUYS

Again, you've got a healthy assortment of units to deal with in this scenario: two sizable groups of Warriors, a nice bunch of Archers, a couple Dwarves, and even a Journeyman. This should be a cakewalk with troops like this, right? Wrong. This is what you get:

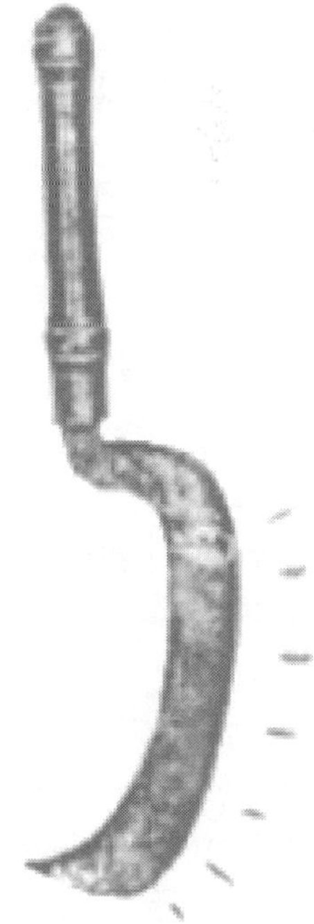

-  Dwarves
-  Warriors
-  Archers
-  Journeyman

THE EVIL HORDE

The Undead minions have a motto in this scenario: more is not enough. They seem to have an infinite number of Thrall, Wights, and Myrmidons on the map. This is what they get:

- Thrall (and plenty of 'em)
- Myrmidons (if you even see these guys, you're dead)
- Wights
- Soulblighter (he's just an observer)

LAY OF THE LAND

There are several breaks in the Covenant city wall. Unfortunately for you, all of them have large mobs of Thrall guarding the exits. Although it may not have been one of your first choices, the marshy area on the left side of the map will provide the best

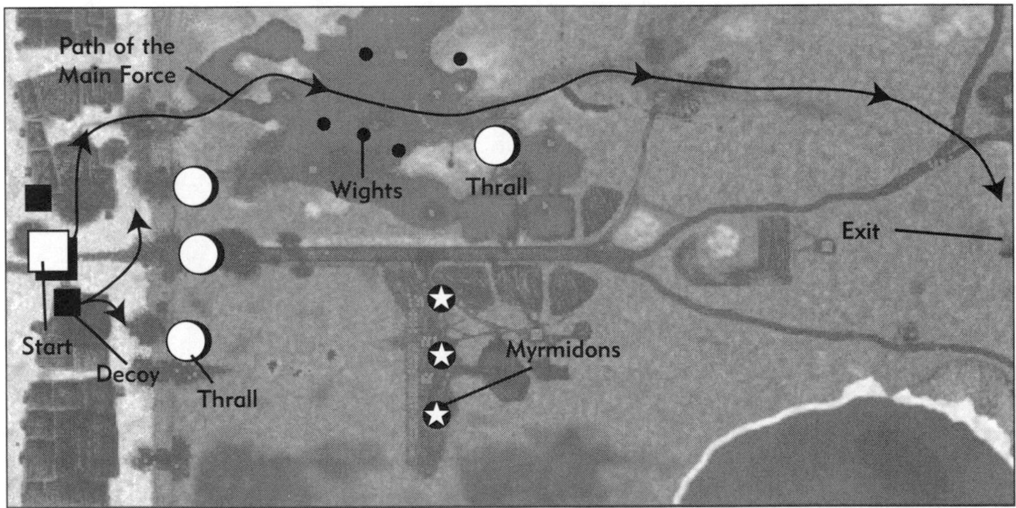

escape route for your troops. In the marsh you will avoid the main enemy force, and the wetness will help to cushion the blow of the Wights when they approach you.

The road that runs down the middle of the map should be avoided at all costs. You can see why in the above graphic. Normally we don't show the enemy units

(represented by dots) on these maps, but in this case I thought it would speak volumes. Note that if you follow the central road, you'll meet a very, very large group of Myrmidons and Thrall. If you meet up with these Undead units, you WILL be finished for sure, so stay as far away as possible. The tunnel that will take you out of this level is at the back of the map, right between the two forks in the road. The tunnel can only be seen from a couple of angles; it's easy to miss.

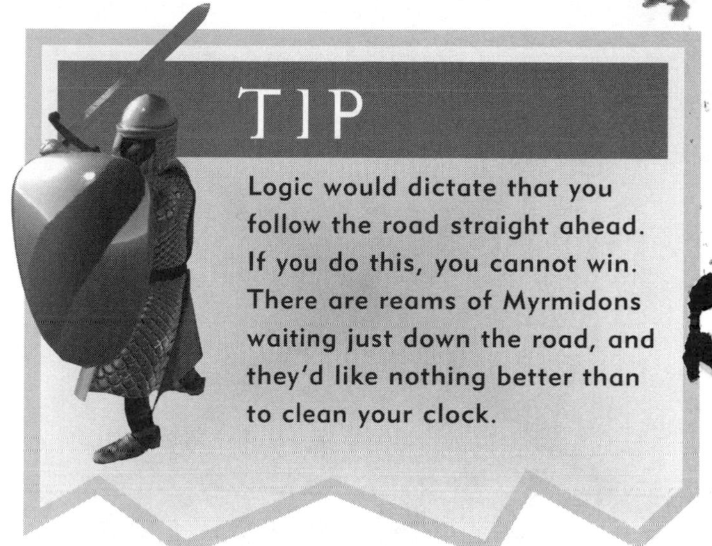

TIP

Logic would dictate that you follow the road straight ahead. If you do this, you cannot win. There are reams of Myrmidons waiting just down the road, and they'd like nothing better than to clean your clock.

BATTLE PLANS

This scenario begins with your troops moving slightly forward, and then stopping just before the broken walls of Covenant. There are three main holes in front of you, each with a large group of Thrall heading straight for you. Your first instinct might be to start madly throwing down Satchel Charges and preparing your Archers to try to pick off the Thrall as they advance, but this is not the way to win big. You can survive the onslaught this way if you're very careful, use your Dwarves perfectly, and get a little lucky. However, you'll be left with only a handful of badly damaged units. Have hope, because there's a better way.

The other option for surviving the first onslaught of enemy troops is to create a decoy force of six or seven Warriors and maybe one Archer. This force can spread out and get the attention of many of the advancing Thrall (see Figure 4.3). In the meantime, group the rest of your units together and make a run for the leftmost opening out of the city. You should be able to move right past the Thrall that came through the opening and move through it yourself. You'll have a bunch of Thrall on your tail this whole time but they should number only about one-quarter to one-third of the total Thrall that initially attacked you. The units you left behind will divert the other Thrall. Out of sight, out of mind.

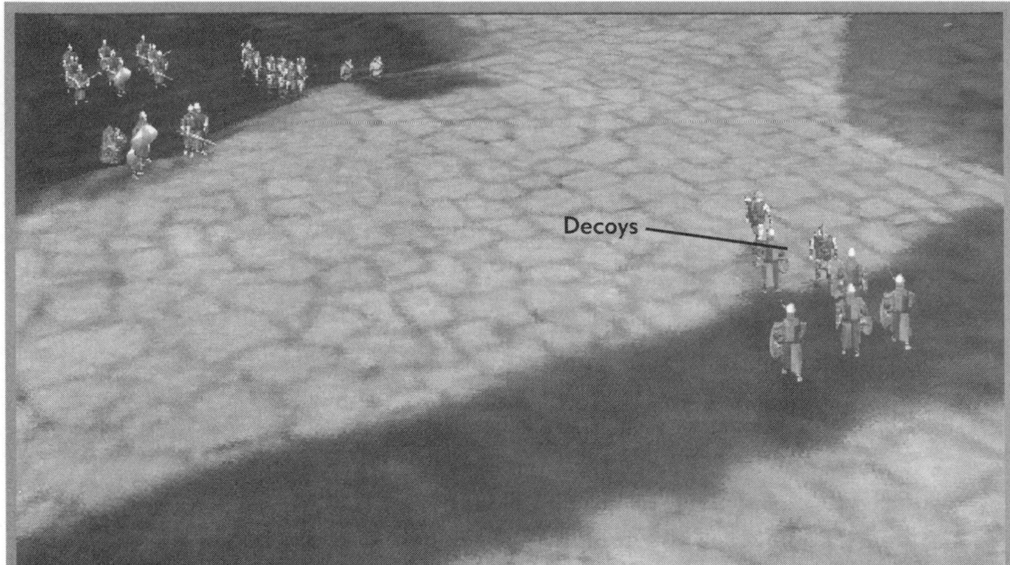

FIGURE 4.3: Break off a few units from your main force to act as a decoy for the tons of Thrall that will be pouring through the wall.

You can take out all the Thrall following your troops at the same time if you show a little patience. Once on dry land, many of the Wights will fall in line with the Thrall and join the chase. If you can hit just one of these Wights with an Explosive Bottle or with three arrows, the resulting chain of explosions will dispose of all the enemy units for you.

As you move along into the marsh, you'll occasionally need to let a couple of arrows fly at the Wights as they approach you from all angles. You need to move toward dry land before you can take out the pesky Thrall that still follow you. Stay along the left side of the map and keep heading north. Use your Dwarf to take out as many Thrall as possible as you move along. As you approach the back of the map, you need to move toward the middle area where the secret tunnel is. Have a look at Figure 4.4 to see the best path to follow in this scenario.

As you approach the tunnel, you'll come across a group of Thrall with a few Myrmidons. Try to get a couple of lucky bottle shots from your Dwarves and make a run for the tunnel. Don't waste time; the enemy will soon be *right* behind you. Protect your Journeyman in this scenario; he's the one you have to get through the tunnel safely.

FIGURE 4.4: The tunnel can be hard to see from all angles, so orbit around the general area until you spot it.

Blow by Blow

- Divide your units into two groups: one with five or six Warriors and one Archer, and another (your main group) with all the rest of your units.
- Move the main group off to the leftmost exit while being careful to not get caught in a bunch of Thrall. The Thrall may come close to you, but all of your units are faster, so make a run for it.
- Move into the marsh. Keep moving to stay ahead of the Thrall behind you, but also watch out for Wights coming toward you. Use your Archers to take out the Wights.

Continued on next page

Continued from previous page

- Move up onto dry land at the end of the marsh.
- When the Thrall exit the marsh, bomb them into the Stone Age with your Dwarves.
- Keep moving along the left side and head toward the back of the map.
- Once you're far enough along, move toward the tunnel, all the while keeping an eye out for errant Wights and roving Thrall.
- Get your Journeyman and any other units you have into the tunnel as fast as you can.

5

Into the Cold

You're no longer in the early part of *Myth,* so you can't expect to be treated like a beginner anymore. Nope, the folks at Bungie have got a few missions that will push your abilities to their limits. Worst of all, they do it in the cold and hostile environment of the snowlands. You can look forward to having your Explosive Bottles fizzle in the snow with Thrall marching on your position and licking their partially decomposed lips. Depending on Dwarves in Bagrada is a ticket to death; on the other hand, you *must* depend on Dwarves in the Challenging Stage if you want to defeat the 100 Soulless that swoop down on you. No matter what, when you finish these three scenarios, you're gonna be a better *Myth* player; though you may have aged 10 years in the process.

FORCE TEN FROM STONEHEIM

This is your first trip into cold, snow-covered lands. The climate doesn't actually affect gameplay in any way other than that Explosive Bottles have a much greater chance of snuffing out instead of blowing the pants off the enemy. The objective of Force Ten is to destroy one of the four World Knot pylons (purple things), thereby preventing any more nasties from ruining your frosty Friday. This World Knot lies a fair hike away and, dag nab it, it's defended very heavily! There'll be plenty of hack 'n slash for you on this one, baby.

MISSION OBJECTIVE

Destroy one of the World Knot pylons, thereby securing the western side of the Couldspine Mountains. If you lose all your Dwarves, your mission is over. You need at least one Dwarf to detonate the Satchel Charges that will destroy the pylon.

YOUR GUYS

If there's one thing lacking in Force Ten, it's hand-to-hand combat units. You've been left downright vulnerable in this scenario, but what you don't have in brawn, you make up for in finesse. Use your Archers and Dwarves carefully, and this level can be a cakewalk. Here's what you get:

- Dwarves (at least eight)
- Archers
- Berserks (only a handful)

THE EVIL HORDE

There's nothing fancy about the Undead slimebags in this level. You're gonna face what you're used to: Soulless, Thrall, and Ghols, with a Wight or two thrown in just for good measure. As usual, there's plenty of them, so use your Dwarves to blow the crud out of them. Here's what they get:

- Soulless
- Thrall (in mass)
- Ghols (only a handful, but annoying)
- Wight

LAY OF THE LAND

This map (like many you've seen so far) is divided by a river. Although the river is ice-covered, it's not passable except for in two areas. The first area (in the middle of the map) is the suggested way to get across the river. It is heavily guarded, whereas the second area is not. However, the second area (in the south by the waterfall) makes positioning your troops for attack a little more difficult, and you face a greater risk of being flanked (in other words, squashed).

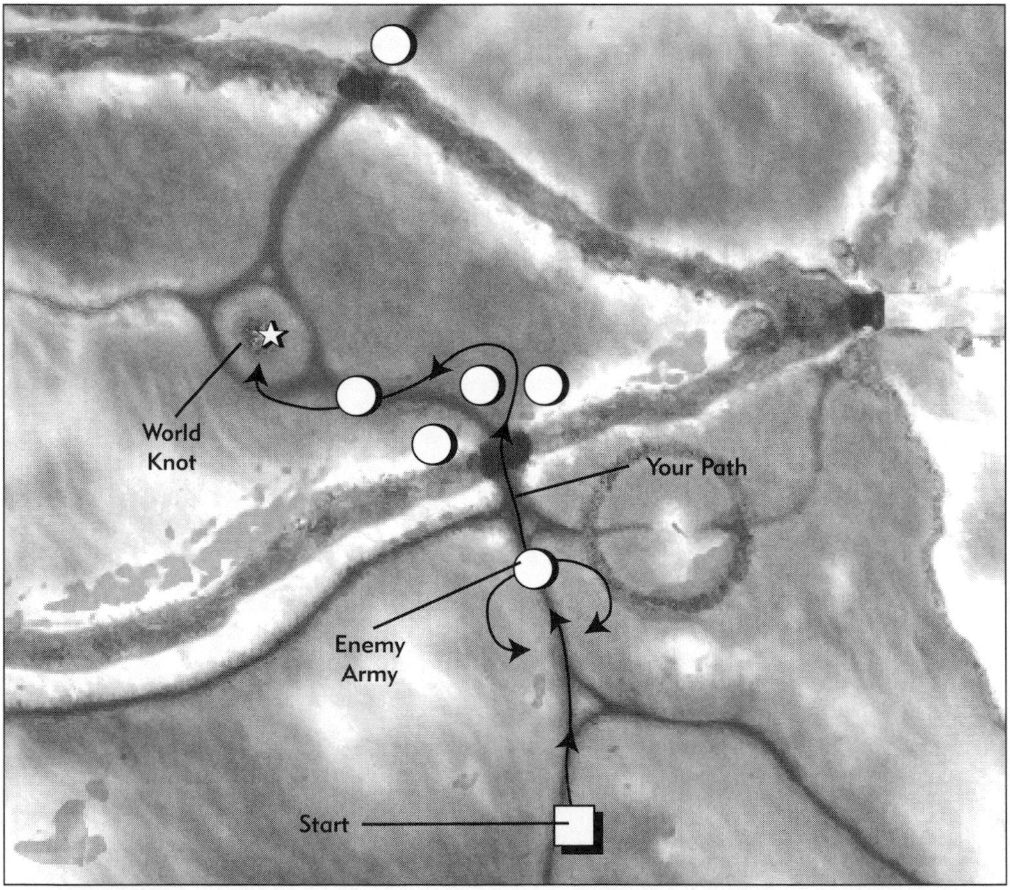

The snow does not cover the entire map, so you can use your Dwarves confidently in most places. Just remember that around the river the Explosive Bottles are hit-and-miss, and they will not work in heavily snow-covered areas. There are plenty of trees on this map as well. Use them as cover from the advancing Soulless. Finally, there's a

monument to the right of the main road, but it has no real significance in this scenario (in case you were interested).

WARNING

The frozen river looks passable, but the ice is too thin. You can pass anywhere where there is no ice.

BATTLE PLANS

You begin this scenario in the middle of the road with a bunch of Pilgrims, who are traveling to visit a shrine. This is going to sound cruel, but the Pilgrims are expendable. Yep, you can let them die their horrible deaths at the hands of the Ghols if you'd like, or you can pull a few Berserks out of your ranks to help protect them. It's up to you. You should group your units into Berserks, Archers, and two groups of four Dwarves.

Keep your groups of Dwarves away from each other, because if even one bottle goes off accidentally, the resulting chain reaction can end your scenario before it even gets started. Check out Figure 5.1 to see what I mean.

FIGURE 5.1: Watch your Dwarves carefully and keep them side by side. Otherwise, they tend to throw bottles like this, and I think you can see where this is headed.

Now move your troops down the road straight ahead of you (east), a small distance at a time. Soon you will come up against an enemy army. Before they have a chance to rush you, get into a formation with your Archers in the middle and the two Dwarf groups on either side (see Figure 5.2). Have the Berserks hang back a bit until they're needed.

As the enemy approaches, have your Archers shoot at the Soulless, while your Dwarves come up and lob Explosive Bottles eight at a time toward the advancing Thrall. It's really a sight to behold, all those Thrall parts flying through the air with the greatest of ease, but I digress. I need to stress again that when you have three or more Dwarves together, you must keep them in a parallel line to the enemy. This way there's no chance that a Dwarf in the back will lob a bottle that will blow the tar out of a Dwarf in the front. If you need proof of this, take a look at Figure 5.2 again.

Once that group of enemy is toasted, move up to within a short distance of the river. You'll see that there's a pretty healthy force of Undead waiting for you, and that's not anywhere near all of them. By now the Pilgrims are enjoying their stay at

FIGURE 5.2: This formation is an excellent way to deal with all the enemies you'll face in this scenario. The Dwarves are the "hammers" and your Archers are the "anvils."

the stone monument under the protection of your Berserks, or they've been horribly mutilated by roving bands of Ghols. Either way, you're going to have to keep an eye out for the pack of Ghols that (I promise you) is behind your forces. The way to save your hide is simply to always keep a couple of Berserks behind your main force. They'll catch any attack that comes from the rear.

To lure the enemy across the river, you'll need to get your Archers wet. Move them into the middle of the river and open fire on the Undead (preferably the Soulless). When the Undead army starts to approach, run like heck back to shore. Move your Archers right back, but not so far that the Undead troops turn around. Then bring up your eight Dwarves (four on each side) and bomb the living daylights out of everything that steps ashore. Expect to see some Ghols make a run at your Dwarves on the right side of your formation. Keep a couple of Berserks ready to take them down. Heck, if you need the extra troops, pull them off the Pilgrim protection detail—what have those Pilgrims ever done for you?

You should still have the bulk of your Archers, a few Berserks, and at least three or four Dwarves left at your disposal. Cross the river now and move up on the shore (to the right) to get your breath before attacking the next group of Undead. There should still be two main groups of Soulless and Thrall ahead of you to the north, so get ready to have a little fun before blowing up the World Knot. Move your Archers up to attack the group on the left, and set the Archers to hit the Soulless. At the same time, move a pair of Berserks up to attack the Soulless in the right formation. The Undead will initially run from the Berserks, as shown in Figure 5.3, but then they'll turn and fight. If you're quick, you can often take out three or four Soulless and still get one of your Berserks back to safety before the enemy bears down on you.

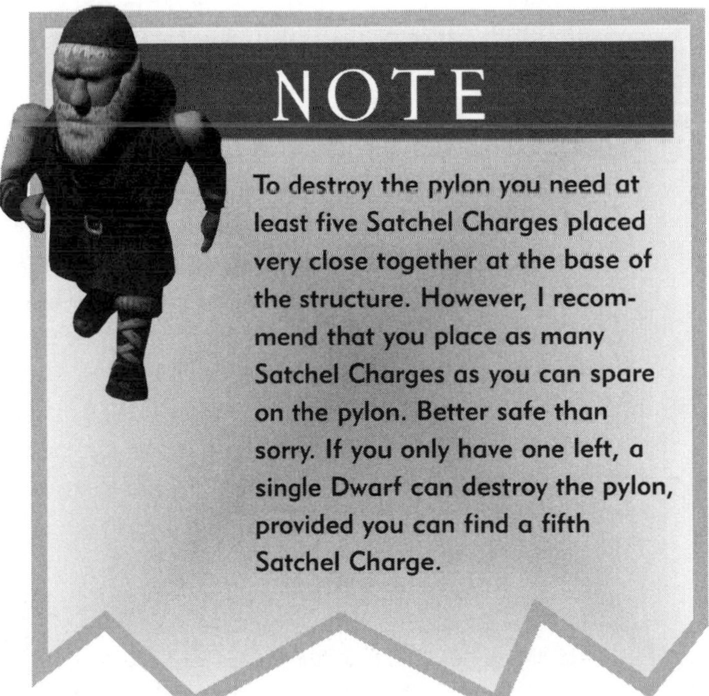

NOTE

To destroy the pylon you need at least five Satchel Charges placed very close together at the base of the structure. However, I recommend that you place as many Satchel Charges as you can spare on the pylon. Better safe than sorry. If you only have one left, a single Dwarf can destroy the pylon, provided you can find a fifth Satchel Charge.

FIGURE 5.3: Sacrifice a couple of Berserks to thin out the ranks of the Soulless before you bomb them into the Stone Age with your Dwarves.

As the Undead advance on your Archers and Dwarves, fall back, but don't stop launching arrows and bottles at the enemy. You should be able to eliminate the enemy force completely and still preserve all of your Dwarves and two or three Archers. If you were careful, you might even have a couple of Berserks standing by. Continue to move north. Watch out for Wights and for the occasional Soulless that will come out of the woods. When you get to the World Knot, don't go in it right away—a Wight will teleport in, and then blow itself up. Immediately after this explosion, a group of Thrall and Soulless will teleport in. Yet another group of Thrall and Soulless will begin to attack you from the east. This may seem like a challenge, but trust me, your Dwarves are more than capable of destroying all of these units. You'll just need a little support from your Archers to keep the Soulless occupied while your Dwarves move around and throw Explosive Bottles.

Now that you have destroyed most of the enemy forces, take two Dwarves and move to the World Knot pylon that's farthest away from the nearest enemy. Get as close to the pylon as possible. Have each Dwarf drop all four of their Satchel Charges as close to the pylon as you can get. Now back away from the pylon, and have the two Dwarves throw a pair of bottles at it simultaneously. As you can see in Figure 5.4, this combination of Satchel Charges and Explosive Bottles is enough to destroy the pylon.

Once the pylon is destroyed, that's it. Congrats!

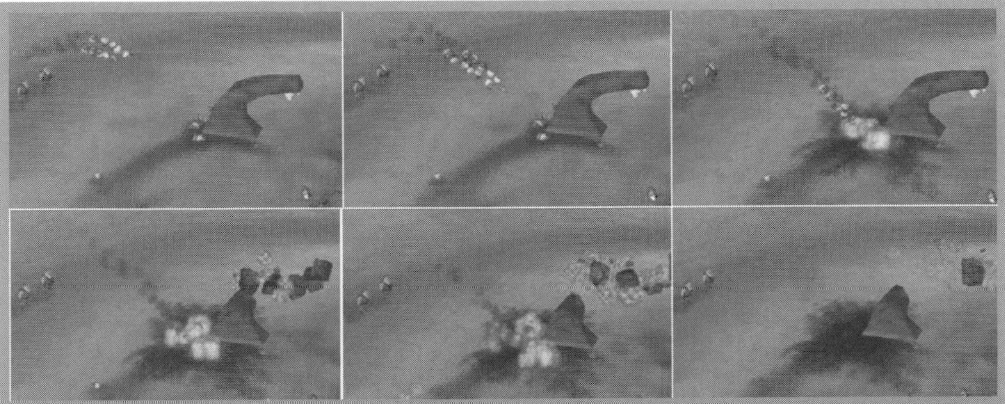

FIGURE 5.4: This collection of six screen shots shows how to blow up the pylon. I can watch this again and again—it never gets old.

Blow by Blow

- Group your units into Archers, Berserks, and two groups of four Dwarves each. Remember to keep your Dwarf groups away from each other.
- Move straight ahead on the road (east), keeping an eye out for the first Undead army.
- When you see the Undead army, move your Archers up in a loose line and have your two Dwarf groups flank the enemy on either side. Keep your Berserks nearby as well.
- Have your Archers fire on the Soulless, and bring your Dwarves up to sandwich the advancing Thrall between walls of fire.
- After the first group is polished off, move to the river, but not right up to the bank. Repeat your previous formation; it will also serve you well here.

Continued on next page

Continued from previous page

- Optional: If you want to save the Pilgrims, send a couple of Berserks to the stone monument to your right. However, you should know that these Berserks will be busy guarding the Pilgrims for a while, and you may need them elsewhere. You don't need the Pilgrims to win, so you can let them die if you want.
- Move your Archers up into the river and open fire on the Undead to draw them to you. Move your Archers out of the water and back to your shore
- Now bring up your two sets of Dwarves, and punish the Thrall and Soulless as they cross the river. Keep your Archers firing on any Soulless that are in range. At this point, watch out for a Ghol attack on your right flank.
- After you've demolished that group of Undead, move across the river and turn north.
- Use your Archers to fire on the western (smaller) group of Undead. At the same time, run a pair of Berserks up to pick on the Soulless in the eastern (larger) group. Bring your Dwarves up and get them ready for the onslaught.
- When the Thrall begin their rush, again use your Dwarves to make them pay. Fall back with your Dwarves and Archers as much as possible to minimize casualties.
- Move up to the World Knot (north), and on your way look out for Wights and Soulless that come out of the forest.
- When you get to the World Knot, don't enter it immediately, because a Wight followed by a group of Thrall and Soulless will appear. You need to use your Dwarves and Archers to deal with this World Knot crew quickly. Then turn east because another group is on its way to get you.

- Once you've disposed of most of the enemies, with any luck you should still have a few Dwarves at your disposal. Place at least five Satchel Charges (or more if you have them) in neat piles as close to the pylon as you can.
- Once this is done, back away, throw a couple of Explosive Bottles at the Satchel Charges, and watch the Knot pylon crumble. Sweet.

BAGRADA

Bagrada is a maze of tiny canyons crisscrossing the mountains between the Plain of Scales and Forest Heart. This is your first encounter with a completely snow-covered map.The incessant snowfall can be a major factor also because your Dwarves' bottles may go out even before they hit the ground. This makes it hard to use your Dwarves as effective weapons. Bagrada is the scenario where you'll meet the giant Trow for the first time. The Trow can crush your troops in a matter of seconds. Learning how to deal with the Trow is an important part of this scenario, so read carefully. You also get some reinforcements in Bagrada. Buck up, it won't be so bad.

MISSION OBJECTIVE

Cross the snow-covered passes to the area in the north-east (there's a marker there), making sure to destroy all enemies along the way. When you meet the Trow, kill it.

YOUR GUYS

You've got a healthy complement of units in this scenario. You have the fast and powerful striking power of the Berserks, the solid performance of the Warriors, and the long-range abilities of the Archers. You even have a Journeyman to help you heal your wounds. Best of all, when you reach the marker, you get some reinforcements. Here's what you get:

- Journeyman
- Warriors
- Berserks
- Archers
- Dwarves

Reinforcements

- Dwarves
- Journeyman
- Archers
- Warriors

THE EVIL HORDE

The Undead will come at you in waves in Bagrada. They have the usual Thrall and Soulless, and this time there are also marauding bands of Myrmidons, which are roughly equivalent to your Berserks. These spell trouble. And of course, there's the Trow: a giant that can kick your troops to death in seconds. Here's what they get:

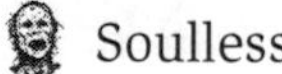

- Soulless
- Thrall
- Myrmidons
- Trow

LAY OF THE LAND

As you begin Bagrada, there's a small area that's not covered with snow. This makes it fairly easy to bomb the first wave of Undead. However, after you venture farther onto the map, you're in for a snowy good time. The Explosive Bottles are doubly likely to go out prematurely because either the falling snow or the snow on the

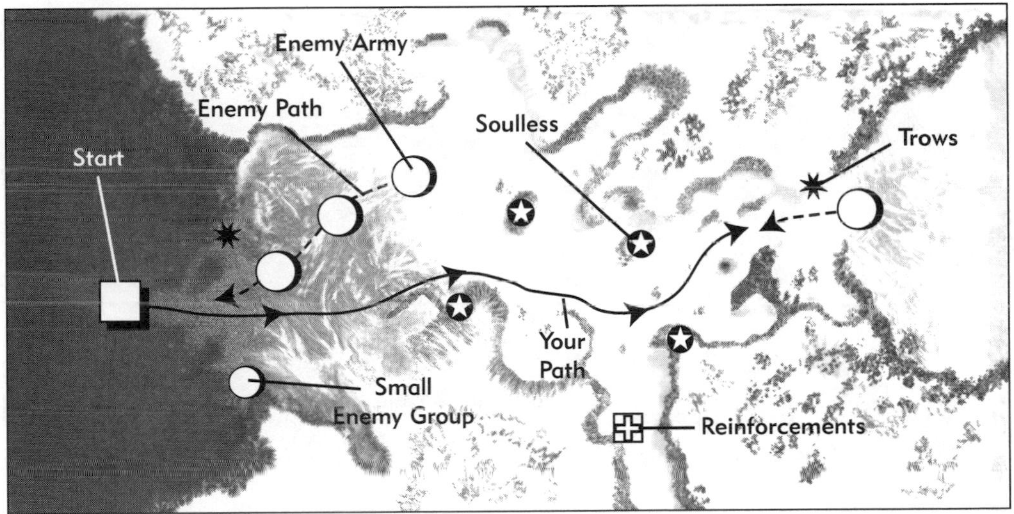

ground can extinguish them. Don't rely on bottles in this attack. The defining features on the map are the inaccessible mounds that lie all around you. These mounds often have one or two Soulless on them (see Figure 5.5); they cannot be reached by any of your troops except your Archers. Keep your Journeyman handy to heal any damage your Archers may take.

BATTLE PLANS

You begin the scenario facing east (to the right side of the map) in front of a set of broken city gates. You'll ultimately want to go in this direction, so group your units into their respective categories, and move forward just a little. Move your Dwarves up to where the gates were and lay down some Satchel Charges. Position a few Berserks and Warriors to the left and right of the Dwarves to protect them from the Myrmidons that will approach from either side (see Figure 5.6). A pair of Myrmidons charging a couple of Dwarves will almost always win because the Dwarves'

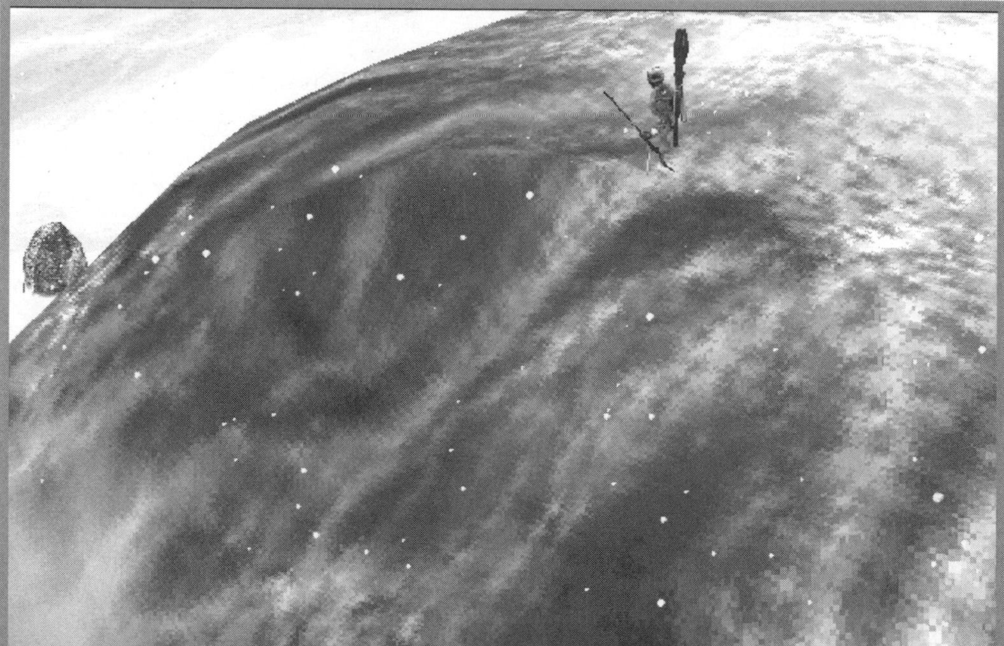

FIGURE 5.5: Watch out for the Soulless that sit on lofty perches and pick you off down below. Use your Archers to take these guys out.

bottles cannot kill the Myrmidons in one shot. I often send the rest of my Berserks to hunt down any Myrmidons that may have gotten behind me.

It's best to use your Dwarves at this point in the game because this is the only area where you can use Explosive Bottles with any real reliability. Now that your charges are set up, just sit and wait. The enemy forces should come up to attack shortly. When they do, use your Archers to target the Soulless and your Dwarves to try to take out the Thrall. If you're careful, you can catch the Thrall right over the Satchel Charges and blow them up all at once. Your Berserks make excellent Soulless chasers, so send them out if you're having any trouble with them.

After you've cleaned up the first group of Undead, move forward a bit until you see the second wave coming at you. Take out these units in the same way you dealt with the others. When you're done with them, there will be yet another wave. This third group might just be making a run for the exit, but you'll need to kill them as well. By this time you should have come across at least a couple of bands of Myrmidons scouring the landscape. It's easy to deal with these louts if you can just keep a few soldiers (Berserks or Warriors) near your Archers and Dwarves at all times.

FIGURE 5.6: Keep a group of Berserks or Warriors on both flanks while you lay down your Satchel Charges. There are Myrmidons out there just waiting for their chance to pounce.

Keep moving east, and follow the directions on the map at the beginning of this section. Eventually you will come to a stone marker. You'll probably meet some more Myrmidons and a Soulless or two, but nothing you can't handle easily. Keep your Archers healthy by using your Journeyman to heal their wounds. For that matter, keep your Berserks healthy, too. Move forward to the second marker (see Figure 5.7). When you get there, a group of reinforcements will appear on the bottom of the map.

Now continue to move east until you find a campfire that's still burning. Remember this campfire from the cutscene? Yep, this is it. Remember how the guys in the cutscene died? Yep, a Trow kicked the crap out of 'em. Get ready to meet Mr. Trow. Move past the marker, but keep your troops spread out with your Warriors on one side, your Berserks on the other, and the Archers in a long line in the middle. Dwarves won't be of much use against the Trow because of the snow and because the Trow move *very* quickly. Before you meet the Trow though, you've got another group of Soulless and Thrall to shred. Don't waste your troops on these units; try to take out as many of them as possible with your Archer.

FIGURE 5.7: You must pass this marker to get your reinforcements.

As soon as you've finished off most of the Undead units, the Trow will show up. This guy is really tough, and you'll need to have all of your Berserks and Warriors ready if you want to take it down. To kill the Trow, you need to attack with all of your Berserks and Warriors at the same time, and from all angles. When the Trow is completely surrounded and has a pile of units hacking away at it, that's when it's most vulnerable. Use this technique

TIP

The Trow is a powerful creature, but it has its weak spots. The only way to kill a Trow without losing piles of units is to attack the Trow from all sides with as many Berserks and Warriors as you can. If you attack a Trow in a single-file column, it will kick the crud out of every single one of your units until there's none left.

to destroy the Trow (see Figure 5.8), then move all of your troops over the last marker, and the scenario is yours!

FIGURE 5.8: To kill the Trow you need to surround it and attack from all sides.

Blow by Blow

- Group your units by kind. Move your Dwarves up to the gates to lay down some Satchel Charges (this is the only place on this map where you can reliably use them). Then bring up some Warriors to cover your forward flanks from Myrmidon attacks.

Continued on next page

Continued from previous page

- When the Undead army comes, use your Dwarves and Satchel Charges to take out as many as possible while the Archers shoot for the Soulless. Use your Berserks to clean up, if need be.
- Heal any damaged units. Then move forward and deal with the second wave in a similar manner; however, you may not have time to get the Satchel Charges down before their attack hits.
- After dealing with the second wave, move forward again until you see the third wave. Dispatch it using your Archers, Berserks, and Warriors, and then heal any damaged units.
- Move toward the first and second markers, keeping an eye out for Myrmidons and Soulless along the way. When you get to the second marker, your reinforcements will arrive.
- Group your reinforcements in with the rest of your troops, and use the new Journeyman to heal any Berserks or Warriors that need help.
- Move forward again until you reach the campfire. Use your Archers to take out the Soulless on the hill to your left.
- Just past the campfire, another group of Soulless and Thrall will attack. Use your Archers to lure the Thrall in, but fall back to avoid contact. Soon the Trow will come. At that point move your Warriors in from one side and your Berserks in from the other, and then just hack away.
- If you've managed the attack properly, the Trow will die quickly. Finish off any straggling enemy units. Move forward to the last marker, and voilà! You're done.

AMBUSH AT DEVIL'S OVERLOOK

Remember those old coin-op games like Galaga? Well, so did the folks at Bungie. It inspired the special challenge in this scenario. You depend mostly on Dwarves to kill 100 Soulless. The idea is that these 100 Soulless got separated from their masters and are lost in the canyons. Your job is to use your resources, mostly Dwarves, to kill all of the Soulless. Best of luck.

> **MISSION OBJECTIVE**
>
> Kill the 100 Soulless, or as many of them as you can, before losing all of your units. The number needed to win depends on your skill level. You must kill 60 percent of the Soulless to win at the Normal level, 80 percent at the Major Damage level, and 90 percent at the Total Carnage level.

YOUR GUYS

You start out with a whole bunch of Dwarves and with more Satchel Charges than you can carry. You'll have to make good use of them to win. Here's what you get:

- Dwarves (with extra Satchel Charges)
- Berserks (small group)

THE EVIL HORDE

Well, there just isn't any other way to put this: they're all Soulless, all 100 of them. Here's what they get:

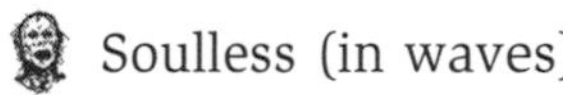

- Soulless (in waves)

LAY OF THE LAND

This map is another frozen area, with lots of snow, which, of course, helps add to the challenge of this level. You are given mostly Dwarves, who throw burning bottles, but the snow puts the bottles out. The good news is that it's not snowing during the game, so you don't have that extra headache to worry about. The majority of this scenario takes place on a nice, flat, frozen lake, so you know that for the most part you'll be on a level playing field. Watch the hills behind you though, because the Soulless have a tendency to sneak around back. There's a large dump of Satchel Charges piled up at the back of the lake; you should start ferrying them out to the lake as soon as you can.

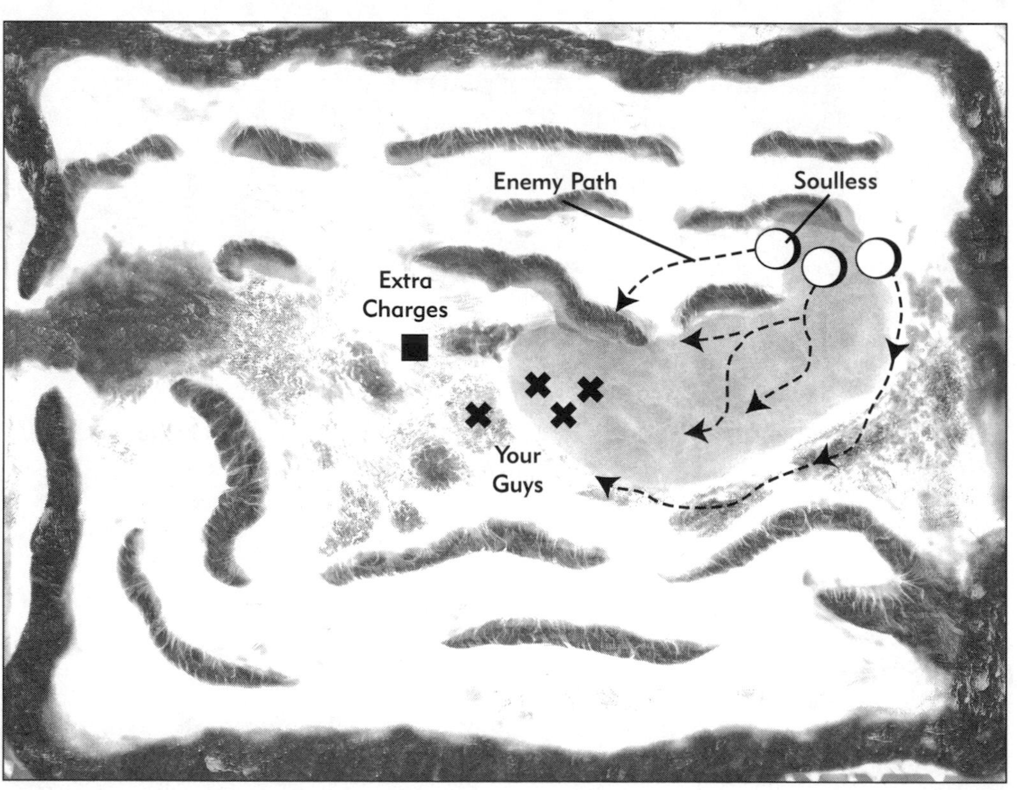

BATTLE PLANS

The game begins with some of your Dwarves setting down a few Satchel Charges along the area where the Soulless are most likely to attack. Have some of your other Dwarves lay a large maze of Satchel Charges around the lake. Ideally, you'll be able to get a large chunk of Soulless to cross over the charges, so that you can ignite one of them and set off a chain reaction to take out the rest (see Figure 5.9).

The first wave of Soulless will come from the right and left sides of the lake, almost in a zigzag fashion. You can bring a couple of groups of Dwarves up to take on each band of Soulless, but be wary of their spears. This is a good time to use the Dwarf Juke (explained in Chapter 3). If you can dodge most of the Soulless' spears, you can eliminate large numbers of them without losing all of your Dwarves. Each

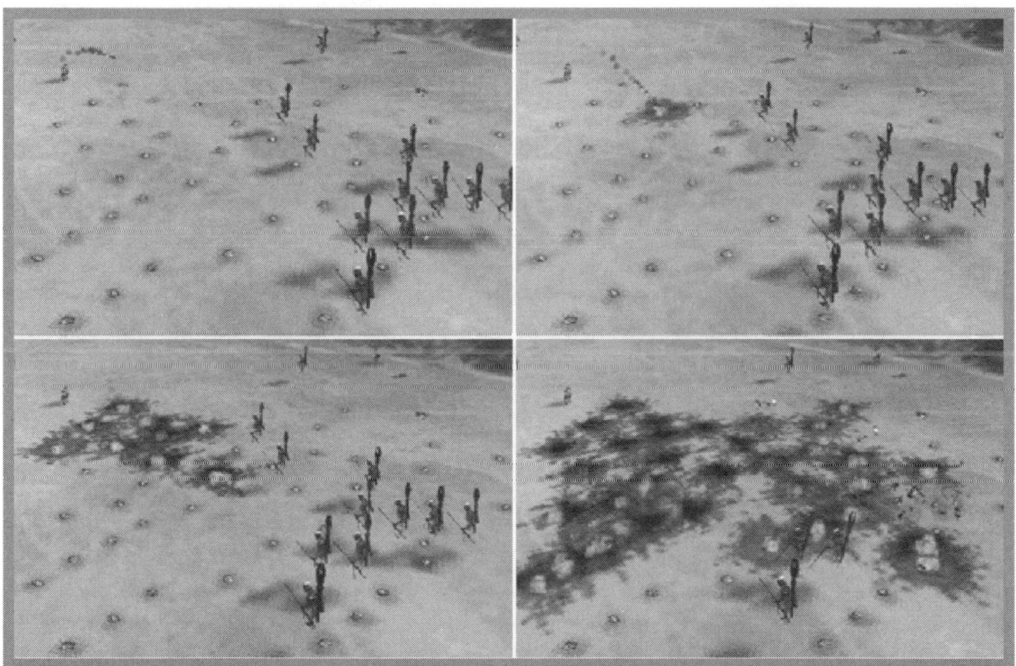

FIGURE 5.9: Lay down the Satchel Charges and try to take out the Soulless with a chain reaction.

successive wave of Soulless will be identified by wave number. The Soulless advance in waves in this manner:

- Wave #1—one group of 10
- Wave #2—one group of 10
- Wave #3—two groups of 10
- Wave #4—two groups of 10
- Wave #5—two groups of 10 plus every Soulless that has survived so far
- There are also 20 Soulless that just wander the map in small groups, hunting for blood (see Figure 5.10)

FIGURE 5.10: The Soulless travel in long lines like this, so it's better to attack from the front rather than the back.

There's not much else to say about this scenario, other than that you've got to keep your Dwarves alive long enough to kill at least 60 percent of the Soulless (at the Normal skill level). Many of the experts at Bungie set out groups of Satchel Charges in various areas along the lake where they know the Soulless will come, but to do this, you have to be very familiar with the scenario. The other strategy that some players use is to group two or three Dwarves together with one Warrior for more protection. When your group approaches the Soulless, you can send your Warrior forward as a decoy while your Dwarves move into position to launch their bottles.

I suggest that you save the Ambush at Devil's Overlook at the beginning and play it over a few times. This way you can learn which way the Soulless come in on each wave and where you should put the Satchel Charges. Refer to the map at the beginning of this section to see the approximate paths the Soulless use to approach you.

Blow by Blow

- Group two or three Dwarves together with a Warrior.
- Get your Dwarves out on the ice, and lay down groups of Satchel Charges wherever you think the Soulless might come. They pretty much all come through the lake, so you don't have to worry all that much about the woods.
- When the first wave of Soulless arrives, use one or two groups of Dwarves and Warriors to attack the Soulless. Use your Warriors as decoys as you move closer with your Dwarves.
- Do the Dwarf Juke to avoid getting impaled by the Soulless' spears.
- Repeat as necessary.
- Try to get at least 60 percent of the Soulless to win.

6

We Are the Champions

In this chapter you'll play a couple of scenarios that introduce you to a new kind of character in *Myth*. Well, they are sort of new, but not exactly. I'm talking about the Champions; they look like regular units, but they're "super" units that can throw, fire, and attack faster, longer, and with more power than any unit you've seen so far. In fact, you'll be absolutely amazed at what a champion Archer/Hero can do to a group of Ghols. It's incredible to watch.

These two scenarios allow you to enjoy these superb units in a desert landscape, with plenty of enemies and interesting pathways to follow. In the Five Champions, you must find Alric on a huge map, and then free him from a protective force field—great fun indeed. Out of the Barrier is the natural continuance of the Champions story, except this time Alric will be with you. Working with small numbers of very powerful units should prove to be an enjoyable experience for you.

THE FIVE CHAMPIONS

You have five heroes at your disposal, each of which has characteristics and abilities that are superior to what you've seen in similar units so far. You must traverse the map to find Alric, an Avatara who's imprisoned in a force field and guarded by many Soulless. Along the way you will encounter many Thrall, Soulless, and Ghols, but your superior forces should be able to make their way across the desert map safely

to locate and free Alric. Remember, if even one of your heroes dies, the scenario is over. Be careful, and use your Journeyman to heal any nicks and scratches that you might receive in a tussle.

> **MISSION OBJECTIVE**
>
> **Wind your way through the map to find Alric and release him from the force field that holds him. If any one of your five champions die, your scenario is over.**

YOUR GUYS

These champions are really great. They're kind of like taking a hot sports car out for a spin. They shoot farther, faster, and can take more hits than even an experienced regular unit. Enjoy them while they last. Here's what you get:

- Berserks (two)
- Dwarf
- Journeyman
- Archer

THE EVIL HORDE

As usual, there's plenty of Undead on this map. Most of them are Thrall and Soulless, with a few pockets of Ghols thrown in for good measure. Here's what they get:

- Thrall
- Soulless
- Ghols

LAY OF THE LAND

This map is a desert with several large canyons running through it. Although you can move about freely on the map, the nature of the canyons and bridges you come across will pretty much dictate the path you'll take to find Alric. The dry surroundings make your Dwarf very effective. You can do some serious damage to the large groups of Thrall you'll encounter without having to worry about 80 percent of the bottles

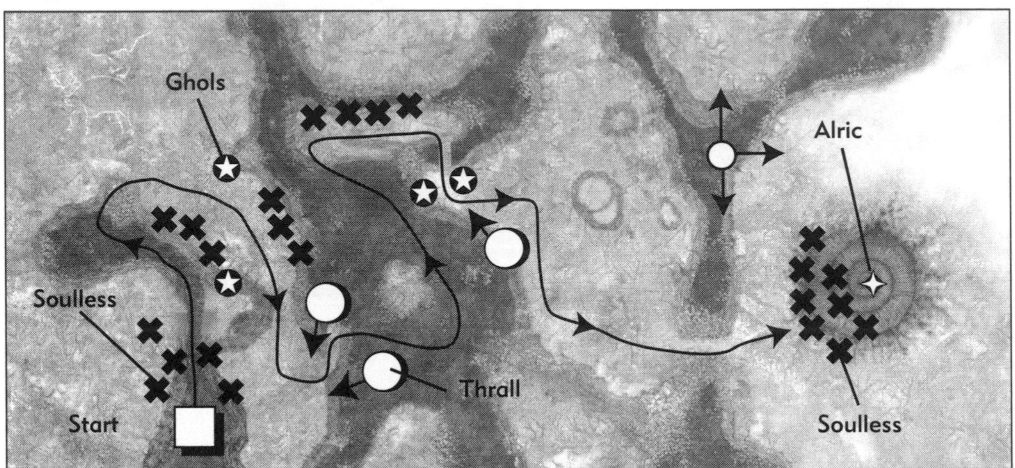

snuffing out like you did in the last few scenarios. The canyon walls would normally present a problem because of the Soulless that like to perch on the edges of the cliffs, but your Archer is so proficient that it's easy to waste any Soulless that even looks in your direction. Nevertheless, be sure to keep an eye out for Soulless that are at the top of the canyon walls, and when you're on the upper plateaus, keep a look out for Ghols that may come up behind you.

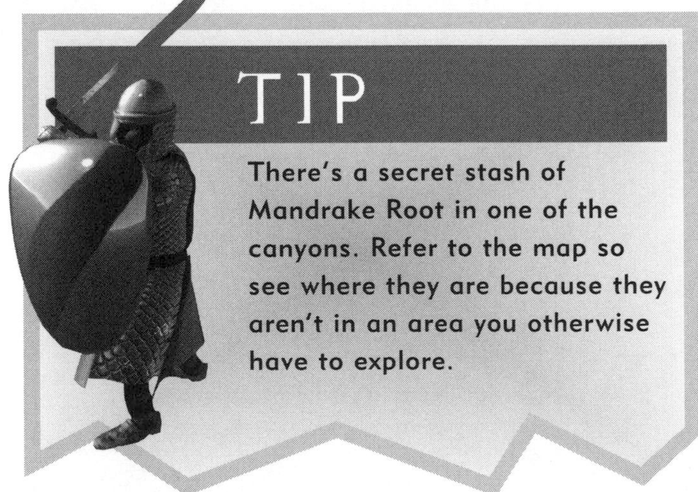

TIP

There's a secret stash of Mandrake Root in one of the canyons. Refer to the map so see where they are because they aren't in an area you otherwise have to explore.

BATTLE PLANS

You begin the scenario parked in a canyon under a large arch. You are able to move forward (the direction you're facing) or backward, but if you turn and move backward you lose the scenario. So, as strange at this may sound with only five units, group them by type. This gives you four groups, with your two Berserks in one group and the other units as three separate groups.

Turn on your overhead map and move forward (through the arch) until you encounter a few Soulless that are taking pot shots at you from above. Take the Soulless out with your awesome Archer, and then continue down the canyon. You'll come across more Soulless, a few Ghols, and a large contingent of Thrall lumbering toward you. Your Dwarf can take out the Thrall with a little help from your Archer, as shown in Figure 6.1.

Now proceed up the ramp and out of the canyon to the plateau above. Once up there, follow the path that's shown in this scenario's map to find your way to the next canyon. Along the way you'll have a set of Soulless harassing you on either side, but you should be able to dispose of them quickly with your Berserks and

FIGURE 6.1: Use your Dwarf to take out large groups of Thrall.

Archer. As you begin to descend the next ramp, a large group of Thrall will start moving toward you along the canyon floor (see Figure 6.2). Use your superior height to butcher them before they can even get close to you. After you've finished with this first bunch, you'll have to deal with yet another large group of Thrall.

After you've waxed the two groups of Thrall, you can pretty much move through the canyon freely. Heal any units that may have a few nicks. Follow the path on the map to the next ramp that will take you out of this canyon. As you are walking through the canyon, note the cool smoking vents along the canyon floor. Move up the ramp with your Dwarf and Archer. Be ready for a group of five or six Soulless that will open fire on you as soon as they see you. Your Dwarf can take out several of them at a time with carefully placed explosives. After this, you may need to heal your Archer, your Dwarf, or both. Move along the path to the suspension bridge, and get ready for a pack of Ghols (see Figure 6.3).

After you cross the bridge, you'll be on a new plateau, where another small group of Ghols will be waiting. As you move forward onto the plateau, you'll be assaulted by another huge group of Thrall. Again, they shouldn't pose much of a problem if you use your Dwarf and Archer properly; however, I had to use my Berserks to help clean up a couple of Thrall that got through my defenses. Now follow the map directions to get to the next bridge—this time it's a land bridge.

Cross the bridge and heal any of your champions that are damaged by more than one-third. Move forward with just your Archer and Dwarf until you trigger the Soulless to come out and fight. The key to this battle is not to let the Soulless kill even one of your units. Remember one death equals failure. I found that the Archer

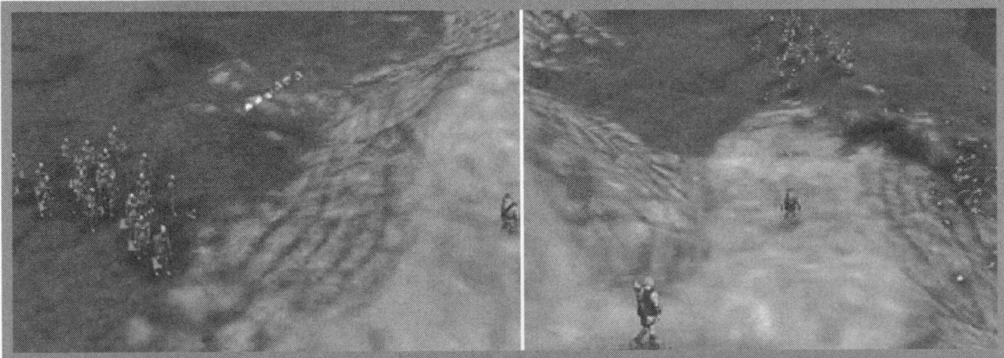

FIGURE 6.2: Two large groups of Thrall will attack before you descend this ramp into the second canyon. Stay at the top and use the height to your advantage.

FIGURE 6.3: This pack of Ghols will come straight at you as you attempt to cross the bridge.

stands up admirably against the Soulless and will only take one or two hits for every Soulless killed. Just set up your Archer to attack the Soulless on one side and concentrate on the other side, where you'll need to hand-control your Dwarf. Do the Dwarf Juke (moving in the opposite direction as soon as you see the Soulless begin their throwing motion) to move in on the Soulless, and then blow them up with your Explosive Bottles. Save your game before

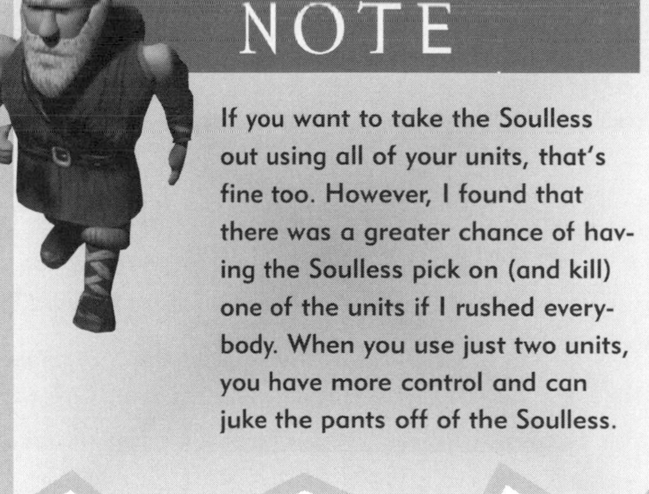

NOTE

If you want to take the Soulless out using all of your units, that's fine too. However, I found that there was a greater chance of having the Soulless pick on (and kill) one of the units if I rushed everybody. When you use just two units, you have more control and can juke the pants off of the Soulless.

you begin this, because it may take a few tries to clean up all the Soulless without losing a unit.

After you've gotten rid of all the Soulless, you can move in and have a look at the force field that's holding Alric in the center of the disc. You'll need to blow up the four corner pedestals (see Figure 6.4) to release him. After you've done that, you've won! Pat yourself on the back, and get ready for an even harder challenge.

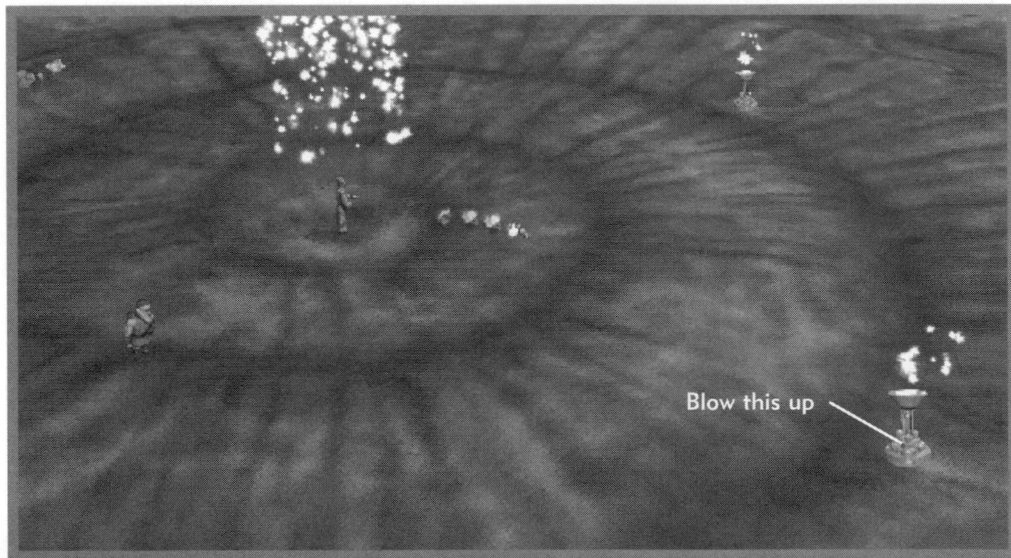

FIGURE 6.4: Blow up the four corners of Alric's detention force field, and you'll release him and win the scenario.

Blow by Blow

- Group your units (I know, I know, there're only five units) by type, and then move forward down the canyon.
- Kill any Soulless that are lingering along the tops of the canyon walls.

- Continue to move down the canyon until you come to some Ghols and Soulless. Take them out and get ready for a large group of Thrall that will come down the ramp. Kill the Thrall.
- Move up the ramp and follow the directions on the map for this scenario.
- Expect to get ambushed by Soulless and Ghols along the way to the ramp that leads into the second canyon.
- As you head down the ramp, two large groups of Thrall will approach, one at a time. Use just your Archer and Dwarf and their height advantage to eliminate the Thrall as they try to climb the ramp.
- Move through the canyon to the next ramp.
- As you climb the ramp, be ready for a group of Soulless that will attack you from the valley beyond.
- Move to the suspension bridge, and cross it. Be aware that a pack of Ghols will try to stop you.
- Heal any units that are damaged.
- After you cross the bridge you'll have to contend with another small group of Ghols and a very large group of Thrall. Use your Dwarf to eliminate them. You may need to use your Berserks to clean up any Thrall that get close.
- Move toward the next bridge, and cross it.
- Take out all of the Soulless that are guarding Alric.
- Blow up the four corner pedestals of Alric's containment field, and you'll win.

OUT OF THE BARRIER

Although you've freed Alric from the confines of the Undead force field, your battle is only half over. You must now lead Alric out of the desert area known as the barrier. Again, you only have the five champions to work with. In Out of the Barrier you will also be treated to a new Undead unit, the Shade. This guy is, as you might expect, really mean, and lives to shred the flesh off your troops. Fortunately, Alric is with you. He'll come in mighty handy.

MISSION OBJECTIVE

Lead Alric out of the canyon and escape the barrier.

YOUR GUYS

Again, you have only the five champions at your disposal in this scenario. This time you also have Alric (although you can't yet control him). Here's what you get:

 Berserks

Dwarf

 Archer

 Journeyman

 Avatara (Alric—not in your control)

THE EVIL HORDE

The Undead forces are thick with Ghols in this scenario, so always keep an eye on your back. There are also plenty of Myrmidons wandering about, and packs of

Soulless, too. The new unit you'll have to deal with is the Shade. Not to worry, Alric will take care of him for you when the time comes. Here's what they get:

- Soulless
- Myrmidons
- Ghols
- Shade

LAY OF THE LAND

Ah yes, more nice, dry desert terrain for your gaming pleasure. Once again, this toasty map is great for letting your Dwarf's Explosive Bottles find their mark and explode. This map contains rolling hills of sand punctuated by several large buttes that rise from the desert floor. For the most part, the buttes are impassable, so you'll have to go around. There is an old mine entrance that has a special bow (the Bow of Stoning) sitting outside its opening. Only your Archer can pick this bow up. When you do pick it up, you'll be in for a surprise. This part of the map, however, is just a distraction. The exit from the map lies in the opposite direction.

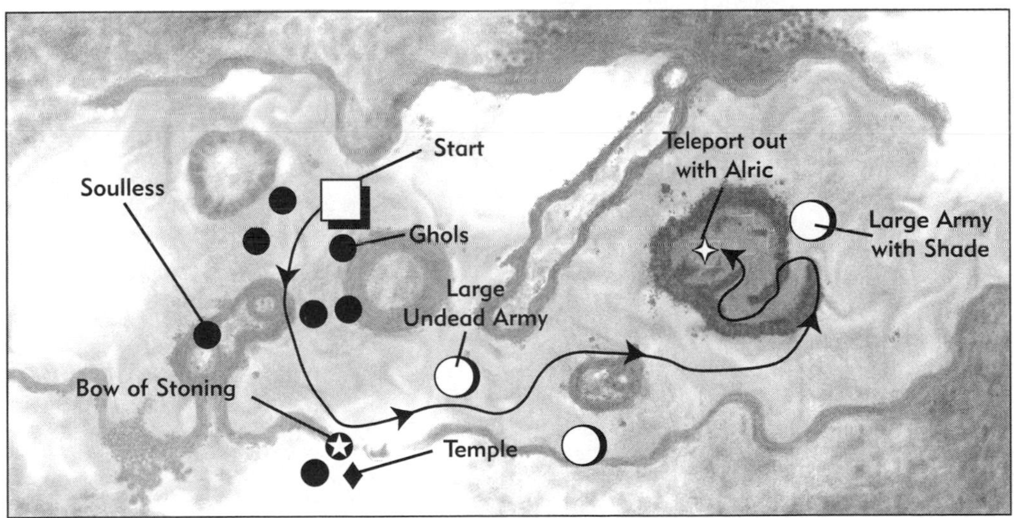

BATTLE PLANS

You begin this scenario with your Archer (and the rest of your troops) chasing a pair of Ghols across the desert. You might as well follow the Ghols and take them out while you're at it. You'll find that your Archer has excellent range and is very highly skilled. After you've taken care of these Ghols and the several more that move in on you, move to the east (see arrow on the map) and dispatch the two Ghols that are waiting there. You also might want to take out the Soulless that are occupying the ridge on your right (see Figure 6.5). These Soulless will run, one at a time, as you shoot them. They do this to draw you into their range, so be sure to keep your distance.

You'll now want to move ahead past the butte and turn to the south. You'll meet up with a group of Myrmidons guarding the pass. As you come around the corner, a group of Ghols will run right past you. Take out as many of them as possible. After the Ghols leave, it's time to think about the Myrmidons to the south. You can dispose of these guys with your Dwarf and Archer, but *always* keep your Berserks

FIGURE 6.5: Your Archer can single-handedly take out these four Soulless. Just be careful to keep your distance so that all four of them can't fire on you at once.

nearby. Remember, Myrmidons are very fast and they have a tendency to outrun the Dwarf's bottles. After you've cleaned up the Myrmidons, you have a couple choices as to what to do next. You can go get the Bow of Stoning, or you can continue toward the finish of the mission. Let's get the bow.

The Bow of Stoning (see Figure 6.6) is a special item that sits just outside the entrance to a half-buried temple in the southeast. You might as well grab it before you move on to complete the scenario. As you approach the temple entrance, an army of Myrmidons and Soulless will line up to the east (your left if you're facing the temple). To deal with these guys, set your Archer to attack the Soulless, have your Dwarf hit as many of the advancing Myrmidons as possible, and have your Berserks hack the rest to pieces. If there are any Soulless left over, have your Berserks chase them down to get them out of your hair.

After you've destroyed most of the Undead army, move toward the temple and stop a short distance away. Have your Dwarf lay out a couple of Satchel Charges leading away from the mine, and then have the Dwarf stand ready to throw. Your

FIGURE 6.6: The Bow of Stoning is a handy item to have. To get it, you'll have to deal with some Ghols that come out of this buried Temple just as you're reaching for the Bow.

fastest unit is your Berserk, so take one of them and move just close enough to the temple that you trigger the Ghols to come running out. Quickly get your Berserk out of there and have your Dwarf lob a bottle at the opening to the mine. This will ignite the Satchel Charges and send little bits of Ghol flying around everywhere. You'll eat tonight! Now take your Archer and pick up the Bow of Stoning.

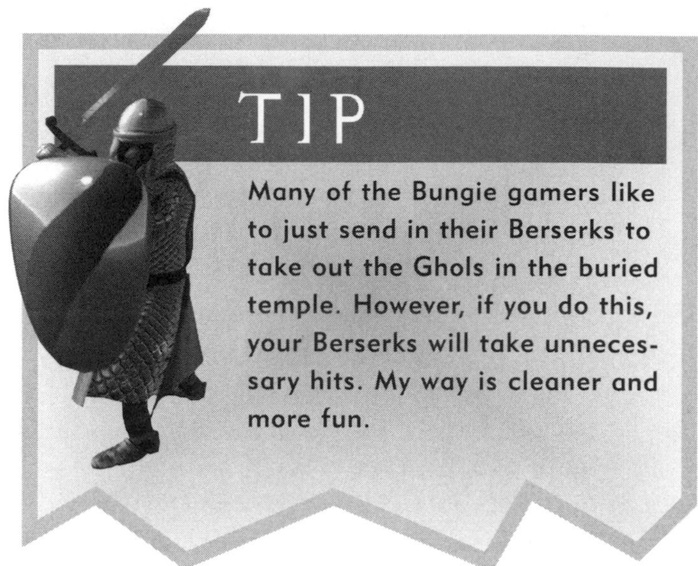

TIP

Many of the Bungie gamers like to just send in their Berserks to take out the Ghols in the buried temple. However, if you do this, your Berserks will take unnecessary hits. My way is cleaner and more fun.

Now that you have the Bow of Stoning, you should know that it only has 12 charges, and it must be activated by pressing the T key before you shoot. If the arrow misses its mark, that's a wasted charge. You should also know that not all of the Undead creatures are affected by the bow. Don't waste your charges on the Soulless or the Shade.

Now move toward the east, but do it carefully. You'll soon come across a large group of Myrmidons and Soulless. Although it may be difficult, you should be able to take out most of them using your Archer and Dwarf. When the Myrmidons get close enough, finish up with your Berserks. Heck, you can even use your Journeyman in a pinch. After you've cleared out the entire group of Undead, move east again until you come to a large hill on your left (it has a ramp that runs up the side). As you approach this area, you'll see a *huge* force of Myrmidons and Soulless and a Shade standing guard at the front of the ramp.

When you see this huge force, you'll probably think, "How in the heck am I ever going to do this?" Good

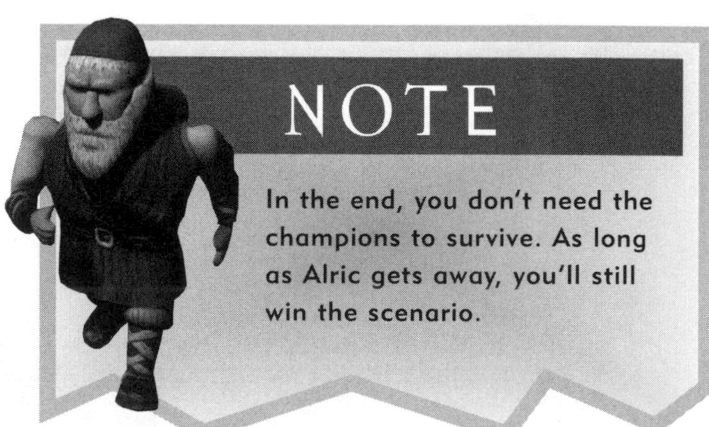

NOTE

In the end, you don't need the champions to survive. As long as Alric gets away, you'll still win the scenario.

question. The answer lies in trigonometry. Well, actually it lies in Alric, but trigonometry sounded better. Simply move one of your units just close enough so that your field of vision covers the entire enemy force. When this is accomplished, Alric announces that he'll take care of things. His Dispersal Dream blows the living crap out of each and every enemy unit. Get some popcorn and a drink because it's really fun to watch (see Figure 6.7). After the other units are destroyed, Alric will take care of the Shade personally.

After dealing with the Undead army, Alric begins to climb the ramp and beckons you to follow. Quickly group your units close together and follow him up the ramp. A new pile of Undead troops will begin to gather from all sides, so you must hurry to get to the top of the hill. Once you get there, move your units in very close to Alric, who will teleport you out of danger (see Figure 6.8). I can't stress enough how important it is to get to the top of the hill quickly. If you wait until the Soulless arrive at the top of the hill, Alric will get distracted, and you'll have to do battle with the Soulless. It's much better if you can just boogie on out of there ASAP.

FIGURE 6.7: Alric puts an end to the Undead army with his Dispersal Dream. It's really fun to watch. Bring a friend.

FIGURE 6.8: You must quickly get close to Alric for him to teleport your units to safety.

Blow by Blow

- Follow the first bunch of Ghols and kill them with your Archer. More Ghols will rush you from all angles.
- Move to the east and take out the Soulless on the butte to your right. Then take out the Ghols straight ahead.
- Turn right after the Soulless butte and deal with the Ghols that are attempting to run by you.
- Move forward and eliminate the Myrmidons guarding the passage to the buried temple.
- Move toward the temple, but be ready for an Undead force to attack from your left.

- Deal with the Undead force, and then return to the temple.
- When you make a grab for the Bow of Stoning, six Ghols will emerge from the temple. There are two ways to deal with this: set a trap with your Dwarf's Satchel Charges, or use your Berserks to go in and hack the Ghols to death.
- Pick up the Bow of Stoning and head east.
- Take out the remaining Myrmidons and Soulless that you will meet in the east. Use your Archer and Dwarf as much as possible before involving the Berserks.
- Move toward the large hill, but don't move close enough to trigger the enemy force.
- Move one unit just close enough to the enemy army that you can see their entire force. Alric will then move in and take care of them.
- After this army has been dispatched, quickly follow Alric up the ramp.
- At the top, move your units close to Alric so that he can teleport you away.

7

A Call to Arm(s)

The next few scenarios all revolve around the severed Arm of the Watcher. You find the Arm (and escape with it) in Silvermines. Then you must defend the Arm against wave after wave of Undead attackers in Shadow of the Mountain. Finally, in Seven Gates, you must clean up any troops that are left in the mountain passes after the Watcher made his escape. The first two scenarios are somewhat different, in that you want to avoid engaging the enemy. However, you bloodthirsty types shouldn't worry, because Shadow of the Mountain has plenty of conflict. Let me give you a, um, hand, through these three scenarios.

SILVERMINES

You're now near the town of Silvermines, where the Watcher's Arm is rumored to be. What is the Watcher's Arm? It's the shriveled-up limb of one of the three most powerful sorcerers to ever live, the Watcher. Presumably this item is of special significance to the side that has it, so your task is to pick it up and take it off the map before you get crushed by one of the patrolling Undead armies. You'll do well to avoid confrontation whenever possible, or you'll end up with a complete set of dead soldiers.

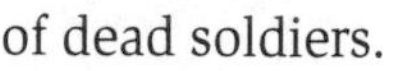

MISSION OBJECTIVE

Your Journeyman will lead you to the Watcher's severed Arm, but beware of enemy patrols. Recover the Arm and escape through the pass in the northwest.

YOUR GUYS

You have only one unit in this scenario, and no reinforcements are coming. You will not have control of your Journeyman (and his healing powers) until *after* you pick up the Arm. Here's what you get:

- Berserks
- Archers
- Dwarves
- Journeyman (you do not control him until after you have the Arm)

THE EVIL HORDE

The Undead are everywhere in this scenario. They patrol the map in packs, and they also act as sentinels and obstruct your passage. Here's what they get:

- Soulless
- Fetches
- Thrall
- Myrmidons

LAY OF THE LAND

This map is a dry wasteland punctuated by buttes that prevent you from traveling freely across the landscape. Usually, the Arm can be found outside the entrance to a mine. The mine is of importance only as a landmark. The land bridge you cross at the beginning of the scenario is the only practical way across the body of water that spans the map from east to west, but there's really no reason why you would want to return to the bottom of the map anyway. The exit to the map lies in the upper-left corner, and you must head up through the graveyard to make it off the map successfully. A group of Undead with two Fetches always waits by the graveyard. You must face them every time.

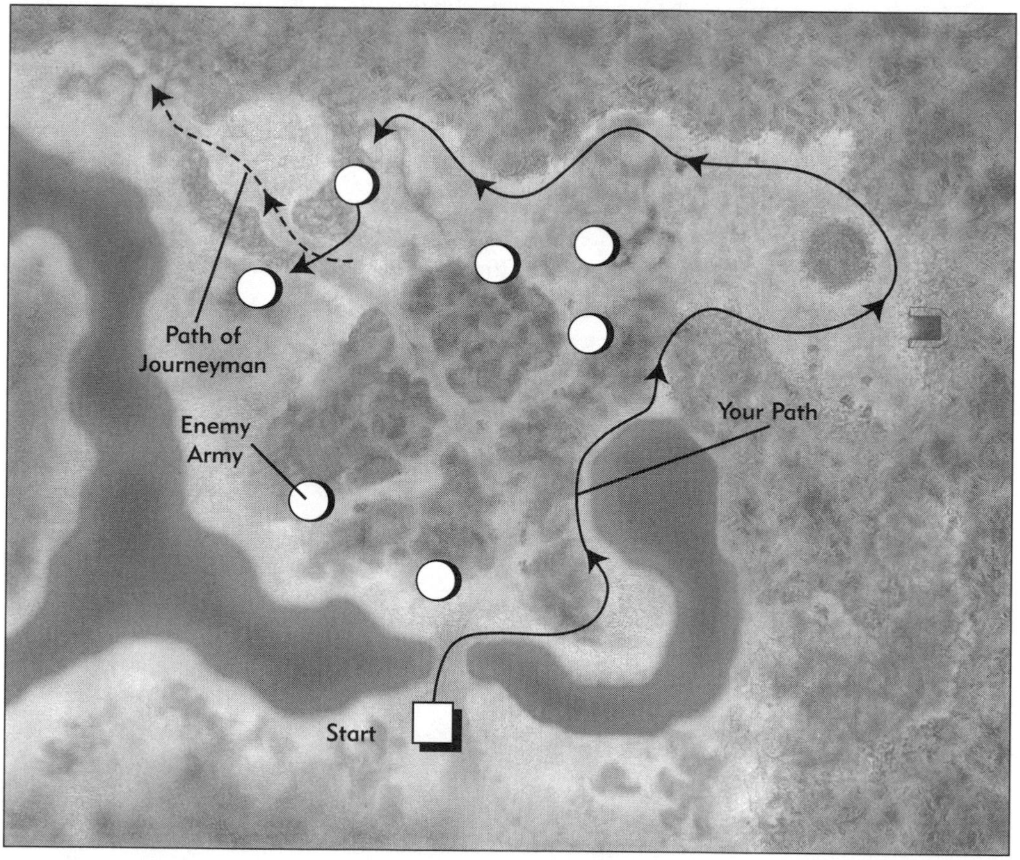

BATTLE PLANS

You begin on a land bridge facing north (up), with the Journeyman (who isn't under your control) urging you to follow him to the Arm. Follow the Journeyman carefully; you don't want to get too close to one of the roving Undead armies and trigger an attack. The name of the game in this scenario is avoidance. If you follow my lead, you can make it through the entire scenario and only engage in two battles.

The Journeyman will take you to the Arm, which may be in one of several locations. The Journeyman sometimes takes different routes to get to the same location, so it's almost impossible for me to tell you which way he'll go. Instead, I suggest that you move your troops over to the right side of the map above the water, and send your Journeyman out with one Berserk to retrieve the Arm. The Journeyman will be happy as long as one unit is following him, so your other units can rest while he and the Berserk get the Arm.

> **NOTE**
>
> Avoiding conflict is the only way to win in this scenario. The Undead armies patrolling the map are very powerful, so if you try to attack them all, you'll lose for sure. Instead, be passive and back off whenever you see an enemy group. You have to get fairly close to the Undead groups to trigger an attack, so just keep your distance and let them pass while you go around their position.

Once you find the Arm, I suggest that you move all of your troops up the right side of the map until you get to the top above the mine entrance, keeping your distance from any Undead that cross your path (see Figure 7.1). Once you're at the mine, just wait there for the Journeyman and Berserk to come after they've retrieved the Arm. Keep in mind that the Arm might be at the mine, thus killing two birds with one stone.

Once you're at the mine and you have the Arm, you'll have control over the Journeyman. This is an added bonus because you can use him to heal any damaged troops. You should *not* have had to fight anyone so far. To avoid the Undead and

FIGURE 7.1: Keep your distance from the enemy units; you don't want to attack anyone unnecessarily.

escape, follow the top of the map all the way to the left side (near the graveyard) as you can see in this scenario's map. When I say that you need to follow the top of the map, I mean *hug* it. If you wander below the very top of the map, you will trigger an attack, and probably lose the scenario.

Move across the top of the map until you trigger an attack by a roving band of Undead. This group of Undead waits just to the south of your location. This is the first of two armies you'll have to face, and it consists of some Soulless, Myrmidons, Thrall, and a Fetch. The key here is to attack carefully using diversionary tactics. Send a Berserk off to one side to take out or occupy the Fetch, and then move up your Archers to also fire on the Fetch (see Figure 7.2). This will trigger the Myrmidons to rush you, so have your remaining Berserks ready to come up and deal with them. Without this diversion, the Fetch would barbecue your Archers and Berserks.

After this group of Undead is taken care of, heal your troops and get ready for a wild and wooly finish. Continue to move toward the upper-left side of the map where there's a ramp that goes up into a graveyard and then off to the upper-left corner of the map. This is where you'll need to get your Journeyman to win. You

FIGURE 7.2: Bring a Berserk in from the side to distract the Fetch while your Archers shoot it down.

must meet the enemy force that waits on the other side of this ramp. It's a large force with plenty of units, including two Fetches, and there's no way to sneak past them, so you're going to have to do some fancy footwork to make it out alive.

I like to create a diversion with my Archers and Berserks while I sneak my Journeyman and Dwarves up the ramp and away to freedom. To do this, set your Warriors and Berserks to rush the enemy position (they'll have to run over the ramp to get there) on two different angles (see Figure 7.3). You definitely want to have two groups so that

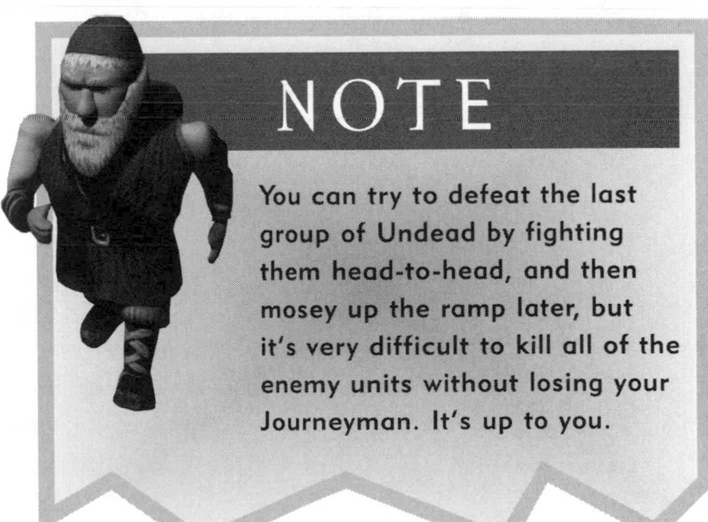

NOTE

You can try to defeat the last group of Undead by fighting them head-to-head, and then mosey up the ramp later, but it's very difficult to kill all of the enemy units without losing your Journeyman. It's up to you.

FIGURE 7.3: Rush the last Undead army with everything you've got while you try to sneak your Journeyman through the graveyard.

the Fetches cannot take your troops out in one shot. Now bring your Archers up to take out the Fetches, and at the same time have your Dwarves and Journeyman move up the ramp and into the graveyard. If any enemy troops come after you, use a Dwarf as a decoy. The Journeyman is the only unit that *must* make it off the map for you to win. This strategy almost always works. Sometimes, your Berserks and Warriors win the battle, leaving you with some extra units when all is said and done. Either way, this is an excellent method for winning a tough scenario.

Blow by Blow

- Follow the Journeyman to the Arm. If you want, just use one Berserk to escort the Journeyman to the Arm while your other troops cool their heels on the right side of the map.

- Get the Arm; then move your troops up to the top of the map near the mine entrance.
- Avoid fighting with any Undead troops for now.
- Hug the very top of the map along toward the left until you come to an obstacle. You'll see several groups of enemies, but if you hug the top, they won't come after you.
- Once you reach the impasse, you'll have to fight the Undead group. Send a Berserk off to one side to distract the Fetch, and then use your other units to attack.
- Heal any units that were damaged in the previous battle.
- Send your troops over the ramp and into hell in two separate groups (two separate groups of Berserks) with your Archers backing them up. As you're doing that, send your Journeyman and at least one Dwarf up the ramp into the graveyard.
- Get your Journeyman through the graveyard and up the path that runs to the upper-left corner of the map.

SHADOW OF THE MOUNTAIN

Okay, so you've got the Arm; now it's time to defend it. You've got an excellent defensive backdrop, but it'll take all your skill to stave off the waves of Undead that are going to climb the hill looking for the Arm and your life. This scenario revolves around how well you can manage the resources you've been given to counter the onslaught of Undead troops.

MISSION OBJECTIVE

Defend the Legion's Standard and the Watcher's Arm.

YOUR GUYS

This time you have a solid core of units, but don't get cocky; you'll need them all. Here's what you get:

- Dwarves
- Archers
- Berserks
- Journeyman

THE EVIL HORDE

You name it, they've got it: Archers (not Soulless), Dwarves, Myrmidons, and even a Trow, but you shouldn't have to fight it. Here's what they get:

- Archers
- Thrall
- Dwarves
- Myrmidons
- Trow (you shouldn't have to fight it)

LAY OF THE LAND

This map is pretty simple. You're on the top of the mountain, and the enemy is on the bottom, trying to get up. You never have to leave the lofty perch where you begin; you just need to defend it. Use this great height advantage to your benefit.

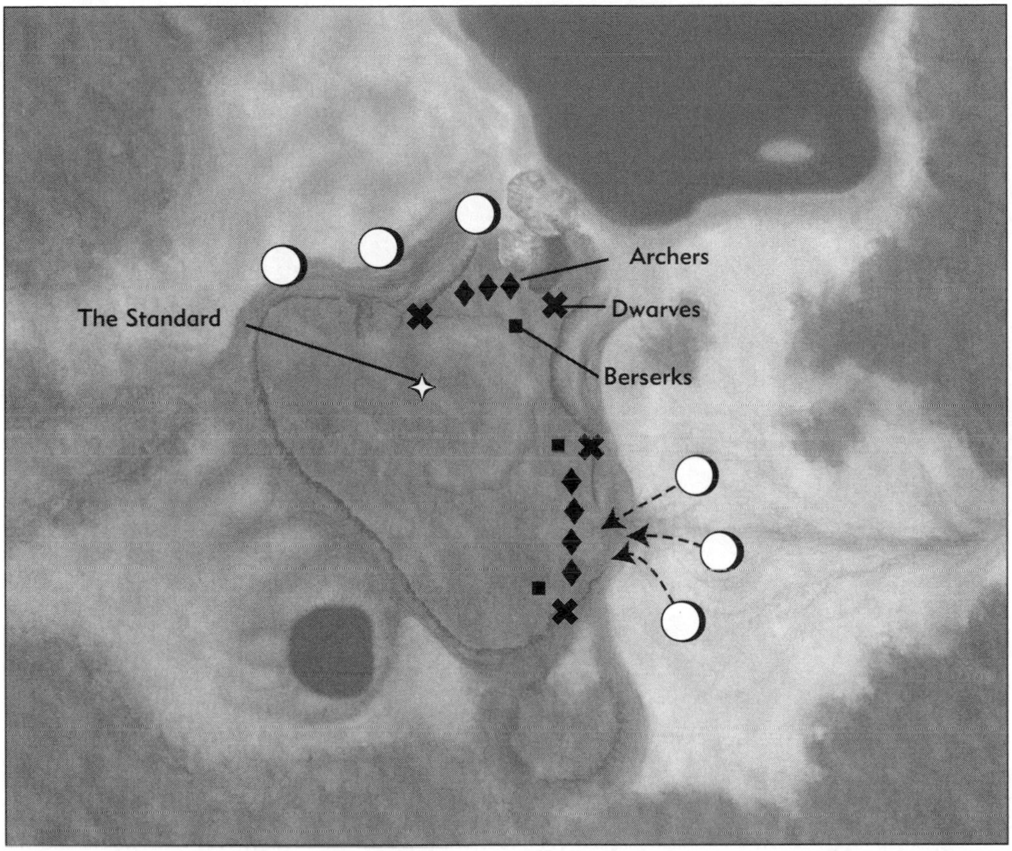

BATTLE PLANS

The first thing you should do is move your Archers forward in a long line at the top of the hill, with Dwarves and Berserks flanking either side (see Figure 7.4). The enemy will come at you with a large contingent of Thrall, Dwarves, and Myrmidons, but they're coming up such a steep hill that you can use your Archers and Dwarves to shred them before they even get close to you.

After the first wave has been eliminated, the next three waves are random, so I cannot tell you exactly where they'll be coming from or what they'll consist of. They will come from one of two locations: the area where the battle was just fought or the left flank. Usually, you'll have to move to the other side of the mountain to defend

FIGURE 7.4: Line up your Archers with Dwarves on the flanks, and make sure you've got some Berserks to back them up.

yourself against the second wave. Whatever you do, don't leave one of the two main flanks undefended.

It's pretty straightforward from here on out—just kill each successive enemy wave. The waves are roughly like this (but not necessarily in this order):

- Thrall/Dwarves/Myrmidons
- Dwarves
- Archers/Thrall/Myrmidons
- Archers/Myrmidons

Once you've dealt with the waves of attackers, you may have to go down and clean up a few straggling Archers, but that's pretty much it. If you do venture down the hill, don't get close to the Trow. It won't attack you if you don't provoke it (on the normal skill level), so don't even get it started. Wherever you are, use a line of Archers flanked by Dwarves and Berserks—this is one of the most effective defensive formations on a hill.

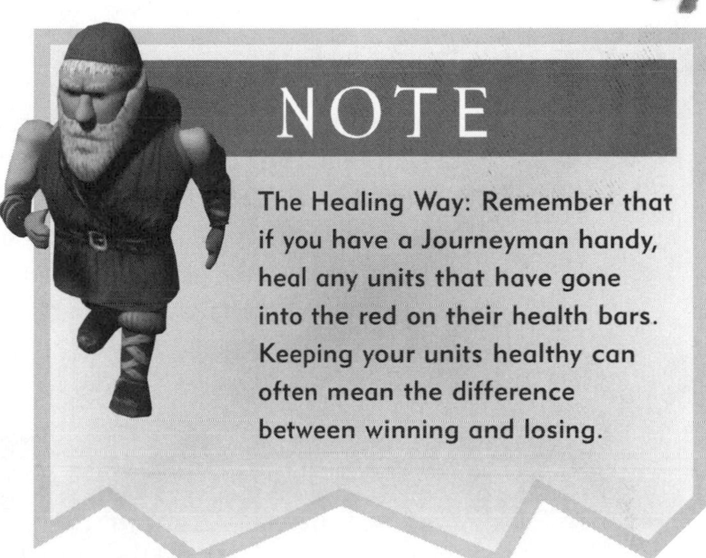

NOTE

The Healing Way: Remember that if you have a Journeyman handy, heal any units that have gone into the red on their health bars. Keeping your units healthy can often mean the difference between winning and losing.

Blow by Blow

- Move your Archers in a line with a Dwarf on each end; position some Berserks near the Dwarves.
- When the first wave hits, use your Dwarves to bomb the enemy into submission. Your Archers should be able to control any units that get past the Dwarfnet.
- After you've handled the first wave, heal your units.
- Get ready to move to whichever side of the mountain the enemy decides to attack from next.
- Repeat as necessary.
- You may have to chase down a few Undead Archers after you've defeated all the waves, but this should be easy. Use Berserks or, if you have plenty of Archers, you can simply shoot them down from a distance.

SEVEN GATES

Sure, you may have the Arm, but that doesn't mean the Watcher is dead. Your task now is to purge any remaining enemy forces from the area around the pass. However, there's a new twist: the Deceiver and the Watcher are at war, and their rival factions of Undead forces are actually more interested in doing battle with each other than with you. Much of the key to the Seven Gates is in letting them take care of each other so that you don't have to. If you play your cards carefully, you will hardly have to do any fighting at all.

MISSION OBJECTIVE

Eliminate any enemy forces that remain in the pass.

YOUR GUYS

You have basic units this time, with a single Journeyman available to heal some of your suffering. Here's what you get:

 Warriors

 Archers

 Journeyman

THE EVIL HORDE

As usual, the Undead are more or less traveling around the map in packs. Some groups contain Fetches, and one has a Shade. Here's what they get:

 Shade

 Fetches

- Thrall
-  Soulless

LAY OF THE LAND

This is one of the most dynamic and interesting maps in *Myth*. It consists mainly of a winding pass punctuated by several hills and some standing water. It's important to be sure which terrain features you can walk over successfully. This map has so many different features that it can be confusing. Veins of rock flow around the entire map, but despite their appearance, you can generally walk over them or use them to gain a height advantage. The water is also passable for the most part, since it is almost entirely shallow. You don't have to worry about explosives, because you don't have Dwarves.

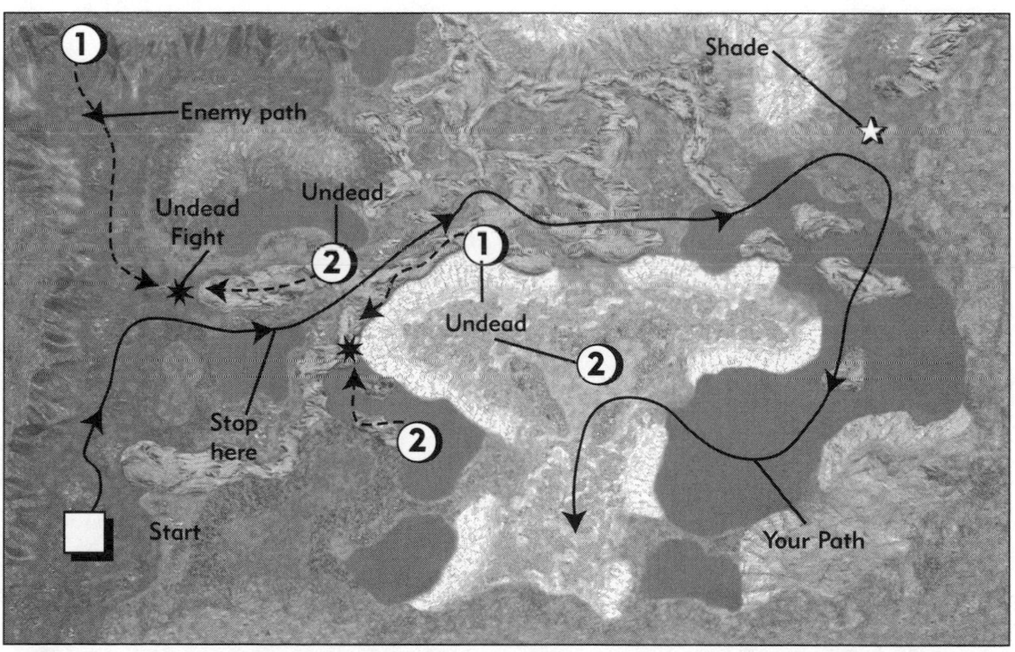

BATTLE PLANS

You start out with a few Thrall and a Soulless coming toward you. Notice that one of the Thrall is a different color, and it is being hit by the other Thrall. This is your first exposure to the rival Undead factions. Their infighting is going to make your job in this scenario a heck of a lot easier. Take out this first group of Undead, and then move forward (up) the pass until you get to a path that leads to the right (see the Seven Gates scenario map for directions). Once there, form one group with your Archers and another with all but two of your Warriors. Then sit tight for a sec.

You will soon notice a pair of Thrall coming along the other side of the hill. Send one Warrior to kill them. At the same time, send another Warrior up to the north; stop when you meet a large Undead Army. After disposing of the Thrall, have the first Warrior move to the east (right) of the map until you come across a large group of Undead. Once both Warriors have gotten the attention of both Undead armies, turn around and run back to where your troops are waiting. You don't want to fight; you want to lead both sides of the Undead together, and then get the heck out of there, as shown in Figure 7.5.

FIGURE 7.5: Use a pair of Warriors to lead the Undead armies right into one another; they'll do the killing for you.

When the two Undead armies meet, they'll hammer the crap out of each other, leaving you to clean up the rest. The only units you have to worry about are the Soulless and the Fetch (if he survives). Prepare your Archers to take out the Fetch before it turns on your troops. After this is done, move your troops down the pass to the right, and have them sit on the rocky outcropping. Be careful not to move your troops too far forward; if you're lucky, you can again introduce two Undead rivals to each other without getting a scratch yourself.

Move your Archers forward to take out a few Soulless coming toward you, and then back off again. This time, take one Warrior and walk off straight ahead (east) until you see an Undead army bearing down. Now turn around and move back (with the Undead army giving chase) toward your troops, but before you get there, hang a left (south/down) around the large hill. This will make the two Undead armies ram smack dab into the middle of each other (see Figure 7.6). After the Undead battle is over, you can move in and finish off any remaining units with your Archers.

Now that you've enjoyed watching two-thirds of the Undead on the map kill each other, you can spend your time tracking down the remaining units. How you finish off the Undead from here on out is pretty much up to you. Only one large group of Thrall poses any real threat to you, and they can be killed off from a distance with your Archers. You will, however, encounter a Shade in the upper-right corner of the map. Look out for this guy, because the Shade has a Dream that's similar to the Avatara's, and it can kill all of your units in one fell swoop. The Shade is badly damaged, so you should be able to take care of it with your Archers.

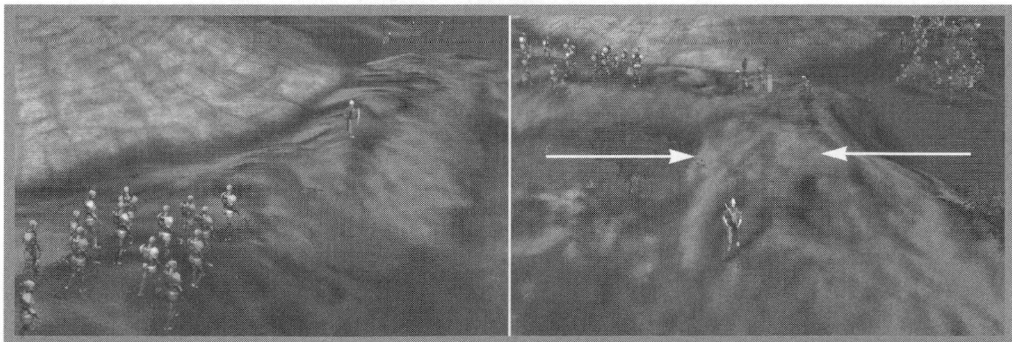

FIGURE 7.6: Once again, a single Warrior can lead two Undead forces into each other, saving you a lot of trouble.

Otherwise, just move around and kill off any remaining Undead units. When they're all gone, you win. I've suggested a path to take (see the Seven Gates scenario map), but it's really up to you how you want to explore the rest of this map.

Blow by Blow

- Put your Archers into one group and all but two of your Warriors in another.
- Move up the pass and kill the few Soulless and Thrall that you encounter.
- As you approach a pass to the right, you'll see two Thrall coming from around a hill. Kill them with a Warrior.
- Send one Warrior up north, and one to the east. They will both meet Undead armies. Move them back toward each other until the Undead armies meet and fight.
- Clean up any Undead that survived the battle.
- Move toward the east (right), and then move a Warrior further to the east. When the Warrior meets an Undead army, get them to follow you around the hill and to the south, where another Undead army will be approaching.
- Finish off any Undead units that survive. Heal your units.
- Move to the upper-right corner of the map; take out the Shade (and any other units) that are there.
- Scour the map to find the remaining Undead units and kill them.

8

Cave Dwelling

In the following three scenarios, you'll do battle with four big, ugly Trow and descend into the realm of caves and Spiders. Forest Heart tests your ability to manage an inferior force against the most powerful opposition you've faced so far. In Heart of Stone and the Smiths of Muirtheme, you must find your way out of a pair of caves. The latter two scenarios show why *Myth* is such an exceptional game. They are more like puzzles embedded in this otherwise highly tactical game, and they're very refreshing as the halfway point in the scenarios.

FOREST HEART

This is without a doubt the most difficult scenario you have played so far in *Myth*. This baby's gonna challenge you tactically, strategically, and emotionally, so grab a large amount of your favorite comfort food before you begin. Your task is to defeat each of Soulblighter's four generals. Unfortunately, these generals are all Trow, and they are heavily guarded by reams of Undead minions. Strap on your helmet—here we go.

MISSION OBJECTIVE

Destroy all four of Soulblighter's generals (Trow).

YOUR GUYS

You have a decent complement of forces, but the lack of a Journeyman will be felt immediately. This is the first time you get Forest Giants. These are roughly equivalent to Trow and go a long way to evening things out. Here's what you get:

-  Archers
-  Berserks
-  Forest Giants

THE EVIL HORDE

As you might expect, the Undead have them all in this one, and plenty of them. Of course, the generals (Trow) are your biggest worry. Here's what they get:

-  Thrall
-  Myrmidons
-  Soulless
-  Trow

LAY OF THE LAND

The limiting factor (for most of your troops) on this map is the great number of rivers and other deep bodies of water. Your units cannot cross many of these; you must use one of the two bridges. However, those bridges are heavily guarded (what a surprise!), so you'll be in for plenty of combat whether you like it or not. Although it might be tempting to trash my advice and try to find a better way around the map, there are quite a few roving groups of Soulless and Myrmidons (and one Trow) that will dash your hopes in a jiffy. In short, I advise you to follow the party line on this one. If you want to fly solo, you do so at your own risk.

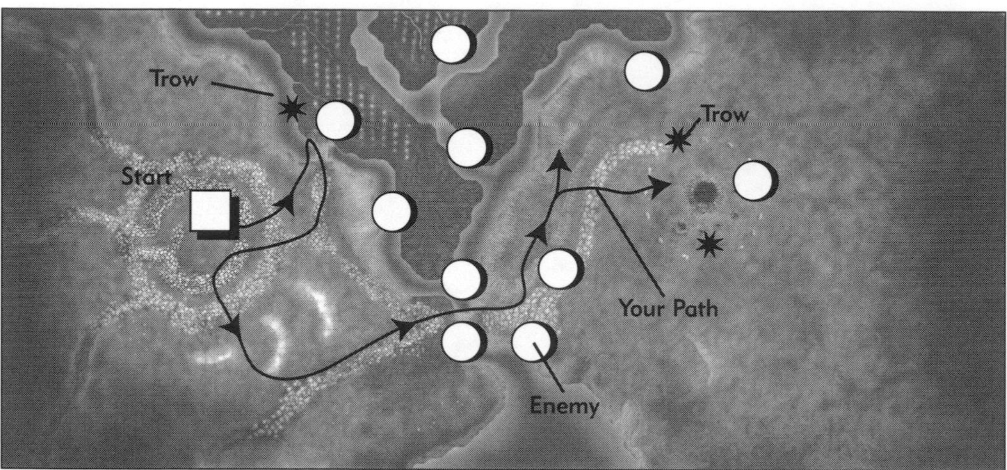

BATTLE PLANS

This scenario begins with a group of Berserks and Archers getting whipped really badly by Myrmidons and a Trow. Your instinct is going to tell you to save these units, but I can tell you that they are *not* intended to survive. They're there more for context and as a prologue than anything else, so don't sweat it if they die. You can, however, use them to do as much damage on the Trow as possible because it will benefit you later on in the game. As soon as those troops are dead, your viewpoint will automatically pop back to your main forces.

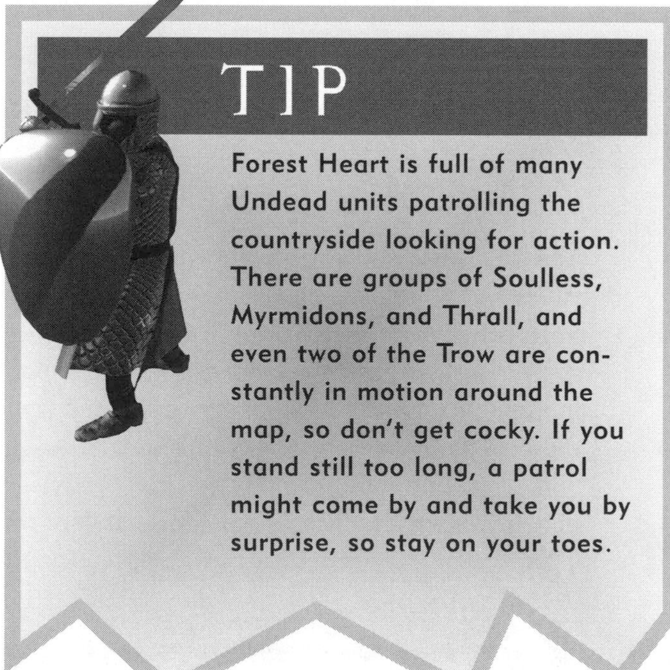

At the main position, three Myrmidons will rush in immediately. Use your Archers to take them down a couple of notches before your Berserks kick them into the ground. The first thing you should do next is

group your Forest Giants together, your Archers together, and your Berserks into two equal groups (for now). Then move your troops up to the north bridge (see the Forest Heart scenario map above) and take out any Soulless that are guarding it.

Whatever you do, don't cross the bridge; heck, don't even step on it, or you'll trigger an attack. There is a row of Myrmidons on the other side, but they won't attack unless you cross the bridge, so just forget about them. Move your Forest Giants to the bank on the left of the bridge, and then move just one of the giants across the river to the other side. (They can cross it even though it's very deep.) Once the Myrmidons have been alerted, turn around and move back to your shore where the other Giants are waiting. By crossing the river you've triggered the Trow to attack, but the Myrmidons won't, so you only have to worry about the Trow. When the Trow crosses the river, kick the crap out of it with all three of your Forest Giants simultaneously (see Figure 8.1). One down, three to go.

Now that you've taken care of the first Trow, stick around this bridge and wait for another one to come along (you can hear them coming). Of the four Trow, there's one that patrols the river as part of its area, and eventually it'll show up. You

FIGURE 8.1: Always try to attack Trow 3 on 1. This way each of your Forest Giants takes minimal damage while the Trow go down.

should have no trouble taking out the second Trow with your three Forest Giants and the rest of your forces. Two down, two to go.

Now I suggest you return to the area where you started, because if you follow the river to the south bridge, you'll attract a lot of attention from Soulless patrols. Once back at the starting point, head toward the south bridge.

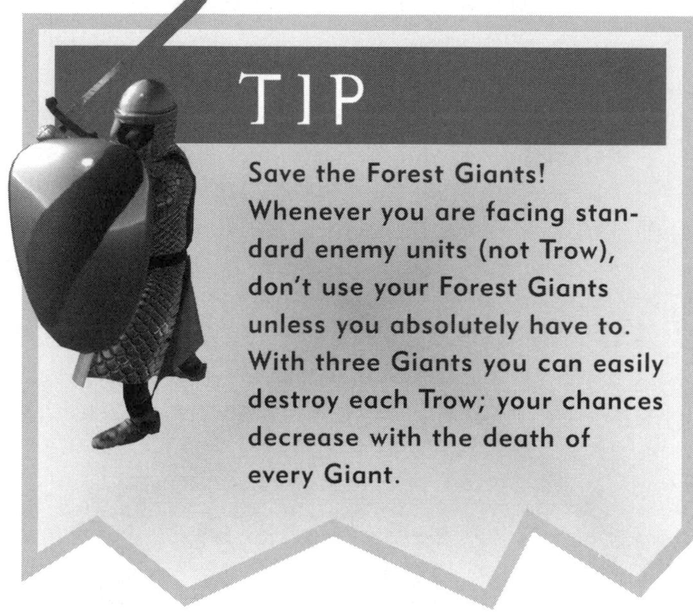

TIP

Save the Forest Giants! Whenever you are facing standard enemy units (not Trow), don't use your Forest Giants unless you absolutely have to. With three Giants you can easily destroy each Trow; your chances decrease with the death of every Giant.

When you arrive at the south bridge, you'll likely have to fend off at least one group of Soulless, but your Archers should be able to make quick work of them. This bridge is tricky because a whole pile of Thrall are hiding in the water below (believe me, you'll be glad I told you) and are triggered when you walk over the bridge. Move your Archers up in a line a ways back from the bridge so that you can get several rounds off before the Thrall are close.

Now move a Berserk up and over the bridge, and then turn back immediately. Voilà! A mess of Thrall emerge from the water and begin their slow walk toward you (see Figure 8.2). You should be able to take out a good 50 percent of the Thrall before they reach your Archers; use your Berserks to mop up the rest. As an alternative, you can take out the Thrall on the left side of the bridge with your Archers and meet the Thrall on the right side of the bridge with Berserks as soon as they climb out of the water.

Now move your troops across the bridge, but not too far forward. Send your Berserks to take out the band of Myrmidons that are nearby, and use your Archers to eliminate the Soulless on the ridge to your left. Once this is done, move your units to the ridge on the left and hug the ridge until you come to a ramp that leads to the top. If you venture even a smidgen away from the ridge, you'll trigger a large Undead army to come after you. Move your units onto the ridge and park everyone

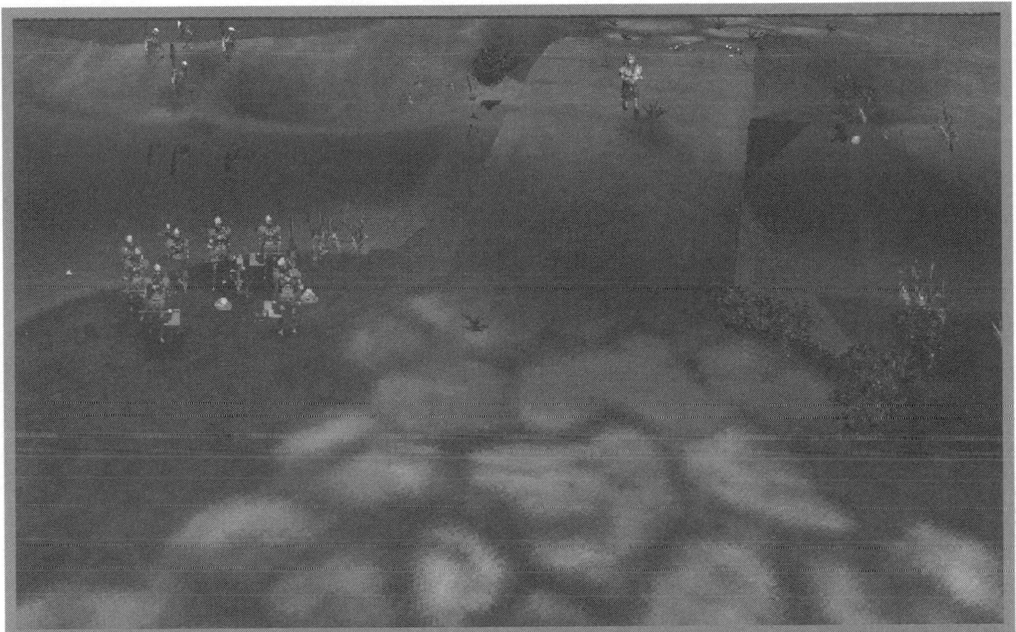

FIGURE 8.2: As soon as you run even one unit over the south bridge, the Thrall will come out of their underwater hiding places.

except your Forest Giants. Move them down off the ridge, again being careful not to provoke any of the Undead armies nearby. If you do, you're dead.

As you approach the statue, the third Trow will come forward and attack. Your three Giants should be able to kill it quickly, but by this time, they are all probably damaged by at least 50 percent. Now move closer to the statue, and you will see the last Trow circling the statue with a bunch of Myrmidons providing protection, as shown in Figure 8.3. Don't hesitate; make a charge for the Trow with all three of your Giants. If you can position your Giants properly, you'll kill the Trow before the Myrmidons finish off all of your Giants. That's it, you've won!

FIGURE 8.3: Don't worry about the Myrmidons; just rush in with all three Forest Giants and kill the last Trow General. That's all you need for the win.

Blow by Blow

- Forget about saving troops at the very beginning of the scenario; they are all meant to die.
- Kill the Myrmidons that attack your main position, and then group your units into Archers, Giants, and two Berserk groups (or one if you prefer).
- Move to the north bridge and kill the Soulless, but don't step on the bridge.
- Move one of your Giants across the river, and then return immediately. The Trow will advance.

- Kill the Trow with all three of your Forest Giants.
- Wait at this bridge for another Trow (which is roving). It will come eventually.
- Move back to the starting point, and then move to the south bridge, but don't cross it, either.
- At the south bridge take out any Soulless, and set up your Archers so that they can attack the Thrall that will come out of the water by the bridge.
- Run one Berserk up the bridge. This will trigger the Thrall; kill them.
- Once the Thrall are dead, cross the bridge and take out any Thrall and Myrmidons that are nearby.
- Hug the ridge on your left and climb up it when you hit the ramp. (Staying close to the ridge will avoid triggering any Undead armies to attack.)
- Move your three Giants off the ridge toward the northeast, again being careful not to trigger any Undead armies. The first of the two Trow here will now attack. Kill it.
- Move toward the statue, and when you see the Trow guarded by the Myrmidons, rush it with all three Forest Giants. When this last Trow is dead, you win.

HEART OF STONE

This is the first of the cave scenarios. Your task is to simply find a way out of the cave, nothing more. The only reasons you know that this is a cave is because you are told so and because you occasionally see a stalactite hanging from the ceiling and blocking your view. This is another original scenario. You probably won't even have to fight the Undead all that much, if you don't want to. You will have to fight, though—you'll see.

MISSION OBJECTIVE

Find a way out of the cave.

YOUR GUYS

You have a good assortment of units, but the nature of this scenario divides them up; and thus diminishing their strength. Here's what you get:

- Berserks
- Dwarves
- Archers
- Journeyman

THE EVIL HORDE

Although there are a couple of Fetches and a few Ghols in this cave, some of them will be killed before you get there. What kills them? Spiders. Spiders are the natural inhabitants of the cave, and they defend their territory. Here's what they get:

- Ghols
- Fetches
- Spiders (enemy, but not Undead)

Reinforcements

Teleport in as you move around the cave. This is what you get:

- Archers
- Berserks

LAY OF THE LAND

This map is an underground cavern with a central island surrounded by molten lava. The island is also your exit, and to get out of this level, you have to find a way to create a bridge across the lava pool. The stalactites that occasionally come into view are pathways for Spiders to crawl down from above, so always be ready in case they drop in.

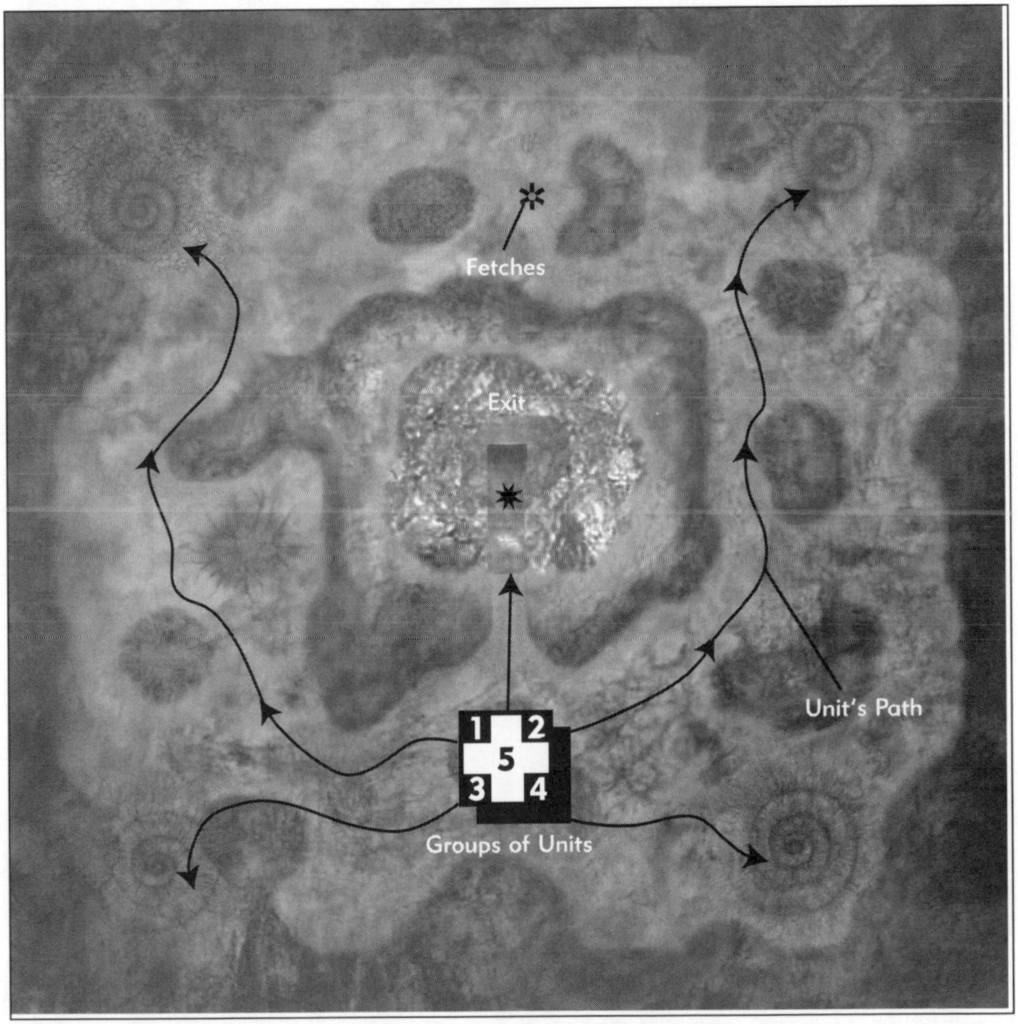

BATTLE PLANS

This scenario is an exercise in managing multiple groups of units at the same time. Basically, the enemy threat consists of a couple groups of Ghols and several Fetches, and for the most part you will only have to do battle with the Fetches; however, there *are* cave Spiders that will hunt you down and attack you. You are supposed to find a way out of the cave; it should quickly become clear to you that the way out lies in the center of the cave in the area surrounded by the molten lava. However, the bridge that leads out is transparent and no one can cross, yet. There are four pylons in the corners of this map, which begin to glow when you get close to them (see Figure 8.4). Sorry to ruin the suspense, but what you have to do is get at least one of your units at each of the four corners at the same time to cause the bridge to become solid. Sounds easy, doesn't it? Think again.

TIP

Spiders can drop in and make your life miserable at any time. Always try to hit them first; this may help you avoid excessive damage.

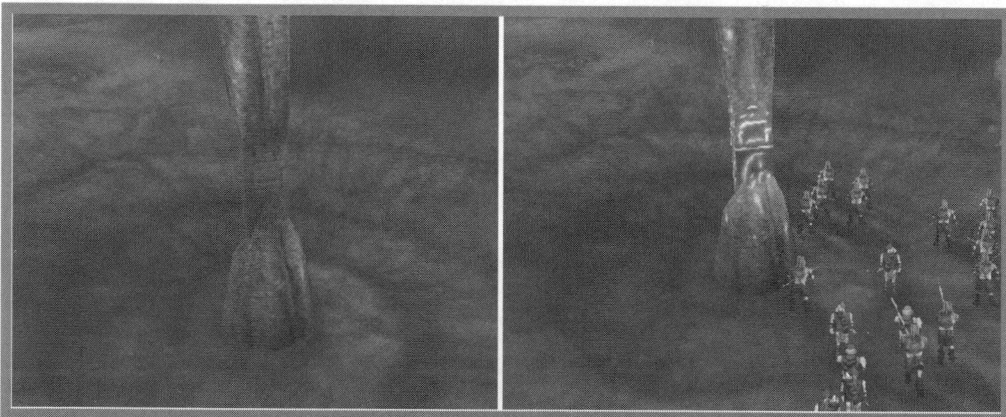

FIGURE 8.4: You have to get your units close to each of the four pylons at the same time to activate the bridge.

You'll need to break up your troops into five segments that can each handle their own defense. I like to put one Berserk and one other unit in each of four groups; then form a fifth group with the remainder of the units. The fifth group should have the Journeyman, and at least one Berserk. Send each of the four Berserk groups to one of the four corners. *Do not* increase the game speed during this process; Spiders can drop from the roof at any time, and if you are not monitoring things, your units will sustain damage before they turn and fight the Spiders.

On the way to the pylons, it's very likely that at least two of your groups will meet up with Spiders, so keep a very close eye on the overhead map. If any of the Berserk groups encounter Fetches, rush at them as fast as possible, and you shouldn't have any trouble with them. Getting to the corners can actually be a heck of a lot more difficult than you might think, and once you're there, you'll be hard-pressed to stay alive for long. When a large group of Spiders attacks, they usually go for the Archers first, so your Berserks are free to come up behind them and hack their legs off. Archers are fairly useless in this scenario anyway, so using them as fodder is okay.

FIGURE 8.5: As soon as the bridge is activated, you'll have some arachnid company.

Once the pylons are activated, the bridge becomes solid and, as you might expect, a new group of Spiders drops down near the bridge to chew up your units. Run your softer units over the bridge as fast as possible while your Berserks kill off the Spiders (see Figure 8.5). After everyone at the bridge makes it to safety, start moving any extra units away from the corners and over the bridge until there's only one unit left at each corner. When you've done this, the scenario is over. Congratulations!

NOTE

Although it will work, dividing your units up can be risky, and in fact many of the guys at Bungie keep their troops together as long as possible in this scenario. By far the easiest way to do it is to keep your units in one large group and move around the map clockwise, leaving a unit behind at each pylon. After the fourth pylon, you simply take the group and head for the exit.

Blow by Blow

- Assemble your units into five groups: four groups with one Berserk and one other unit each and a fifth group with everything else to hang out by the exit.
- If you want to be different, group all your units together and move around the map in a clockwise fashion, leaving one unit at each Pylon.
- Move your Berserk groups out to the four corners of the map, keeping a close eye out for Spiders.
- If you run into a pair of Fetches, run them down as fast as you can with your Berserks.

- Watch out for Spiders dropping from the ceiling.
- Move your units near the pylons in each corner. Once this is done, the bridge will become solid.
- When the bridge activates, a wave of Spiders will attack the bridge, so be ready.
- Move your units across the bridge to safety.
- Move any extra units away from the corners and over the bridge to complete the scenario.
- There's no way to get all your units off the map, because the bridge will not work unless all four corners are covered.

THE SMITHS OF MUIRTHEME

Once again, you need to find your way out of a cave. Although this scenario sounds similar to the Heart of Stone, I can assure you that the path to victory is very different. This time there are new challenges to managing your resources, but you're still going to have to work with multiple groups spread out all over the map. The premise of Smiths of Muirtheme is also novel in that you've got to put the Spheres into the Teleport Gate receptacle in order to escape the cave.

MISSION OBJECTIVE

Find a way to escape the cave. Keep in mind that if you lose all your Dwarves, you cannot finish this scenario.

YOUR GUYS

Again, you have a decent complement of units, and you even have a Journeyman. However, Spider wounds *cannot* be healed by the Journeyman, so he's not a heck of a lot of use in this scenario. Here's what you get:

- Berserks
- Archers
- Dwarves
- Journeyman

THE EVIL HORDE

There really isn't much of an evil horde in this cave. Most of the bad guys you face are Spiders; however, there are a few Undead roaming around. Here's what they get:

- Myrmidons (one group)
- Spiders (everywhere)
- Large Spiders

LAY OF THE LAND

Another cave, complete with stalactites and creepy coloring. Happily, however, this cave doesn't have Spiders dropping in from the ceiling—what you see is what you get. Although you may think a cave is dank and wet, Dwarves' explosives are still effective in this map.

Your task in this scenario is to retrieve the Sphere from each of four paths. The paths are guarded by obelisks, which will electrocute you if you go near them. (Two other paths are the way you came in and the exit.) It doesn't matter which path you explore first, so this is one time when you can make your own choices.

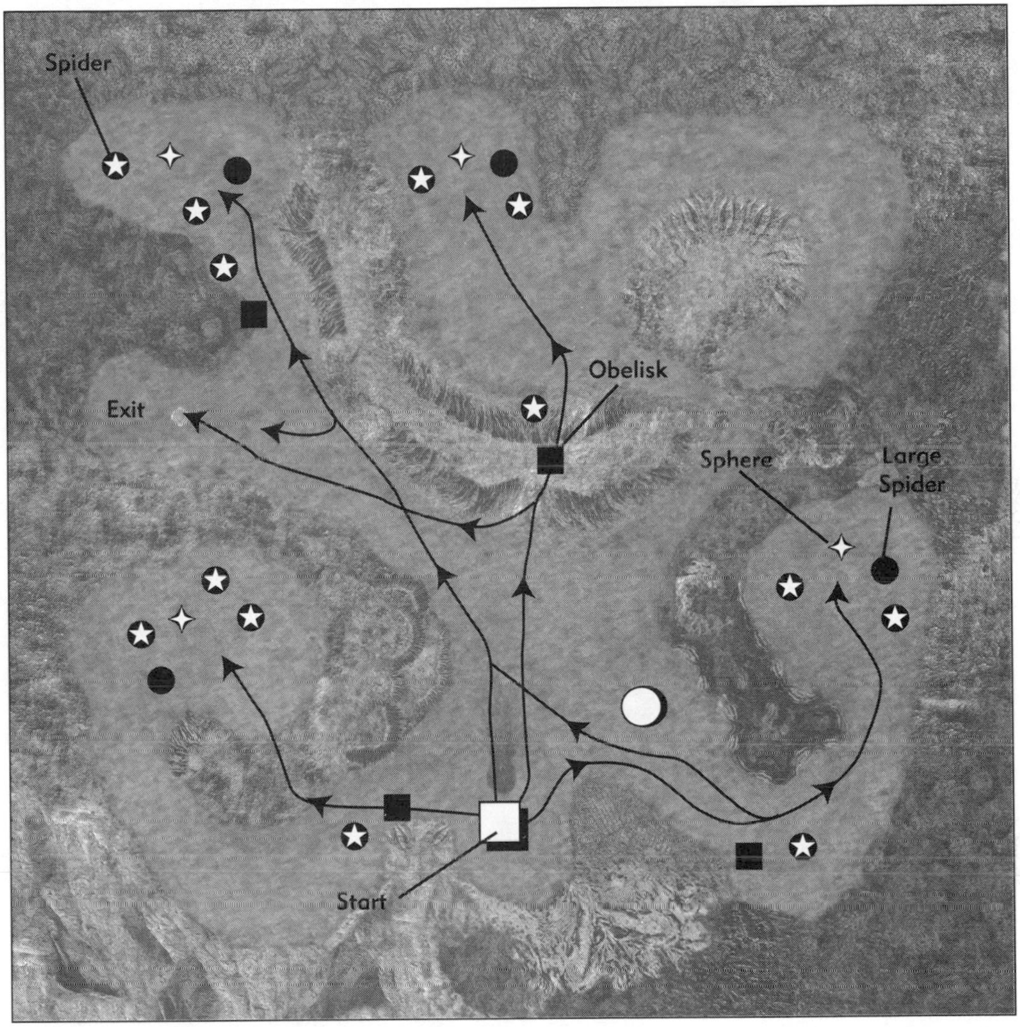

BATTLE PLANS

As you come out of the chute you should probably start grouping your units. I suggest that you group all of your Archers, and four or five Berserks into a "command group." This force will do most of the dirty work while the other units stand guard and protect the Dwarves. If you move to your left, you'll notice the first obelisk standing guard over a pathway that disappears into darkness. If you get too close to the obelisk you'll get fried, à la the Fetch (see Figure 8.6). Lightning streams out of the obelisk, pretty much killing anything that tries to pass. You can try to run by, and some of your

FIGURE 8.6: Don't get too close to these structures right off the bat, or this will happen to you.

units might make it, but you'll never win this way.

So, how the heck are you going to get past these lightning-spewing sentinels? Well, that's easy my friend. Move a couple of Berserks over toward one of the obelisks and inch your way up to it slowly. As soon as you get close enough, you'll notice that it begins to glow, and if you take one step further, you fry. For now just stay put. When one of the obelisks is glowing, move

TIP

Ambushes and sneak attacks are the order of the day in this map. Spiders will sometimes launch a surprise attack on the units that are making the obelisk glow. If those units get drawn away or die, any troops that are near one of the other obelisks will fry. It's a good idea not to hang around the obelisks; get past them as fast as you can.

your command group over to one of the other paths guarded by an obelisk. No reaction at all. As long as you have at least one unit in close proximity to one of the obelisks, you can move freely past the others.

Take your command group up one of the paths, inching forward slowly. Have your Archers take out the Spiders along the way. Continue following the path until you find a glowing white Sphere. There will be a Large Spider here as well; use your Archers to take it out before it can get close to you. Kill all of the Spiders in the area, and then bring the Dwarf in to pick up the Sphere (yes, only a Dwarf can pick it up). Repeat this with the other three pathways on the map. Always keep any eye on the units that are disabling the obelisk defense system to make sure they're okay.

Take the four Spheres to the upper-left corner of the map, and throw them in the archway by pressing Control + click (Command = + click on the Mac) on the spot beneath the arch. You'll notice that with each successive Sphere the sparkles in the arch will grow brighter. Once all four spheres are in place, simply walk your units through the arch, and they will be teleported out of the cave, as shown in Figure 8.7.

FIGURE 8.7: You'll have to place all four Spheres into the circle on the ground to activate the World Knot.

That's all there is to this level, but I have to stress that attacks by the Spiders can take you by surprise and cost you a fair number of units. Try to use your Archers to take out the Spiders whenever possible, because your Berserks can't be healed after receiving Spider bites. Last but not least, there *will* be a surprise attack by a group of five or six Myrmidons if you keep your units in the middle of the map for very long. The Myrmidons are easily handled by your Berserks, and any damage they inflict can be healed, so don't worry about them in this scenario.

Blow by Blow

- Group your Archers and five or six Berserks into a command group.
- Move three Berserks to one of the obelisks; get just close enough to make it glow.
- Send the command group up one of the paths. Use the Archers to take out as many Spiders as possible and the Berserks for mop up.
- After all the Spiders on the path are dead, move a Dwarf in to grab the Sphere.
- Take the Sphere to the archway in the upper-left corner of the map, and throw it under the archway.
- Continue up each of the four paths, killing the Spiders and retrieving the spheres. Keep an eye out for surprise Myrmidon attacks.
- The Spiders will nearly always try to attack the small group you have disabling an obelisk, so be ready for this attack, and keep your units away from the other obelisks on the map.

- Take all four Spheres to the archway and drop them under the arch.
- The World Knot is now activated. Walk through to escape the level.

9

Dwarf Revenge

The first two scenarios in this chapter deal with the age-old conflict between the Ghols and the Dwarves. In the Sons of Myrgard, you are an invisible Dwarf, and you must place a landing marker so that more of your kind can parachute into Myrgard and blow the crap out of the Ghols. You see, Myrgard used to be a Dwarf city, but long ago it was taken over by the Ghols.

In a Long Awaited Party, your task is to get your Dwarves into the area of Myrgard where a sacred Ghol statue sits so they can blow it up. A Long Awaited Party is the "secret" mission in *Myth*. You can only get to it through the Sons of Myrgard level, and if you don't follow the correct path, you'll bypass the level all together and never know it exists.

The last two scenarios in this chapter have you struggling against overwhelming enemy forces. In the Road North you must retrieve the Bow of Lightning, and then run for your life. In Across the Gjol you attempt to hold a bluff against massive Undead assaults.

THE SONS OF MYRGARD

The Ghols long ago captured the Dwarf town of Myrgard and made it their own. This heinous act by the Ghols has never been forgotten, and the descendants of the inhabitants of the old Dwarf town are poised for revenge. You must move through the area unnoticed and put down a signal grenade for your comrades to parachute in for the attack. Once this is done, you need to rid your forebears' home of Ghols.

MISSION OBJECTIVE

You are invisible. The enemy cannot see you, but they can hear you. Sneak past the defenders and find a suitable flat area to throw the signal grenade that summons the Dwarf Paratroopers.

YOUR GUYS

You have nothing but Dwarves in this scenario, which poses several logistical problems. You also have a super-Dwarf called the Pathfinder Dwarf. This Dwarf is invisible at first and can throw faster and more accurately than other Dwarves. Here's what you get:

- Dwarves (they parachute in once the signal grenade is placed)
- Pathfinder Dwarf (invisible at first)

THE EVIL HORDE

The Undead are almost exclusively Ghols in this scenario. However, there are a few groups of Soulless that will keep you on your toes once the paratroopers arrive. Here's what they get:

- Ghols
- Soulless

LAY OF THE LAND

The map runs from left to right and has three distinct areas. The first area has several large pools of water that you could easily walk through, but if you do the Ghols will spot the ripples in the water and cut you to shreds. The middle section of the map is a military compound with a target range and an ammo dump full of Puss

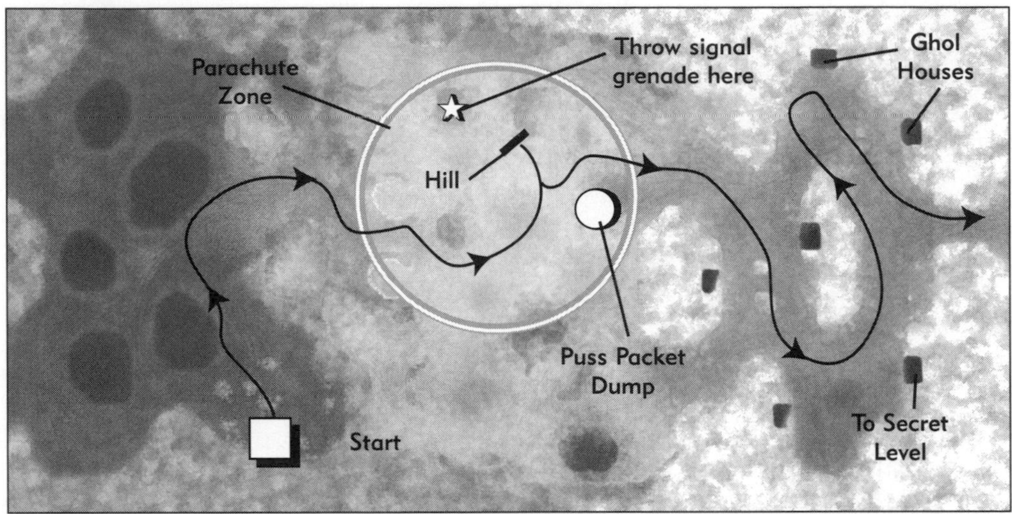

Packets. This is where you want to throw the signal grenade. The third area is higher in the hills and is checkered with many Ghol houses carved into the canyon walls. This is a very dangerous area, but you'll have to pass through it to make it to the exit. There are several hills you can use to your advantage whenever you need to defend yourself.

BATTLE PLANS

You start out in a marshy area with a ton of Ghols circling around everywhere. The Ghols know there's something up because they can hear you when you move, but they can't see you. Occasionally you'll see a Ghol get close to you and take a swipe at the air. If they get lucky and happen to hit or run into you, you're dead. Whatever you do, don't go into the water. If you do, the Ghols will be able to see the ripples you create as you wade through, and they'll come and chop you up in a jiffy. Keep moving through the maze of Ghols, and head for a path that's on the right side of the marshy area, about halfway up the map.

If any Ghols get a little too close for comfort, one thing you can do to throw them off is just stop dead in your tracks. The Ghols are listening to you move around, and if they can't hear you, you're safe (unless one of them bumps into you by accident). Move up the pathway and weave your way through the spiked gates (guarded by Soulless and Ghols), as shown in Figure 9.1. Continue on past the gates and into the open area where you'll see some Soulless engaged in target practice on

FIGURE 9.1: Keep on going, even when you see this. Because you're invisible, they can't hurt you.

the left and a few Ghols guarding a large pile of Puss Packets.

As you approach the Puss Packet ammo dump, you'll notice a small hill to the left. Climb up this hill (the Soulless will then be just downhill from you) and align yourself so that you're dead center and in good position for starting a fight. Wait for all of the Ghols to get a fair distance away from you, and then throw the signal grenade. You will now become visible, and the enemy will rush you at once. However,

TIP

If you press "T" then throw a bottle (with your Pathfinder only), you'll be launching a Airstrike Signal Grenade that will cause a bunch of Satchel Charges to drop in and explode. Using these bottles can be a great help if you get your timing right. You'll know the explosions are coming just after the red signal smoke stops.

your Pathfinder Dwarf can throw Explosive Bottles faster, harder, and more accurately than any other Dwarf. Use this ability to take out any Ghols or Soulless that come close. Soon you'll see a bunch of Dwarves parachuting in (see Figure 9.2) to help you in your cause.

As the Dwarves parachute in, they drop Satchel Charges to try to clear the area where they plan to land. Once the Dwarves

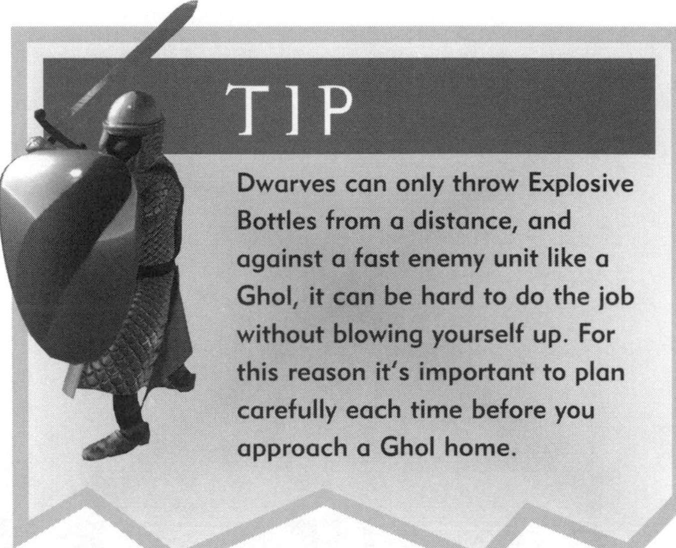

TIP

Dwarves can only throw Explosive Bottles from a distance, and against a fast enemy unit like a Ghol, it can be hard to do the job without blowing yourself up. For this reason it's important to plan carefully each time before you approach a Ghol home.

FIGURE 9.2: Once your friends drop in, you'll have to work quickly to save as many of them as possible from the Ghol guards. Gather the Dwarves on a high point for protection.

are on the ground, get control of them, and move them quickly up the hill where you've been waiting. There will be many Ghols coming after the Dwarf Paratroopers, but if you are careful, you should be able to save six or seven of them. Once you're on the hill, you can move off and blow up the Puss Packets (and the guards around them), while keeping an eye out for any extra Soulless that may be moving around.

Now that you've got your Dwarf strike force ready, move toward the east and blow up the two Ghols guarding the gate that leads to the homes. From here on out, move very carefully. You'll have to take great pains to ensure that your Dwarves don't blow each other up. You need to kill all the Ghols as they come out of their houses in this area. There are six houses, and each one holds a bunch of Ghols (see Figure 9.3). More Ghols are just roving around this section of the map. I won't lie to you, this part of the scenario is exceedingly difficult, and it will probably take you several tries to finish it, so save often. After you've taken out all of the Ghols, you can exit up the path on the east side of the map. You can exit the map the "normal" way, or you can head to the secret level—A Long Awaited Party—through the southeast Ghol's house (see scenario map). If you do choose to go to the secret level, you won't have to defeat it to progress to the rest of *Myth*.

FIGURE 9.3: Each of these holes houses a bunch of Ghols. There will often be more than one wave of Ghols. You've been warned.

Blow by Blow

- Move your Dwarf toward the path on the east side of the marshy area. Don't walk through any water.
- If any Ghols seem to be following you, stop until they go away.
- Move up the path, through the gate, and into the Undead military area.
- Position yourself on the hill next to the Puss Packet pit.
- Throw the signal grenade and get ready for some serious action.
- Kill anything that approaches you while you wait for the Paratroopers.
- When the Paratroopers drop in, work quickly to get as many of them as possible up the hill to join your Pathfinder Dwarf.
- Blow up the Puss Packet dump and the Ghols that are guarding it.
- Move up the path on the east side of the map.
- Clear out any Ghols in the houses carved into the sides of the canyon. This sounds a lot easier than it is.
- Carefully plan each attack on the houses, and save often.
- After all the Ghols are dead, you win.
- As an alternative, you can also move to the secret level through the southeast Ghol's house.

A LONG AWAITED PARTY (SECRET LEVEL)

Okay, so you've killed all the Ghols in the residential part of your ancestral home of Myrgard, isn't that enough? I guess not, because in the Long Awaited Party you must take a party of Dwarves and blow up a sacred Ghol statue. This is the secret scenario in Myth. You don't have to play it, but if you do choose to play it and lose, you can continue on to the next scenario without repeating it (unless you want to). This is a nice bonus for those who find the level too difficult, and believe me, many will.

MISSION OBJECTIVE

Find the Ghol godhead and blast it into fragments.

YOUR GUYS

This scenario is not unlike the last, except that you don't have a Pathfinder Dwarf. Here's what you get:

-  Dwarves
-  Dwarf Parachutists (reinforcements)

THE EVIL HORDE

Ghols are once again the order of the day in this scenario. Here's what they get:

-  Ghols
-  Soulless

LAY OF THE LAND

This map is dry, so you don't have to worry about your bottles going out any more than usual. However, the dryness of this map doesn't make up for the dangerous nature of it. To get to the godhead, you must traverse the map up, down, then up again, each time traveling the entire height of the map. There are many roving bands of Ghols all over the place, and with only one path to take, your options are limited. It's a good thing this is an optional scenario.

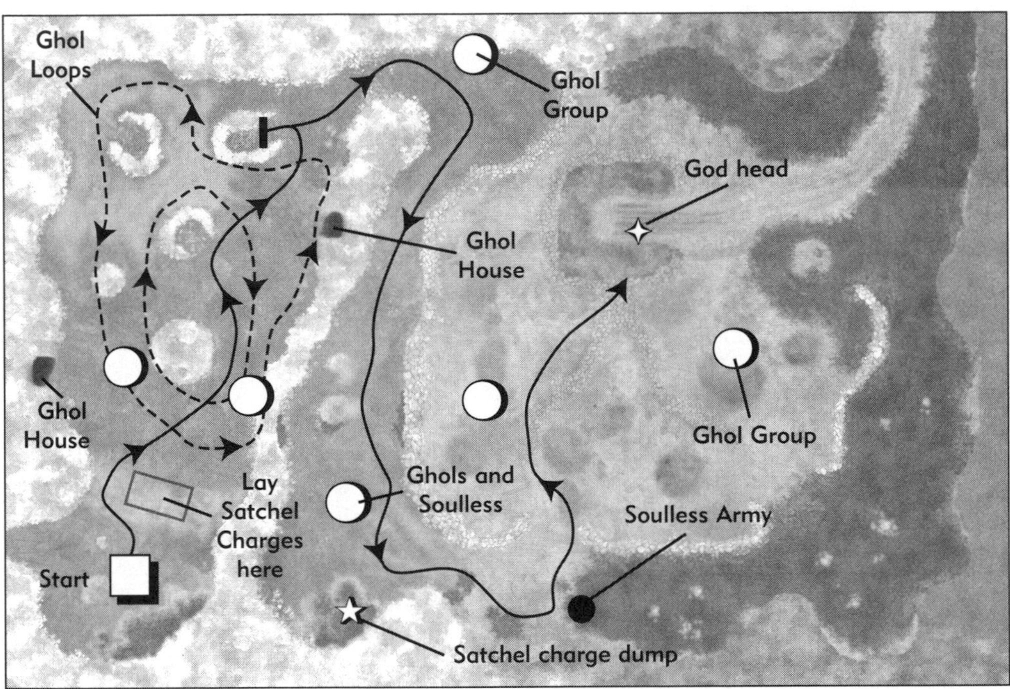

BATTLE PLANS

I'm not going to sugar coat this for you—I found this to be one of the hardest levels in the entire game. What makes it so difficult is that if even one of your Explosive Bottles snuffs out at the wrong time, it can mean the loss of most, or all, of your forces. I suggest that you save very often in this scenario.

You begin with a complement of Dwarves (usually eight or nine) coming out of a Ghol's house with a Ghol right in front of you. One of the Dwarves should take the

Ghol out with a bottle. The first thing you'll want to do is split your force in two and back them up to both sides of the canyon. Two waves of Ghols will come by within a short period of time, and you don't want to tangle with either yet.

After the Ghols have circled by, move out and lay down a few Satchel Charges in a line (see Figure 9.4). Don't use too many because you'll need some later. Then fall back and set up two banks of four Dwarves each. Eventually the Ghols will appear again on their patrol. This time, however, they'll see you and rush your position. When they get close to the Satchel Charges, have one bank of Dwarves fire, and a second later, have the other bank fire. This is important because if all the Dwarves fire at once, then any Ghols that don't die in the explosions will have clear sailing to your units. This way (with two banks) you can always have a backup set of Dwarves loaded and ready to fire on approaching Ghols.

FIGURE 9.4: Don't waste a lot of Satchel Charges on this; just use enough to help you deal with this Ghol patrol.

You should be able to escape the first patrol without any damage. Now move your troops up the right side of the map. Soon you will see another pack of black Ghols coming toward you. Again, use the double bank method to take them all out. You may lose a unit or two here, but if you play it carefully, you should be able to escape without too much carnage on your side. Now that you've taken care of the two main patrols, the key is to avoid the two Ghol houses on either side of the canyon. Move up to the top left of the map, and then inch forward to the pass that takes you to the east.

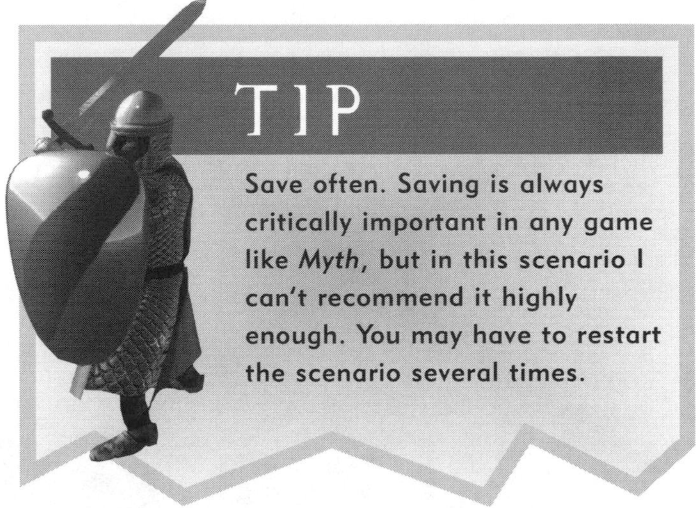

TIP

Save often. Saving is always critically important in any game like *Myth*, but in this scenario I can't recommend it highly enough. You may have to restart the scenario several times.

As you come down the pass, you'll face another group of Ghols. These ones are armed with Puss Packets and will lob them toward you before you can get a shot off. You can usually take them out by sacrificing one Dwarf. Run the sacrificial Dwarf up the left side of the canyon until the Ghols are triggered, and then have him lob a bottle at the Ghols. Now have three or four Dwarves hit the Ghols from the right side of the canyon. This will cost you one Dwarf, but it will destroy this group of Ghols without more bloodshed.

Move around the pass and out into the new area. The plateau you're on overlooks the godhead, but you'll have to follow the path to the south, and then loop back up to the godhead on the other side of the plateau. As you follow the path down to the bottom of the map, you'll come to a group of Ghols and Soulless guarding a pile of Puss Packets. This is yet another formidable challenge that may take you several tries to overcome, so don't give up if you get kicked on the first pass. This time just rush the enemy position in a spread-out formation. If you place your shots carefully, you should be able to take out the Ghols in two rounds. Do the Dwarf Juke to take out the Soulless.

After you're done with that, you'll notice that there's a pile of Satchel Charges waiting for you. Don't blow them up. You'll need to get them to pile up around the godhead. As you approach the Satchel Charges, a new set of Dwarves will parachute in. As

you move to the ramp down off the plateau, you'll come up against a huge bunch of Soulless. Take them out, and then head down the ramp. To eliminate the Soulless, attack from several angles, and keep one or two Dwarves under your control so that you can juke them. From here on out, ferry Satchel Charges to and from the godhead (see Figure 9.5), planting all of the charges on one side. Watch out for Ghols along the way. Once that's done, blow it up! You win.

FIGURE 9.5: Blow up this stone monolith to win the scenario.

Blow by Blow

- Back your Dwarves off in two groups until the two Ghol patrols have passed.
- Lay out some Satchel Charges along the route where the Ghols will most likely attack.

Continued on next page

Continued from previous page

- Bring your Dwarves up in two groups (or banks) on either side of the Satchel Charges. When the Ghols approach, sandwich them.
- Move up the map (as shown in the Long Awaited Party scenario map) being careful not to get the attention of the Ghol houses.
- Take out the second (black) band of roving Ghols.
- Move into the pass in the upper-right corner of the canyon.
- Take out the Ghols in the pass.
- Move down the path until you meet resistance.
- Take out the Soulless and Ghols in your way.
- As you approach the Satchel Charges, new Dwarves will parachute in.
- Take out the Soulless that you'll meet by the ramp.
- Ferry the Satchel Charges from the large pile ahead of you to the base of the godhead, and then blow it up. Watch out for Ghols along the way.
- Keep an eye out for any other resistance as you're approaching the godhead.

THE ROAD NORTH

An Archer hero has been vanquished in the northern portion of this map. It's up to you to find the Bow of Lightning and retreat to the south while avoiding the legions of Thrall. This scenario seems like a cinch at first, but it quickly turns into an ugly run-for-your-life situation when you grab the bow. The Bow is like a extra-strong Lightning Attack on the end of an arrow! Believe me, it comes in very handy.

MISSION OBJECTIVE

One of your Archer heroes has been killed somewhere in the north. Find the Magic Bow and return south with it.

YOUR GUYS

Again, a small party, not well-balanced either. Fortunately, there are reinforcements. Here's what you get:

-  Archers
-  Warriors

THE EVIL HORDE

Thrall are the main enemies in this scenario, but a few others will show up if you stick around long enough. The twist is that the Undead spring up right out of the ground when you grab the bow. Here's what they get:

-  Thrall
-  Soulless
-  Fetches

LAY OF THE LAND

The map is a rainy one—good thing you don't have any Dwarves. This map is very dark, and the relentless rain will make it difficult for you to see the detail you are used to seeing in other maps. There are plenty of obstacles: rock formations, trees, and so forth, but you still shouldn't have a huge amount of trouble maneuvering around on this map. The water is generally shallow; however, it slows your units down (which is bad if there are Soulless following you).

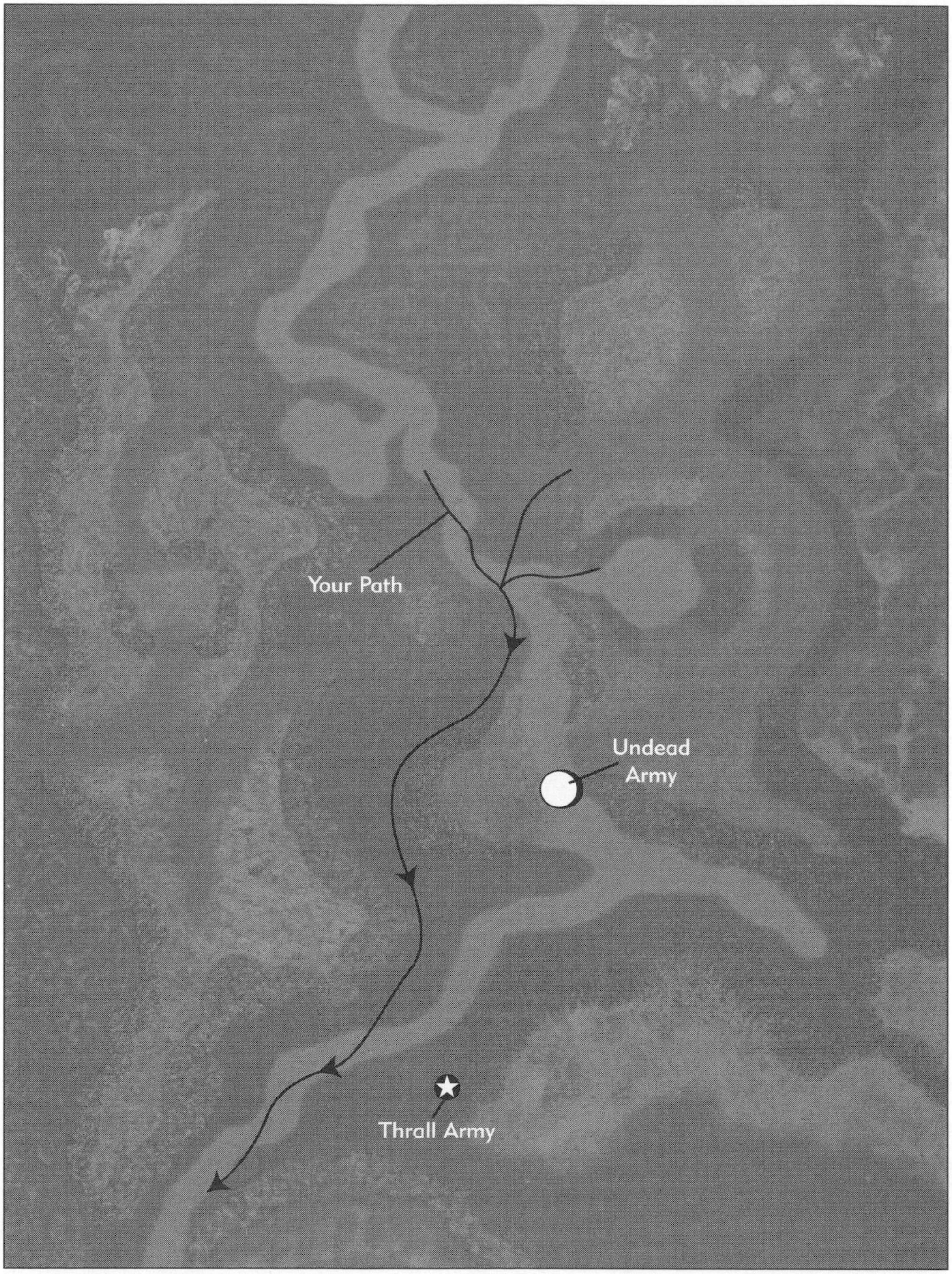

Your Path

Undead Army

Thrall Army

BATTLE PLANS

You start out with three Archers and only a pair of Warriors, but until you actually grab the bow, you won't have to face more than one or two Thrall at a time. Start out by simply heading north. I can't tell you where the bow's going to be, because it's randomly placed somewhere in the upper portion of the map. So, just head up to the top of the map. Keep an eye out for where you are and what sort of pathways you have at your disposal to get back down to the south (once you have the bow). Keep moving around the upper region of the map until you see the bow spinning and glimmering, just waiting for you to pick it up (see Figure 9.6). If you want, you can follow the trail of blood that appears occasionally; it will lead you in the direction of the bow.

Before you grab the bow, you'll need to prepare carefully. Once you have it, there's no turning back. Move one of your Archers and two Warriors close to the

FIGURE 9.6: Don't pick up the bow until you've mapped out your escape route.

bow. Keep the two Warriors near your planned escape route. Once you grab the bow, a circle of Thrall will spring up (out of the ground) around the bow and immediately close on your Archer, as shown in Figure 9.7. Use your Warriors to take out the Thrall, and boogie out of there with your Archer ASAP. You will also notice that another large group of Thrall has appeared, and is heading right for your Archer. Use your superior speed to get around the Thrall and begin your run for the southern part of the map. If you get in a pickle, your Archer can use the Magic Bow's special power (lightning) to take out the offending Thrall.

As you work your way down the path to the south, the Thrall will continue to follow you, so don't let up for a second. If you want, you can try to send an Archer in another direction as a decoy, but this may not work. As you progress toward the south, many Thrall will get in your way. Use your Bow of Lightning to clear out as many of them as possible to make your passage safe. Sacrifice the rest of your units to get the Archer with the Magic Bow off the end of the map; that's all that counts.

The Undead have more than just Thrall behind you. Don't try mounting a counter-attack, or you'll end up with Soulless and Fetches nearby. Just boogie to the end of the map as fast as possible, and use your Lightning Bow to deal with the Thrall that get in your way. Once you're off the map, you win.

FIGURE 9.7: Use your Warriors to cut a hole through the Thrall for your Archer to escape.

Blow by Blow

- Follow the trail of blood to the bow, or just explore the northern portion of the map until you find the bow.
- Move two Warriors and one Archer near the bow, and then move your other units away to the south.
- Grab the bow. When the Thrall emerge from the ground, hack them up with your Warriors so you can escape with the bow.
- You'll have to do some fancy maneuvering to get away from two or three groups of pursuing Thrall, but you're faster so you should be able to do it.
- If you get in a pickle, use one of your other units to distract the enemy, or use your Magic Bow on the Thrall.
- Run like hell to the south.
- Use the Lightning Bow to occupy the armies of Thrall that pop up in front of you on your trip south.
- Again, you may have to get creative with your Archer (with the Magic Bow). Remember, you can use the Lightning Bow power of the bow if you need to.
- Run off the end of the map.

ACROSS THE GJOL

This scenario is similar in some ways to Shadow of the Mountain in that you've got a finite force with which to defend a specific area against overwhelming Undead forces. I personally find these scenarios the most fun because they're pure tactical prowess. No puzzles, no timing issues, just army against army in pure battle. This time you're trying to prevent Soulblighter's army from crossing the Gjol (a river) and punching a hole in the Light side's lines of defense. You are in for a tough battle, but it can be won, and I promise you, it'll be fun.

MISSION OBJECTIVE

You are the rearguard, left behind to hold the enemy at the river (the Gjol). Retreat is *not* an option—you must hold the bluff overlooking the river at all costs.

YOUR GUYS

You have a solid complement of units, complete with a handful of Dwarves. Use them and your Journeyman to turn the tide in your favor. This is what you get:

- Archers
- Warriors
- Dwarves
- Journeyman
- Reinforcements (same as above)

THE EVIL HORDE

The Undead army is well-endowed, and they'll come in waves, one after another. Just when you think they're done, they'll come again. This is what they get:

- Thrall
- Soulless
- Fetches
- Wights

LAY OF THE LAND

This map is very simple. You must protect the bluff as the enemy units stream across the river. Use this high ground to your advantage whenever possible, and you shouldn't have too much trouble winning this scenario. The only thing I must caution you about is the rain. As the scenario reaches its climax with piles of Thrall, Wights, and Soulless bearing down on you, your most effective weapons, your Dwarves, won't be very effective. The skies inconveniently open up to a full downpour just when you could use your Dwarves the most. Oh well, at least *some* of the bottles will go off.

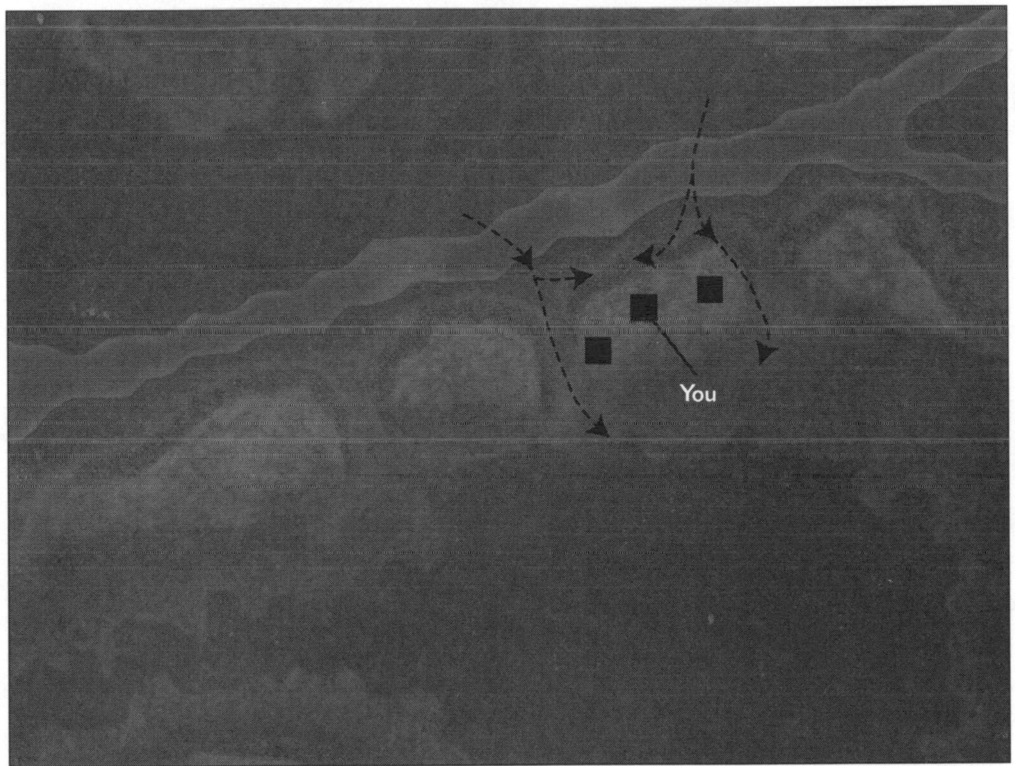

BATTLE PLANS

You start off just behind the bluff you are expected to defend from the onrushing Undead troops. Move your Archers up to the top edge of the bluff in a line, and move your Dwarves to the corners of the bluff, three per side (see Figure 9.8). Put two groups of Warriors (five each) on the back corners of the bluff, and the rest of the units can sit at the bottom of the bluff in the middle. The first wave of Undead will come in the form of two large groups of Thrall crossing the river on either side of the bluff.

Before the first wave of Thrall comes, you may want to take a Dwarf or two and lay down some Satchel Charges along the front of the bluff. This may help to take out a few extra Undead, but it shouldn't be necessary. The weather, for now, is dry, so your Dwarves' bottles should find their mark and explode without incident. When the first wave comes, split your Archers up on either side at the top of the bluff and fire at will on the oncoming Thrall. I like to fire at the Thrall at the back of the pile because the Dwarves' bottles will vaporize the Thrall at the front. If any of the Thrall make it past the edge of the bluff and start to come after your Dwarves, send in the Warriors that you left sitting at the corners of the bluff to mop up the rest.

The second wave is likely to be a stream of Wights meandering across the river. If you can hit the first one of them with your Archers, the rest will go off like a row of explosive dominoes (see Figure 9.9).

FIGURE 9.8: I've had a lot of success with this formation; in this scenario, you should too.

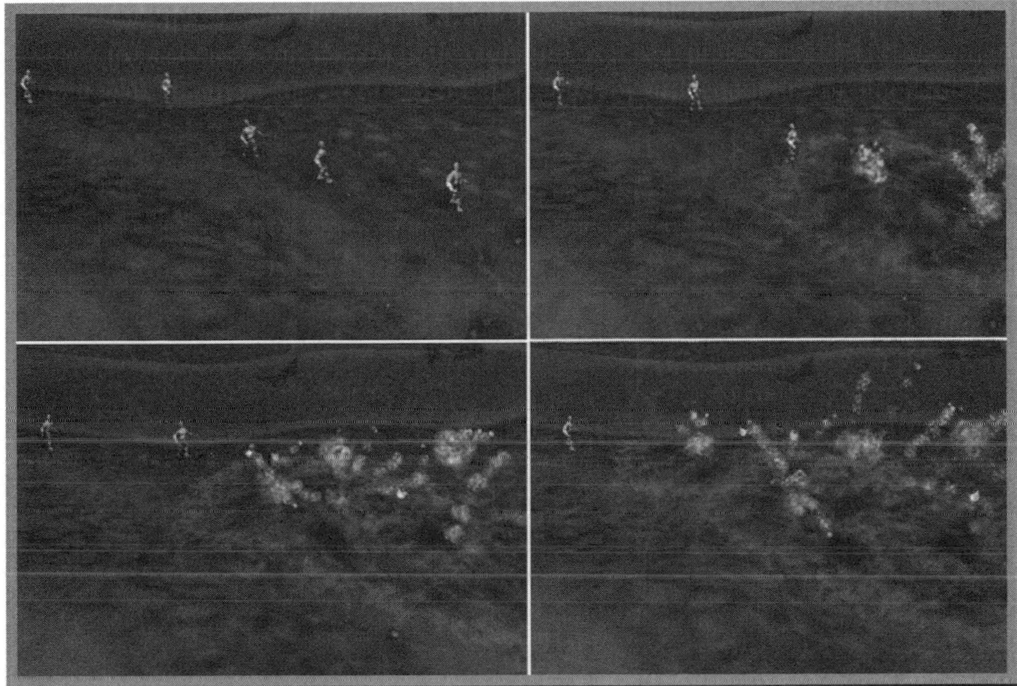

FIGURE 9.9: You only need to hit one of these Wights to make a show of it.

The third wave contains a couple of Wights, several Fetches, and a pack of Thrall that come at you from the top of the map (to your right). Set your Archers to deal with the Fetches, and have your Dwarves handle the Thrall. Keep in mind that the skies may begin to open up a bit here, making Explosive Bottles more temperamental.

The fourth wave is the last, and by far the most threatening (for a couple of reasons). It contains large packs of Thrall supported by a medium-sized contingent of Soulless. This by itself would probably be manageable; however, as soon as the Undead troops draw near, the rain begins to fall, and heavily at that. This makes your usual bomb-them-into-the-ground tactic moot, and ultimately your defenses will be stretched to their limits.

As the fourth wave approaches, move your Archers to the left side of the bluff and have them attack the Soulless. Bring a Journeyman up behind the Archers to heal them as they sustain damage. The Thrall will continue their usual course, so keep firing Explosive Bottles at them even though it's raining. The bottles that don't go off will act like Satchel Charges once they're hit by bottles that *do* go off. By now

a Wight or two will move in with the Soulless and Thrall by the river. Hit the Wight, and the resulting explosion will do most of your work for you. At this point, you should notice that a couple of Wights are sneaking past your lines. You need to destroy at least one of these Wights to get your reinforcements, so send out a couple of Archers on each Wight.

If you're like most players, the Thrall will break through your lines. Your Warriors will be in a free-for-all-fight, while your Dwarves and Archers run for their lives. At this point, a group of reinforcements arrives with Dwarves, Archers, Warriors, and two Journeymen just in time for you to face the final wave. The final wave is usually another bunch of Thrall coming at you in two large groups from either side of the bluff. The new troops should be all you need to take care of 'em. Once they're all gone, you win. Wasn't that fun?

Blow by Blow

- Set up your troops with your Archers in a row at the top edge of the bluff and three Dwarves on each side at the corners. Also put two groups of five Warriors each on the bottom corners of the bluff. The rest of the troops should sit in the middle ready to support whichever side needs the most help.
- If you want, you can lay out Satchel Charges along the sides of the bluff.
- When the first wave comes, use a combination of Archers and Dwarves to take care of the Thrall. If any get by you, clean them up with your Warriors on the corners.
- The second wave should be Wights. Take them out with your Archers. Killing just two Wights should trigger chain reactions that take the rest out.
- The third wave will be Fetches, Wights, and a group of

Thrall that come straight at you from your right (the top of the map). Use your Archers to snag the Fetches before they can get close enough to do any damage.

- The fourth wave will contain plenty of Soulless (all concentrated on the left side of the bluff) and Thrall coming in large groups. Use your Archers to try to control the Soulless, while your Dwarves battle the rain with their bottles.
- If a Wight wanders into the Thrall and Soulless, train *all* your Archers on him until he blows. This will save you a lot of trouble.
- To get your reinforcements, kill any Wights that sneak past.
- Your reinforcements will show up; kill the rest of the Thrall and then celebrate.

THE WATCHER

After heroically holding Soulblighter at the Gjol, you must be emotionally and physically exhausted. Luckily, your stand at the Gjol was long enough to let Alric spring his trap on the Watcher. Alric used bone chips from the Watcher's Arm to create special arrows to turn the Watcher into stone, and sure enough it worked! Now it's up to you and your team of crack Berserks to see if you can finish off the Watcher before Undead help arrives to restore him. You're going up against a pair of Shades in this scenario, so be prepared for some wild magic.

MISSION OBJECTIVE

Find the Watcher (who has been turned to stone), and shatter him before help can arrive.

YOUR GUYS

Berserks, that's all you have in this scenario. But there'll be some reinforcements coming if you're extra good. Here's what you get:

- Berserks
- Reinforcements (same as above) × 2

THE EVIL HORDE

The Undead on this map are not particularly aggressive, so you'll have the advantage of taking the battle to them rather than vice versa. Here's what they get:

- Thrall
- Ghols
- Shades
- Soulless

LAY OF THE LAND

The Watcher can be found in the upper-right corner of the map, which has large areas of marsh and occasional rain. The map is riddled with secret Undead units that pop up as you move around. These units are triggered by your passing, and when they come up they try to surround your units and close in. Always be alert for these surprise units, and use the hills and obstacles to your advantage as you try to avoid the Undead armies.

BATTLE PLANS

You start out with three groups of Berserks gathering at the bottom of the marshy area. Group your Berserks into three equal groups and have them spread out over the marsh while heading toward the upper-right side of it, as shown on the Watcher scenario map. As you move through the marsh, you'll be attacked by small groups of Thrall that pop up out of nowhere, as shown in Figure 9.10. If you attack one Thrall at a time with five or six Berserks, you won't have to worry about sustaining too much damage. This may seem unimportant right now, but believe me, you'll need to have all the health you can muster later on.

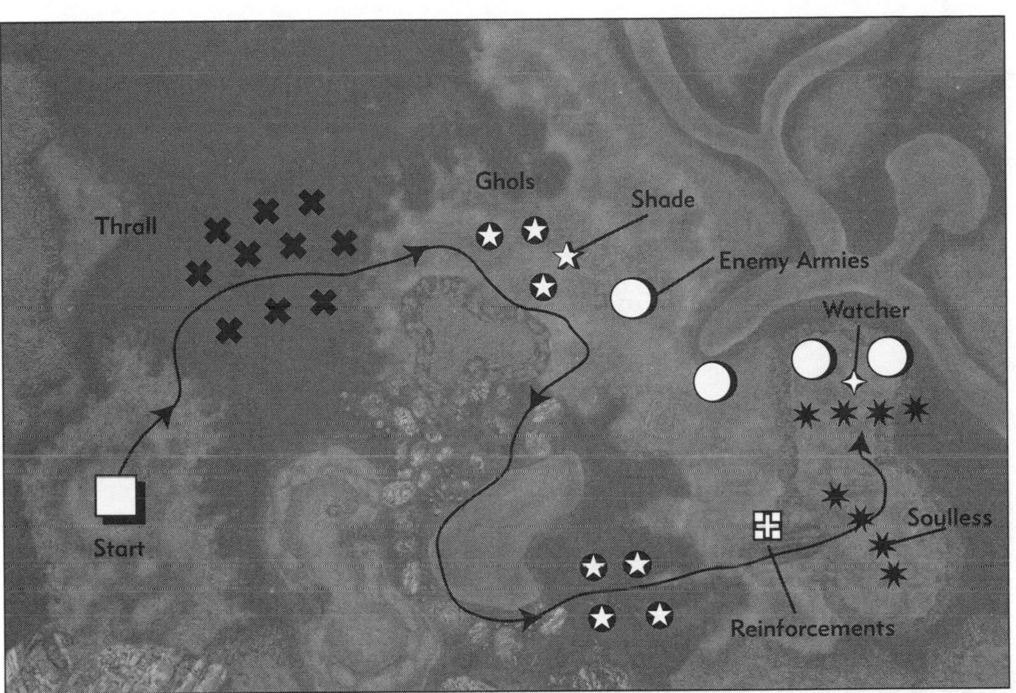

After you've taken out the Thrall in the marsh, move toward the dry area in the upper-right corner of the map. Be careful not to get the attention of the Ghols and the Shade waiting there. The Shade's Dream is very similar to Alric's Dispersal Dream, so you want to make sure that your units aren't grouped close together. Otherwise, the Shade will cast a Dream and all your units will blow up like popcorn in hot oil. However, the Shades do have a weakness. Like Alric, they can't cast their Dreams if units are close enough to them to launch

TIP

You can avoid most (if not all) hits from enemy units (like Thrall) if you attack with three or four of your units to one of theirs. The enemy cannot respond when multiple units are striking it because their wind-up to shoot is stopped when they get hit. This way a bunch of Berserks hacking at a Thrall can kill it without taking a single blow.

FIGURE 9.10: Thrall will pop up in the marsh as you move through it. If you attack one Thrall at a time, you can escape unharmed.

a melee attack. The hard part is getting close enough to the Shade without having all your troops wiped out. If you can do this with enough Berserks, you should be able to kill it.

The best way to approach the Shade is to divide up your Berserks into six groups of three Berserks each, and then move the groups around the Shade (and the nearby Ghols) in a half circle. Next, move half of your groups in to attack the Shade, making sure that each group is far away from each other (see Figure 9.11). When the first round of groups get close enough to the Shade to prevent it from casting its Dream, move in the rest of your Berserks and take care of the Ghols that are still roving around. Remember, always attack enemy units with at least a two-to-one ratio.

After you've killed the Shade, move east (right) until you come up against a group of Soulless and Ghols. You can try to sneak around these units, but it's just as easy to go ahead and kill them. After they're dead, follow the ridge on the right side of this pass to avoid another even larger group of Soulless and Ghols. There's no need to engage those units—unless you're feeling masochistic.

FIGURE 9.11: Keep your groups of Berserks far enough apart that the Shade's Dream won't take out all of your units at the same time.

Move to the lower-right section of the map, where you'll have to face another Ghol-guarded Shade. Kill the Shade and then climb up to the plateau in front of you. Just before you reach this point, you'll get five or six Berserks as reinforcements. You'll need them. Next, move north (up) toward the stone Watcher. He's guarded by a bunch of Soulless and Ghols, as well as another ring of Ghols and Thrall, which are permanent fixtures around him (see Figure 9.12). Move your Berserks forward in two or three groups and chase down and quickly kill the Soulless around the Watcher. After they're gone, move forward and hit one side of the Watcher's defense group. Surprisingly, the defense group won't give you too much trouble. Have two or three of your units attack the Watcher while the others keep the defense units occupied. You may lose most of your Berserks, but if you keep hacking at the Watcher, he'll soon turn to dust.

FIGURE 9.12: This looks fairly daunting, but if you take out the Soulless first, you should be able to crack the defenses.

Blow by Blow

- Organize your units into three separate groups.
- Move into the marsh and get ready to have some Thrall pop up and attack you.
- Move to the upper-right side of the marsh until you get close enough to see the Shade and the Ghols.
- Group your Berserks into five or six small groups, and then attack the Shade from multiple angles with three groups.
- Soon after the first units get close to the Shade, bring the next three groups in to clean up.

- Follow the ridge around and down along the bottom of the lake until you meet another pack of Ghols. Kill them, and your reinforcements will show up.
- Head up onto the plateau, kill the Soulless, and then turn north.
- Kill the Soulless guarding the Watcher first, and then move in on the Watcher himself.
- Destroy the Watcher and you win.

10

The Final Push

This is it—you've fought through the Undead minions with great bravery, solved puzzles, rescued comrades and items, and even killed the Watcher. Now you must follow your accomplishments into the final four scenarios. River of Blood is perhaps the toughest of the four. It is the first of two levels that revolve around Trow. The second, Pools of Iron, lets you use Alric, the Avatara, for the first time. Both these first levels take place in or near Rhi'anon, so the terrain is largely desert. The Last Battle takes place in a similar landscape, but this time you'll have to fight side by side with Alric and try to separate Balor's head from his body. The Great Devoid is the final level in *Myth*, and you've got to get by Soulblighter with Balor's head, and then throw it into the Great Devoid. These four scenarios show why *Myth* is one of the best games ever made.

RIVER OF BLOOD

You start just outside the old Trow city of Rhi'anon, which was abandoned centuries ago after a war that nearly exterminated the Trow race. You must enter the city and find a bridge behind enemy lines without getting yourself crushed by the Trow. The bridge is an important piece in the military puzzle Alric is trying to assemble for the Light side's cause. You'll have to use a combination of power and stealth to ensure victory.

MISSION OBJECTIVE:

Fight your way into the city and locate a bridge over the old canal inside. Secure this location and wait for reinforcements.

YOUR GUYS

The three Forest Giants at your disposal may make you think that you've got tons of power. Don't be fooled; the other guys have more. Here's what you get:

-  Dwarves
-  Berserks
-  Archers
- Forest Giants

THE EVIL HORDE

The Undead are very well equipped here. This old city was once the home of a Trow civilization, so I think you can imagine what you're up against. Here's what they get:

- Soulless
- Thrall
- Myrmidons
- Trow

LAY OF THE LAND

This map is desert, pure and simple, with a nice crimson river of blood at the back of it. I'm sure you'll find the river of blood fairly disturbing at first. The main thing to be wary of on this map is that huge numbers of Myrmidons, Trow, and especially

Fetches are wandering all over, making it very difficult to win the game. Any time you see a large rectangle on the ground, there's probably an Undead army nearby. The edges of the map are good places to be most of the time, but if you get cornered you could be toast.

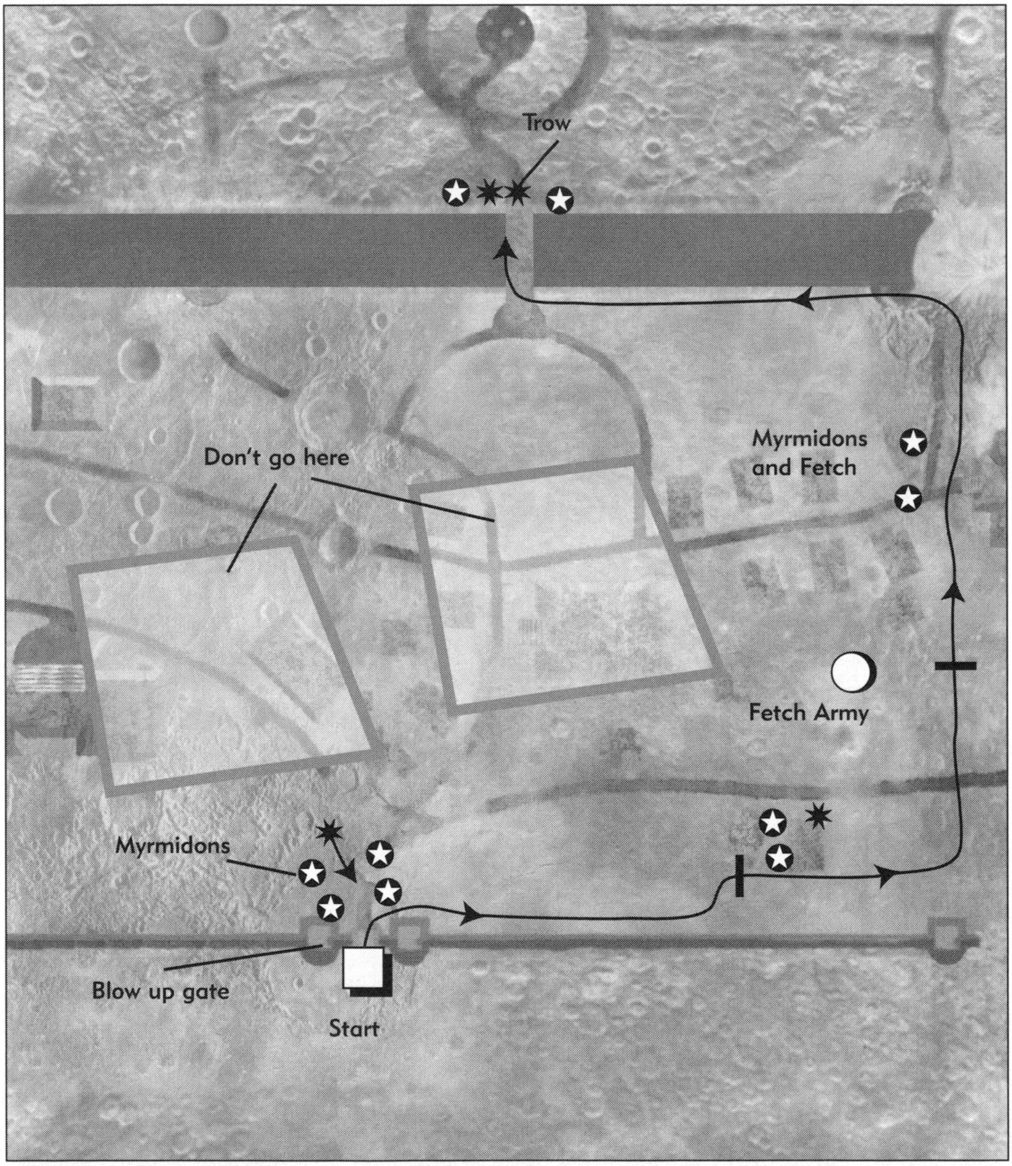

BATTLE PLANS

The first thing you need to do is find a way in through the city gates of Rhi'anon. To do this, get your Dwarves as close to the wooden pylons as possible and drop Satchel Charges right up against them. This can take some time because the Dwarves don't always move the way you want them to in such a crowded area. Take the time to do it right, so you don't waste any charges. After the charges are laid along the first row of pylons (use three to four charges), stand back and have all the Dwarves fire bottles at the charges simultaneously, as shown in Figure 10.1.

After you've opened the gates, move your Berserks inside the city in two groups—one group on either side of the gates. Then move your three Forest Giants inside the gates and right up the middle. The Myrmidons waiting just beyond the gates will rush you. Take on each of the two Myrmidon groups with your two Berserk groups. Then bring your Archers up through the gates and get ready for the Trow. Soon after you've taken out the Myrmidons inside the gates, a Trow and another large group of Myrmidons will approach. Again, use your Berserks to handle the Myrmidons while your three Forest Giants kick the stuffing out of the Trow.

After that's all done, group your units by kind, and then move them along the wall to the east (right). Keep moving along the right side of the map, leading with your Berserks and Forest Giants until you come to some wooden spikes rising out of the sand. When you get to the spikes, move your Archers forward and begin firing at the Fetch, and then bring your Berserks up on the right and your Forest Giants up on the left. Use your Giants to take out the Myrmidons on the left and your Berserks to take out the Myrmidons on the right. Always make sure that your Berserks and Archers stay out of range of the Fetch. The Forest Giants will make quick work of the Myrmidons on the left; once that's done, move them in to take out the Trow.

FIGURE 10.1: Have your Dwarves throw simultaneously to get a bigger bang when you blow up the front gates.

With three on one, it should be a breeze. When all the Undead are mincemeat, move toward the right side of the city wall.

Now move north, up the right side of the map. Move carefully, leading with your Giants. Keep your Archers right behind the Giants, and watch out for a Fetch on your left. You'll soon notice that it's actually a group of at least 10 Fetches! Deal with these guys by having your Archers keep targeting the closest Fetch (see Figure 10.2). The Fetches use a strange sort of rotating formation, and the unit closest to you is always changing. If you just target one unit, it'll run away from you while another unit moves closer and zaps you. This is definitely a hands-on process, and you'll have to be right on top of it in order to kill all the Fetches without losing your Archers. If you're careful, and your Archers are shooting well, you can eliminate the entire group of Fetches using just your Archers.

Now continue up the right side of the map. As you do so, you'll face two groups of Myrmidons, each accompanied by one Fetch. Use your Archers to take out one of the Fetches (while your Berserks protect the Archers). Use your Giants to swat the other

FIGURE 10.2: You can take the Fetches out with your Archers, but you've got to keep switching the target to the closest Fetch as they rotate around.

group into dust. Once they're gone, move straight up toward the river of blood.You must hug the right side of the map because if you venture toward the middle, you'll be DOA. Move along the riverbank toward the bridge (which is in the middle of the map). When you reach it, get ready to rumble.

How you deal with taking control of both sides of the bridge is a matter of personal taste. I like to run my Forest Giants over the bridge and take out the Fetches right away, with my Berserks following close behind. The Berserks can either help fight the Trow, or they can battle the Myrmidons (see Figure 10.3). While this is going on, bring your Archers and Dwarves onto the bridge for support. It's very likely, depending on how your previous scenario went, that you may lose this battle. As long as you take out the Trow and Fetches, you should be OK. If you *do* lose all of your units, there should be reinforcements waiting not far from the bridge, and they should be able to wipe out any remaining Undead units. Once all the Undead units on both sides of the bridge are gone, you win.

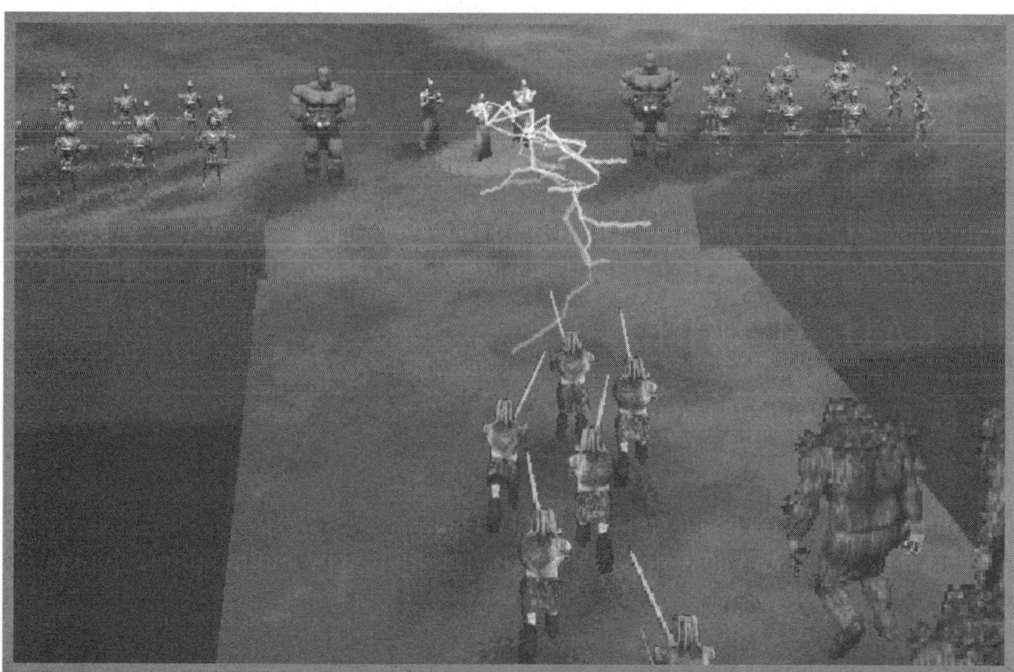

FIGURE 10.3: You may lose this battle on the bridge, but your reinforcements should be able to finish the job.

Blow by Blow

- Lay down Satchel Charges along the gates, and then blow them up with your Dwarves.
- Move through the gates with your Berserks and Giants, and take out the Myrmidons waiting for you.
- When the Trow comes, use your Berserks to take out the Myrmidons so that the Giants can concentrate on disposing of the Trow quickly.
- Move along the wall of the city toward the right side of the map until you come to some wooden spikes (and a small army that includes a Trow).
- Move up your Archers to take out the Fetch, and then use your Giants and Berserks to put away the Trow and Myrmidons.
- Now move up the right side of the map with your Archers and Giants, keeping a close eye out for a large group of Fetches.
- When you see the Fetches, use your Archers to take them out.
- Continue to move up the right side of the map until you meet two groups of Myrmidons and Fetches. Annihilate them and move up to the river.
- Move along the river toward the bridge in the middle of the map.
- Attack the force on the other side of the bridge. If you lose the battle, bring in your reinforcements and finish the job. Once the Undead are gone from the bridge, you win.

POOLS OF IRON

Finally, you get to take control of an Avatara (Alric) in a real live scenario! In Pools of Iron, you use Alric to locate the long-lost World Knot that's rumored to exist in Rhi'anon and find a way to teleport a hand-picked group of Berserks, Journeymen, and Archers over to your location. After you've done that, you must find your way to the lake of blood and wade in. There are many enemies in the way, including a pair of Trow. Alric has an incredibly powerful dream called the Dispersal Dream, which can take out entire groups of Undead with a single use. Unfortunately, you only get four chances to use the dream—use them wisely.

MISSION OBJECTIVE

Lead Alric to the nearby World Knot where he will bring through the rest of your force. Then head west, across the lake of blood, to Balor's fortress.

YOUR GUYS

Again, this is where you finally get to use an Avatara, so enjoy it. The Dispersal Dream is powerful, but don't forget about your Berserks and Archers. Here's what you get:

- Avatara (Alric)

Through World Knot

- Berserks
- Journeymen

- Archers

THE EVIL HORDE

You're still in Trow-land, so be prepared to do some Trow battling. The Undead also have large bands of Myrmidons that roam the countryside mercilessly. Here's what they get:

- Trow
- Myrmidons
- Thrall

LAY OF THE LAND

This is a beautiful desert map with nice rolling sand dunes through the first half. The open nature of the map provides excellent sight lines, so you can see from long distances what's coming at you. I recommend that you leave your map on at all times because when a band of Myrmidons hits, they come fast. The World Knot is not far from where you start out—it's down and a little to the left. There's a giant

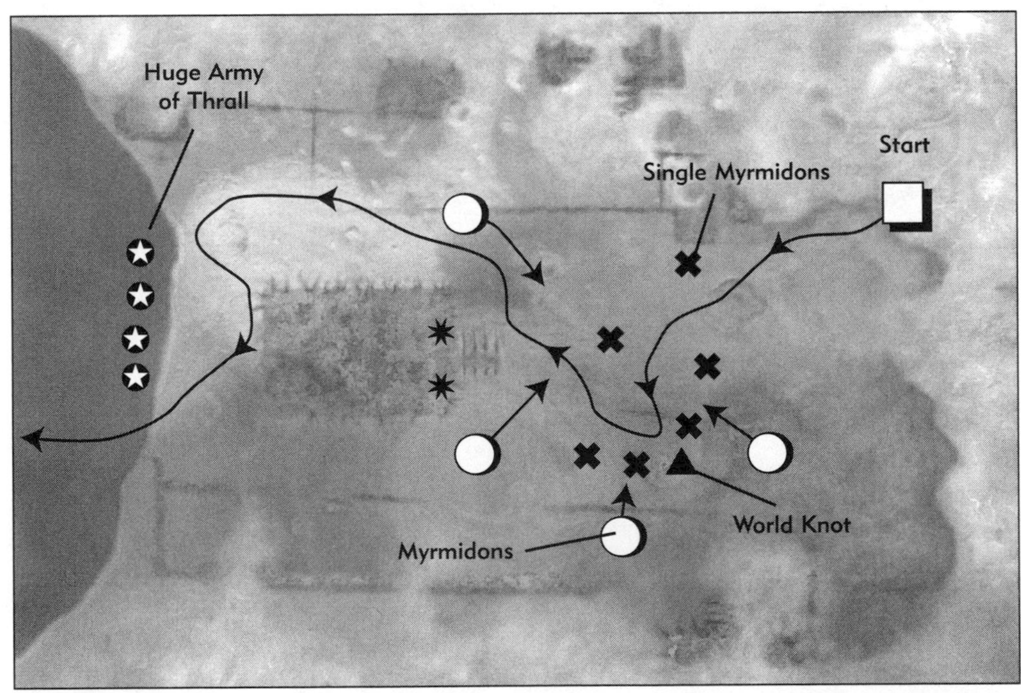

temple closer to the lake, and that's where you'll find those friendly, fun-loving Trow, so be careful when you start to see the structure.

BATTLE PLANS

You begin the scenario with Alric as your lone unit. He has four Dispersal Dreams, and though you're going to be *very* tempted to see how it works, I must caution you that wasting even one of the dreams can be detrimental to your cause. Move Alric to the south and a smidgen to the west (left) to find the World Knot, and along the way kill any lone Myrmidons you come across. As you approach the World Knot, you'll see a huge force of Myrmidons running right at you. You guessed it—it's time to use that Dispersal Dream (see Figure 10.4).

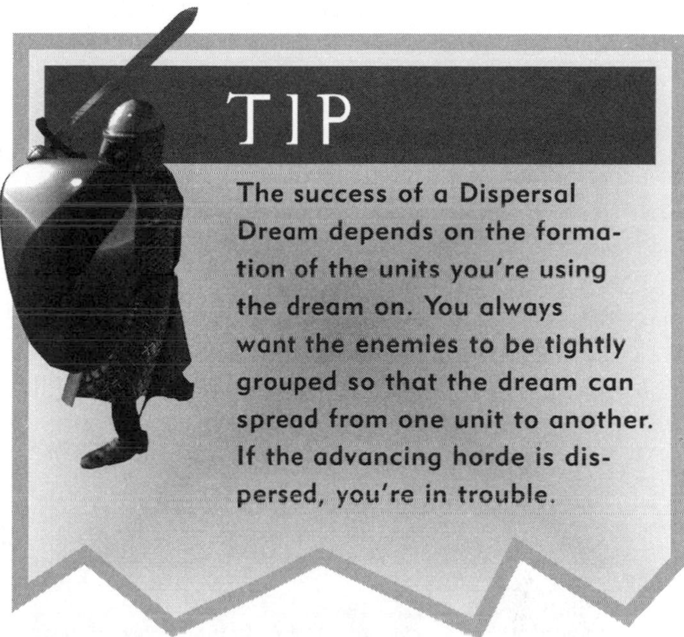

TIP

The success of a Dispersal Dream depends on the formation of the units you're using the dream on. You always want the enemies to be tightly grouped so that the dream can spread from one unit to another. If the advancing horde is dispersed, you're in trouble.

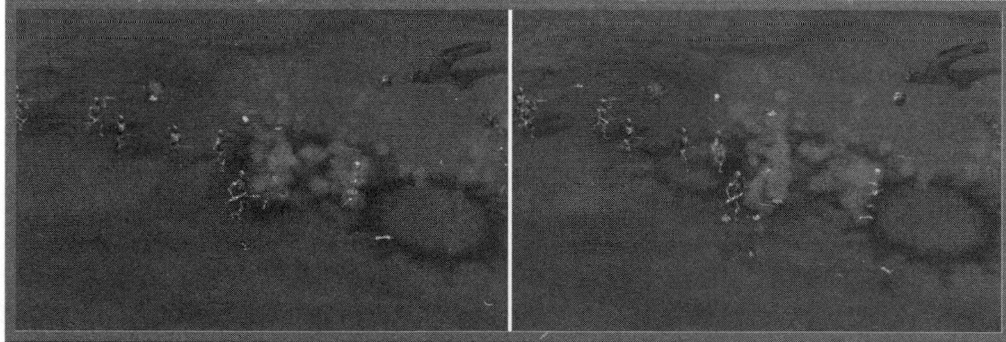

FIGURE 10.4: Alric's Dispersal Dream is really fun to watch, and it's effective as all get out.

After you've cleaned up the first bunch of Myrmidons, head straight for the broken arm of the World Knot. The Avatara completes that part of the World Knot so that your forces can come through. You are now faced with a choice because, as you approach the Knot, a second group of Myrmidons will rush you. You can run for the Knot and try to bring your troops in to help out, or you can use a Dispersal Dream to take out the second wave of Myrmidons. It's totally up to you, but I will say that you may need that extra dream later on in the scenario.

After you've killed the second wave of Myrmidons, gather up your troops and head to the temple (which is nearby) and park yourself there for a sec. This is where you need to get organized before you head into battle. First, you want to divide up your Berserks so that they can take on the Trow effectively. Remember that if you attack the Trow straight on with a long line of Berserks, you'll lose. The key is to surround the Trow, and you'll end up victorious (see Figure 10.5). Second, get your Archers lined up and ready to contribute wherever they're needed. I like to keep a group of four Archers back at the World Knot so that I can bring them in after the carnage is over.

FIGURE 10.5: Try to surround the Trow with your Berserks whenever possible. The Berserks in this picture are heading for a very hard time.

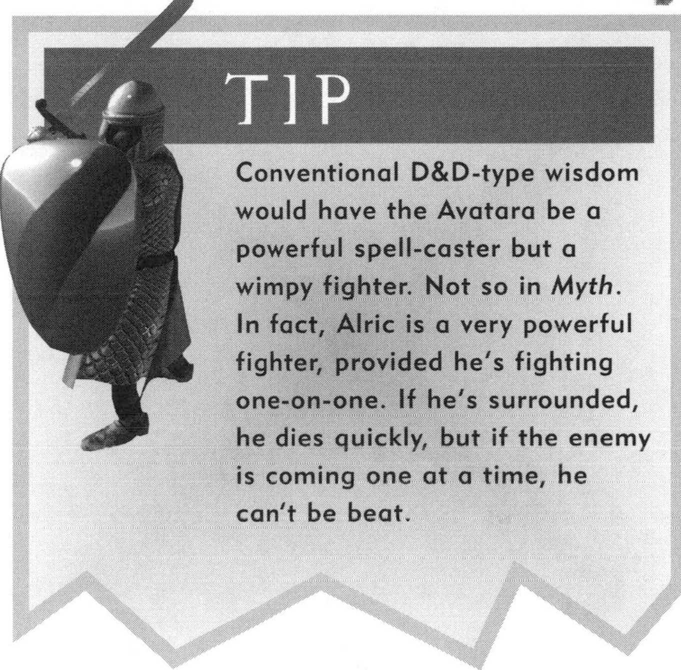

TIP

Conventional D&D-type wisdom would have the Avatara be a powerful spell-caster but a wimpy fighter. Not so in *Myth*. In fact, Alric is a very powerful fighter, provided he's fighting one-on-one. If he's surrounded, he dies quickly, but if the enemy is coming one at a time, he can't be beat.

Now you're ready to provoke the onslaught. Send one Berserk up the temple's ramp, and get ready to rumble because the Trow will take notice and make a run for your troops. As soon as they get within range, open up on them with your Archers and rush your Berserks in from two or three angles (and say a prayer). As this is happening, there'll be two more huge groups of Myrmidons running in from either side of the temple, and you won't have the troops to deal with them. Time for Alric to use a Dispersal Dream on each of the onrushing groups of Myrmidons. Any leftover Undead will be badly injured, and Alric can clean them up himself.

By now you should have killed off the Myrmidons and Trow. If you're like me, you've also lost 75 percent of your units. If you were frugal with the Dispersal Dreams, you'll still have one left, so get ready to use it on some Thrall. Move Alric toward the lake, and when you get close enough to see the Thrall streaming out of the lake toward you, hit them with the dream. Now simply hop in the lake and you're done. If you *don't* have a Dream left, you can still make it into the lake by outrunning the Thrall. Use any units you have left over as a decoy to allow Alric to escape (which is all you need to win).

Blow by Blow

- **Move toward the World Knot, killing any lone Myrmidons that wander by.**

Continued on next page

Continued from previous page

- When the first wave of Myrmidons comes at you, let the Dispersal Dream fly, and sit back and enjoy.
- Hop in the World Knot and bring in your troops to fight the second wave of Myrmidons, or just use another Dispersal Dream to take the second bunch out.
- Move up to the temple and take out the Trow and Myrmidons that rush you. You'll have to use everything you've got to survive.
- Head for the lake.
- When you see the Thrall coming at you out of the lake, use your last dream if you have one left. If you don't, run for it.
- After you're clear of the Thrall, wade across the lake with Alric. He's the only one that needs to cross for you to win.

THE LAST BATTLE

Alric can now sense victory. All he has to do is separate Balor's head from his body. Your first task is to find Alric (he's by the standard with some Berserks and Archers). Once you do this, you'll have a confrontation with Balor. Then you'll have to defeat Balor's armies on your way to chasing him down. To win this battle, you'll have to be very prudent in the use of your troops. If you get to the end of the scenario without sufficient forces to destroy first the Fetches and then Balor, you're history.

MISSION OBJECTIVE

Lead your reinforcements to Alric and the other survivors of the previous level. Then follow Alric and work toward a chance to kill Balor.

YOUR GUYS

You are well-equipped in this scenario, with plenty of firepower, but don't get complacent because the enemy is formidable. Here's what you get:

- Berserks
- Archers
- Dwarves
- Avatara (Alric—not in your control)

THE EVIL HORDE

Balor has a well-rounded army, including a bevy of Fetches, to squash your dreams. Here's what they get:

- Myrmidons
- Fetches
- Thrall
- Balor

LAY OF THE LAND

This is the last of the desert maps (heck, it's the second-to-last map of the game), but the dry desert won't be forgiving as a going away present. Indeed, in the first portion of the map, the flatness leaves you open to Fetch attacks, and when you reach the end of the map, the bowl traps Alric in what can only be called Fetch hell. Fortunately, you have a good defensive position on top of the hill.

BATTLE PLANS

You begin on a sand bar that extends into the lake of blood. Follow the sand bar to the left (west), keeping a very close eye out for Fetches popping up in front of you and behind you (in the lake). The red dots on your map may be difficult to see with the red lake as a background. Take it slow, or you'll end up with a bucket full of crispy-fried Berserk parts. Move along until you see your fellow units and Alric by

the standard (see Figure 10.6), and then move your units up to the top of the hill. *Do not* leave them anywhere near the standard. I suggest you leave at least six Berserks in the river below the hill, and just forget that they're there until later. That way, they'll be like reinforcements when you really need them.

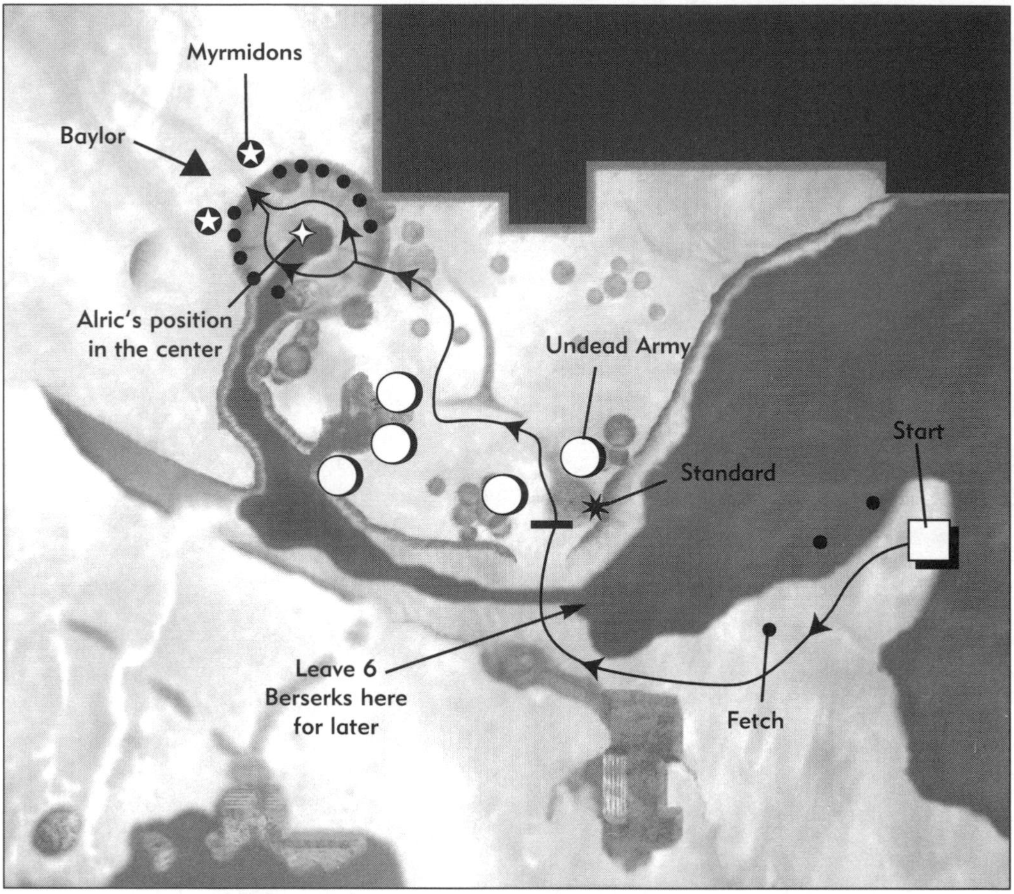

As you're getting settled on the hill, Balor will come up and have a conversation with Alric. Then he'll blow up the standard, as shown in Figure 10.6. Next, the Undead forces in front of you will attack. They should be easy pickings for your Archers and Dwarves. Keep a few Berserks around in case any Myrmidons get close.

Once you're done killing the first Undead army, Alric will lead you to another army down the hill. You'll be bombarded by a bizarre rain of Dwarf heads streaming down from the sky. As if to answer this atrocity, Alric will take out a large row of Myrmidons with a Dispersal Dream and leave the Thrall and Fetches up to you. Use

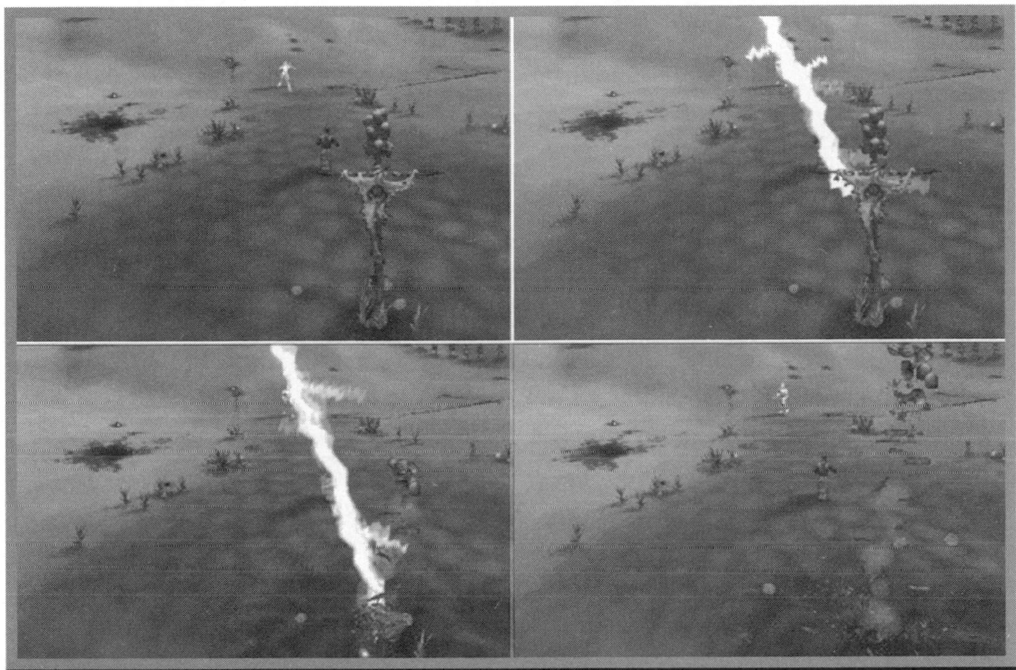

FIGURE 10.6: Stay away from the standard—it's about to be blown up by Balor.

the tactics you've become familiar with to take out the Fetches (using your Archers) and use your Dwarves to bomb the Thrall.

Now that the two main Undead forces have been dealt with, bring the Berserks from the river back up for active combat. Alric will head toward a large bowl-like crater. When he stops and waits on the lip of the crater for a few moments, bring in all of your troops.

This is fairly important now, so follow these directions

TIP

Save your Berserks! You should not only keep six Berserks in reserve in this scenario, but also make extra sure that you: 1) don't take any friendly fire from errant Dwarf bottles, and 2) keep your distance from the Fetches. You'll need as many Berserks as you can muster at the end of the level.

carefully. Put your Archers on the lip of the crater to the right of Alric, and start them firing at the closest Fetch. Keep a close eye on them to make sure that the Fetches don't lure them to their deaths. As soon as you've done that, move two Berserks down to the bottom of the crater, one group on the left side, and one on the right side (see Figure 10.7). When the Fetches come down to attack Alric (who will descend into the crater himself), they will be single-minded in their attacks and for the most part won't bother with your Berserks. Sweep your Berserks around either side of Alric, and systematically eliminate all of the Fetches. Remember, you can also use your Archers to help the cause.

After the Fetches have been eliminated, a large force of Myrmidons will stream down the hill and attempt to kill Alric. Alric is very tough, but he can't defend himself if he gets surrounded by Myrmidons. Be ready to quickly move the rest of your Berserks into the battle (see Figure 10.7).

After the Myrmidons have been disposed of, Alric will begin to move toward Balor. It's very important that Alric is still fairly healthy at this point because Balor will cast multiple Lightning Dreams on him. The Lightning Dreams are not only

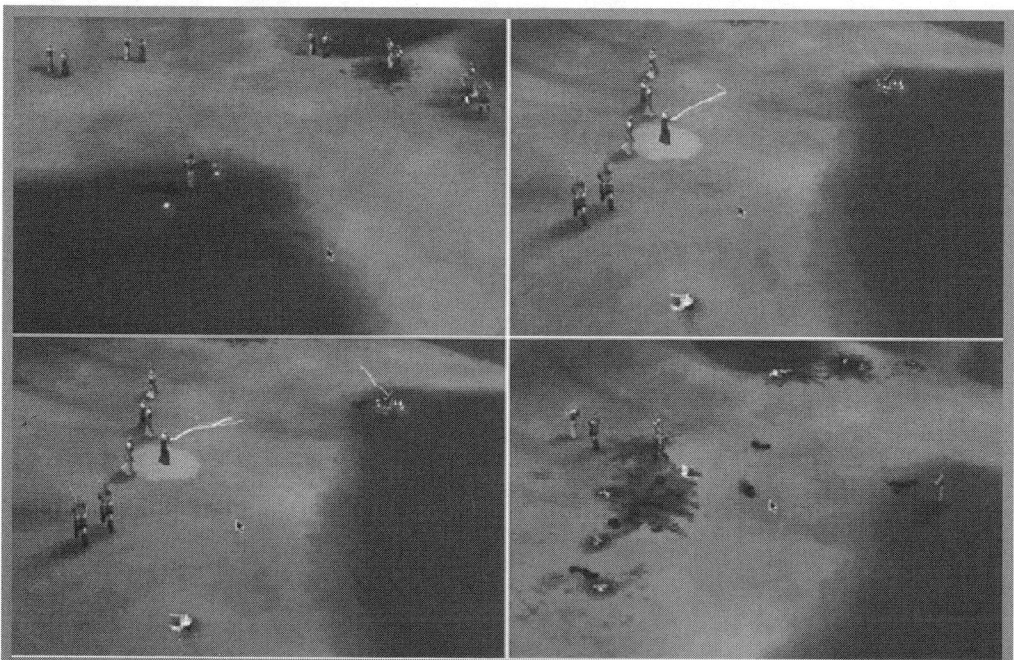

FIGURE 10.7: Use Archers and Berserks to take out the Fetches while they fire at Alric. Be ready for the Myrmidons to launch a counterstrike on Alric.

powerful but rather frightening too. As he gets close to Balor, Alric will cast a dream that will immobilize Balor for a short time. It's during this time that you need to rush with everything you've got and hack at Balor until his head comes off (see Figure 10.8). When this is done, you've won! Congrats.

FIGURE 10.8: When Alric casts the dream that immobilizes Balor, that's your cue to rush in and slice him up. Balor's death is gruesome, but satisfying.

Blow by Blow

- Group your units however you like. I recommend that you put your Archers together in one group because you'll be facing Fetches right off the bat.

Continued on next page

Continued from previous page

- Move west (left) off the sand bar and keep an eye out for the Fetches that will come from the front, behind, and sides of your position.
- Move toward the hill where Alric is (see the Last Battle scenario map), and move your troops up the hill. Leave six Berserks behind in the river (these will act like reinforcements later).
- Get all your troops away from the standard because Balor will blow the darned thing up, and if you have troops nearby, they'll go with it.
- After Balor leaves, line up your Archers and Dwarves for a fight because the Undead are coming.
- After the first Undead force is eliminated, follow Alric to the second force and prepare for a barrage of Dwarf heads from the sky.
- Kill off this second large force by using your Archers to take out the Fetches and your Dwarves to blow up the Thrall.
- Get your reserve Berserk units out to your location, and then follow Alric to the crater.
- Set up your units in the crater so that you can swing two pairs of Berserks around the Fetches and take them all out. Use your Archers on the right side of the crater to pick away at the Fetches.
- Be ready for the counterattack of Myrmidons after the Fetches are deflated.
- Follow Alric to Balor, and when Balor is immobilized by Alric's Dream, surround him with your Berserks and kill him.
- You now teleport out, with Balor's head. One level left.

THE GREAT DEVOID

This is it. You've fought through the entire bloody, exciting, and engrossing game of *Myth: The Fallen Lords,* and you've finally made it to the last scenario. By killing Balor, some say that you have just made him more powerful, as has happened in the past. There's one way to ensure that Balor will no longer be a threat to anyone. You have his head, and if you can manage to throw it into the Great Devoid, the world will be rid of Balor forever, and the forces of Light will have earned the right to rule again. This is what it's all about, so have fun with it.

MISSION OBJECTIVE

Carry Balor's head to the Great Devoid and throw it in. Don't listen to anything the head tells you. The head can only be carried by a Dwarf, so if you lose all your Dwarves, the scenario is over.

YOUR GUYS

It's imperative that you do not lose even one Dwarf in this scenario because the three that aren't carrying the head will be needed to act as very important decoys later on. Here's what you get:

 Archers

 Berserks

 Journeyman

 Dwarves

THE EVIL HORDE

The Undead pull out all the stops in this scenario, throwing an almost inconceivable number of Wights at you. Happily, you don't have to face any Myrmidons or Trow. Here's what they get:

- Soulless
- Thrall
- Wights
- Soulblighter (for all practical purposes, cannot be killed)

LAY OF THE LAND

The Great Devoid map is heavily forested. So densely forested, in fact, that it often prevents you from freely moving from one area to another. It's not entirely restrictive, but you should always be aware that there might not be a way out where you think there is. The trees also provide cover for the many Wights that'll be seeking you out in this scenario. Besides making it hard to see the Wights coming, it's also very difficult to get a proper shooting angle for your Archers, and you can't afford to waste any units on suicide Wight missions. The Great Devoid is pretty cool—it looks like a black hole that fell into a forest. Don't spend too much time admiring it, though, or Soulblighter will come and turn you inside out.

BATTLE PLANS

First, have one Dwarf pick up Balor's head before you forget it. This Dwarf will be known as the "head Dwarf." As a nice change, you start out without any dangerous enemies close by, so you can relax and group your units in whatever fashion you like. However, I'd still recommend that you keep your Archers together in one or two groups because they'll be working overtime trying to nail down Wights.

Move your troops to the east (right) toward the river, and when you get there park yourself on the west side of the riverbank (the side you're already on). You can press forward if you want, but I strongly encourage you to sit tight and kill off all the Wights that will begin to come toward you any second now. When you've killed a couple without taking any damage, save the game.

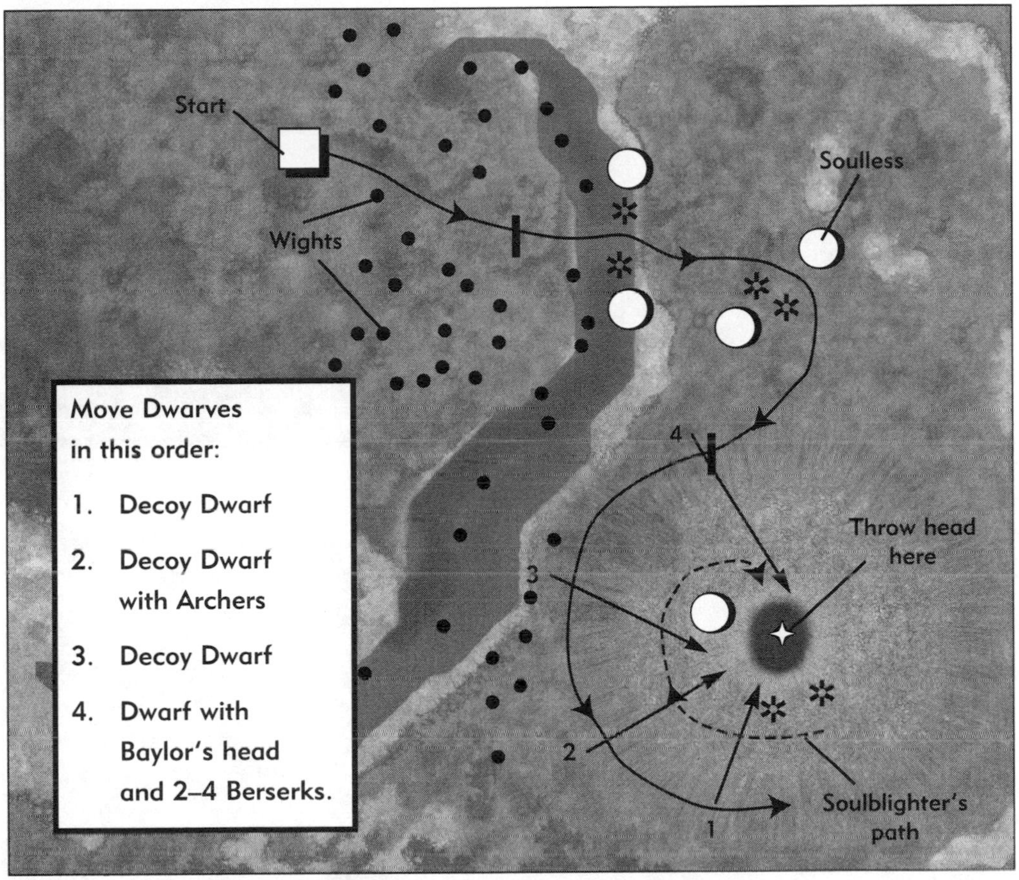

Start
Soulless
Wights
Move Dwarves in this order:

1. Decoy Dwarf
2. Decoy Dwarf with Archers
3. Decoy Dwarf
4. Dwarf with Baylor's head and 2–4 Berserks.

Throw head here
Soulblighter's path

I break my Archers up into three or four small groups and move them to the compass points of the area around my troops, and then just set them to destroy any Wights that come into their line of sight, as you can see in Figure 10.9. This can be a bit dicey at times, and you may have to revert to a saved game, but by this point in *Myth*, you've probably got the hang of managing several small forces at once.

After you've sat there for a while and no more Wights are lumbering toward your troops, you can think about provoking the enemy forces on the other side of the river. Send a group of Archers into the water and start firing on the Fetches on the opposite riverbank. Then fall back to your own bank. The Soulless from the other side will follow you into the water, where your troops on the shore can shred them (see Figure 10.10). Keep your Journeyman right behind your Archers so that he can heal them as they take hits. After you've rid yourself of the Soulless, you can expect to see another round of Wights come for you. It just never ends, does it?

FIGURE 10.9: The Wights creep up on you from all directions, so you have to be very active with your Archers to keep them from blowing up the heart of your forces.

FIGURE 10.10: Entice the Soulless across the river by picking on the Fetches on the other side. Your Journeyman will make the difference in archery battles because he can heal your units on the fly.

When the latest wave of Wights dies down, it's time to head over the river and take out the rest of those pesky Undead dudes. Move your Archers into the water to set the Fetches on their heels, and then run in a couple of Berserks to hack the Fetches and Soulless to pieces. Usually two Berserks can do a surprisingly good job at this. Move the remainder of your troops across the river. After you cross the river and continue heading east (right), you'll run into yet another Undead army consisting of Soulless and Fetches. In this case though, the trees will work to your advantage because they allow your Berserks to get close to the Soulless without taking any hits. Use your Archers to take out the Fetches if possible.

> **TIP**
>
> Satchel Charges might be a problem for the Dwarf with Balor's head. When you are at the edge of the Great Devoid trying to throw the head in, Soulblighter will bear down on you and will likely hit you just after you throw the head. This kills the Dwarf instantly and causes an explosion, which in turn causes the Satchel Charges to go off and blasts Balor's head into orbit rather than into the Great Devoid. If you drop your Satchel Charges first, you can avoid this problem.

After the last group of Soulless and Fetches are dead, you can make your move to throw the head into the Great Devoid. Move your troops very carefully to the very outside of the large circular area that marks the outside of the Great Devoid. Then move three of your Dwarves and your Archers toward the south (down), but still keep them walking very carefully along the perimeter of the circle. Keep an eye out for Wights. You may see some more pop up here, and that's why you brought your Archers. After you've gone a short distance, stop one of your Dwarves and leave him there (see the Great Devoid scenario map). Then continue on along the perimeter of the circle with the rest. After you get about one-third of the way around, stop your

Archers and one Dwarf there. Keep the last Dwarf walking around the perimeter until you get near the bottom of the circle. Save your game now.

This is it. From here on, all you need to do is get the head into the Great Devoid, but it's not going to be easy. Fetches, Soulless, and more importantly, Soulblighter, guard the Devoid. There are a few things you need to know about Soulblighter. He's fast, he will always go after Dwarves (so trying to use a Journeyman as a decoy won't work), and for all intents and purposes, he's immune to attack. This means that you're going to have to find a way to avoid him because if you face him, you'll die for sure. Soulblighter is waiting by the Devoid, ready to pounce on the first Dwarf to violate the Devoid's perimeter. You must be tricky to win.

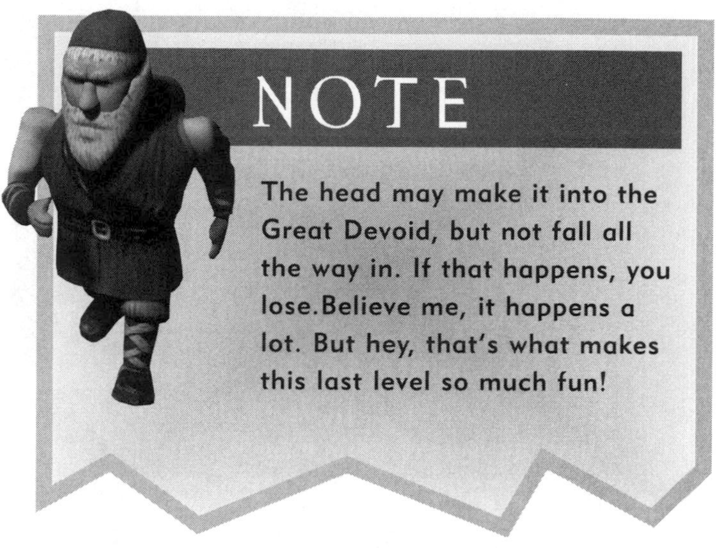

NOTE

The head may make it into the Great Devoid, but not fall all the way in. If that happens, you lose. Believe me, it happens a lot. But hey, that's what makes this last level so much fun!

Have the Dwarf at the bottom of the perimeter walk toward the Devoid, and then immediately send the next Dwarf up the line toward the Devoid. Quickly send the Dwarf with the head and the Dwarf next to him toward the hole. Send the last decoy Dwarf *away* from the Devoid in the opposite direction. Soulblighter is very fast and will run from Dwarf to Dwarf (starting with the one he saw first, at the bottom) killing each one. He can kill each Dwarf with one blow, and then move on quickly to the next, so you have to hurry. As your head Dwarf approaches the Devoid, move up your Berserks to occupy the Soulless that are near the edge of the Devoid so that they can't fire on the head Dwarf.

As you approach the edge, Soulblighter will get close to you. You need to get ready to press the T key and click on the Devoid to throw the head. You have to be fairly close to the edge to get it in (see Figure 10.11), so don't throw the head until the instant before Soulblighter drives his sword through your skull. Again, this is probably going to take a couple of tries, so don't give up. Once the head is in, you win the game. Toast your success with a "Surly Dwarf" Ale.

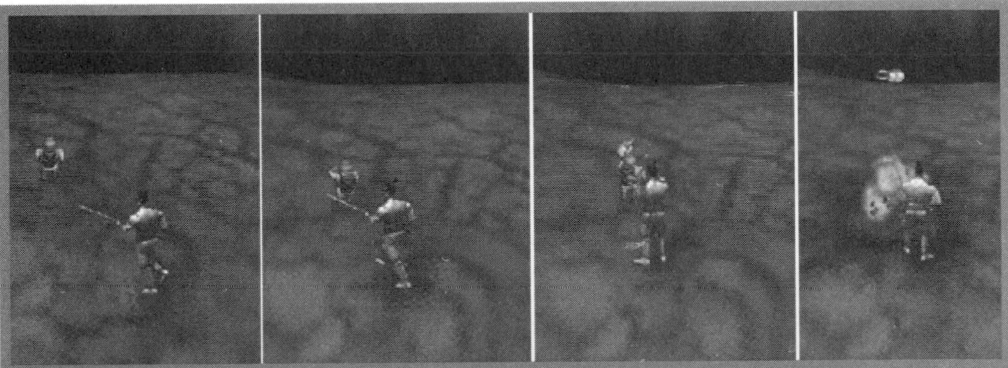

FIGURE 10.11: Wait until the last minute to throw the head. You need to be very close to the edge for it to fall in properly.

Blow by Blow

- First off, have one of your Dwarves (I call him the "head Dwarf") pick up Balor's head (which is still bleeding, yuck).
- Group your units so that you have flexible control of your Archers.
- Move to the east (right) toward the river, and stop when you get to the riverbank.
- Sit at the riverbank and use your Archers to take out the waves upon waves of Wights that come at you. Remember to protect *all* of your Dwarves.
- After the Wights are dead, move into the water to provoke the Soulless to come after you. Then kill them off with your Archers. Don't forget to keep your Journeyman nearby to heal them as they take hits.

Continued on next page

Continued from previous page

- Move across the river and take out the Fetches with one or two Berserks (rushing in) and your Archers.
- Keep moving east until you come to two groups of Soulless and Fetches (they may be close together and look like one group). Use the trees to your advantage as you take them out. Again, protect your Dwarves.
- Move to the edge of the big circle that surrounds the Great Devoid.
- Spread out your Dwarves around the circle. Be careful not to venture inside the perimeter of the circle, or you'll trigger Soulblighter.
- Have the head Dwarf stay at the top of the circle (see the Great Devoid scenario map). Move your Dwarves in toward the center. Start with the Dwarf farthest away from the head Dwarf, and then move the other Dwarves in. There should only be a few seconds between moving each Dwarf.
- You might want to have your head Dwarf drop the Satchel Charges before making a run for it so that the head won't get blown into orbit if Soulblighter hits you.
- Move a couple Berserks up with your head Dwarf so that they can occupy the Soulless that sit near the Devoid.
- As your head Dwarf nears the Devoid, keep an eye out for Soulblighter. When Soulblighter gets three steps away from you, throw the head whether you're close enough or not. You'll die after only one hit from Soulblighter anyway.
- Get the head in the Devoid, and you win. You may have to save the game at the point where your Dwarves are all in place around the circle, and then keep trying until you can get close enough to the Devoid to heave in the head.

11

Moshing with Myth (Network Play)

It's abundantly clear that *Myth* is an awesome game when you're playing against the computer, following the story, and working hard to win the age-old battle against evil forces. Fortunately for all of us *Myth* lovers, there is another even more exciting realm of *Myth* gaming available with your connection to the Internet. In fact, some *Myth* users might purchase the game just to play the online, multiplayer version! Yep, it's that good.

There's something about going head-to-head with another human being that raises the stakes to another level. Sure, the artificial intelligence in *Myth* is extremely competent and supplies hours of nail-biting fun, but it's just not capable of delivering the exhilaration that comes from the human factor. Let's face it, computers are fun to beat up on, but there's just not the same degree of satisfaction when you defeat the computer. Anyone who has beaten a computer opponent after a long, difficult struggle will tell you that jumping up and down in excitement did little to make the computer regret its decisions. There's just something missing—the winner's deeply satisfying opportunity to gloat.

NETWORK OPTIONS

Myth gives you the opportunity to connect with other players through a variety of means, making it easy to enjoy the great fun of multiplayer gaming. If you've played through the entire single-player version of *Myth* (or even if you haven't), you probably want to know where you can get more of this ground-breaking game. Network gaming is the answer to *Myth* withdrawal, and the folks at Bungie have supplied us with plenty of options for connecting to a multiplayer environment.

BUNGIE.NET

`Bungie.net` is the service supplied by Bungie Software, the creators of *Myth*, to allow you to meet and play with other *Myth* gamers from all over the world. You can connect to Bungie's metaserver after you've logged on to the Internet through whatever your connection method is (ISP, T1, or whatever). Once on `Bungie.net`, you can start a new game with your choice of map, type of game, and duration, or you can join an existing game. You can also chat with other players before the game begins. After a game is over, `Bungie.net` is sort of like a locker room for *Myth* fans.

`Bungie.net` works in an interesting way, which maximizes its ability to handle groups of rabid *Myth* fanatics, all of whom are clamoring for the chance to go mano-a-mano against a worthy challenger. Once the game begins, `Bungie.net` hands off the game by designating one player as the server and the others as clients. When the game ends and you see the post-game carnage report, you are automatically returned to `Bungie.net` where your statistics are saved. You can then begin another game. `Bungie.net` is the only multiplayer *Myth* alternative that keeps track of your wins and losses. Your win/loss record will be obvious to everyone because it will be displayed next to your name in the form of a colorful symbol. It's fun to be able to strut your stuff with a powerful symbol. Other players tend to be worried about playing you if your symbol looks like you have kicked plenty of newbie butt!

DIRECT CONNECT

If you have two PCs or two Macs in the same location, you can attach them to each other with a null modem cable (a special cable that connects the two machines using the modem port). Also, with a Macintosh computer, you can simply use built-in AppleTalk networking as described later. Direct connect is probably the cheapest, easiest way to play head-to-head with a friend, but there is a serious limitation: you can only have two players at the same time.

IP ADDRESS

If you have a connection to the Internet through an ISP (Internet Service Provider), you can play *Myth* with a friend on the other side of the city or on the other side of the world by connecting to each other's IP address. Each time you log onto the Internet, you are assigned an IP address (which looks something like this: 204.21.251.11). You can find this information through your Internet connection utility after you log on (the address changes each time you connect). You then need to enter your friend's IP address into the *Myth* connection screen, and your friend must do the same. Then *Myth* will connect you directly over the Internet by way of the IP addresses. The only drawback is that it's easier to set this up on your computer if you can talk to your playmate on the phone at the same time, which is impossible if you only have one phone line. Also, this method is only effective with 28.8 or faster modems.

MODEM CONNECTION

The modem is perhaps the easiest way to connect via the phone lines. All you have to do is put the number you're calling into the correct screen in *Myth*, and dial up your friend. Again, 28.8 modems are pretty much the slowest with which you can play *Myth* successfully, but if you're into frustration you can try it at 14.4. The main drawback with this method is that you will have to pay long-distance phone charges if you plan to play with anyone outside your local area.

T.E.N.

Myth is available on the popular online gaming network T.E.N. (Total Entertainment Network). All you need to do is get yourself a T.E.N. account and away you go. However, T.E.N. does not keep track of your gaming statistics like `Bungie.net` does.

APPLETALK

For almost a decade, all Macs have come with Apple's built-in networking called AppleTalk. This works well, and because it's part of every Mac right from the get-go, it shouldn't give you any trouble. In fact, Mac users have been multiplayer gaming on AppleTalk since 1987! To connect via AppleTalk all you need is a standard Mac printer cable. Another option is available with System 8, called AppleTalk Remote Access. This enables you to connect via modem and have the connection behave like a network. The choice is yours.

NETWORK STRATEGIES

Playing against human opponents is an entirely different gaming experience than what you're used to with a computer adversary. The strategies you learned while playing many long hours of single-player *Myth* can be made moot by a cunning and sophisticated human opponent. For this reason, it's important to have a good look at some of the differences you can expect when competing in the cutthroat world of network *Myth*.

HOW HUMANS ARE DIFFERENT

There's just nothing quite as satisfying as forcing your human opponent into submission. Playing against another person introduces several new elements into the game:

1. Humans will often follow predictable patterns, using certain strategies from game to game. However, the human factor also means that you can never be sure when your opponent might just do the exact opposite of what you expected. This, in turn, affects the way you play your game.

2. Computers don't have good or bad days. In fact, they have the same day, everyday, no matter what. On the other hand, your best friend may not be as good a *Myth* player as you are but could play the best game of their life on the same day that you play your worst game, resulting in a surprising upset.

3. You can taunt the computer all you like, but this will pretty much lead only to your family and friends performing an intervention that results in a two-hour appointment with a psychiatrist. On the other hand, when you play against a person, mind games can add another wrinkle to the fabric of the *Myth*. Unless you're playing with Spock (and I'm sure some of you are), your human opponents will likely react to any boasts, threats, or offers you throw their way. You can sometimes knock someone off their game by playing with their emotions or taking advantage of their faults.

4. You can't make friends with the computer in *Myth*, but if you're playing a large netgame on the desert map, you can often improve your chances of victory by banding together with your buddies, even if you do so informally. This also means that tenuous alliances may be held, broken, or otherwise abused throughout the course of a large netgame, thereby seriously upsetting one or all of the players. Ganging up on a really good player is a great way to cut them down to size. This kind of give-and-take adds a lot of fun to playing *Myth*.
5. Keeping track of how well you're doing compared to your peers is something that means very little when you're playing a silicon chip. However, having your name on a list of the top ten is very exciting when the people below you are your friends. Computers can't give you respect like people can.
6. The challenge of facing a human brain as opposed to computer AI is much greater. It doesn't matter that Kasparov was defeated by Deep Blue, computers just don't have the ability to think three-dimensionally like humans and therefore cannot provide truly inspired opposition(without cheating). If you've only played against the computer so far, you'll quickly learn that facing other humans is truly where it's at.

PLAYING WITH LARGE NUMBERS OF PEOPLE

Although playing against one human opponent can be a great way to enjoy *Myth*, it's also not much different from playing against the computer. The real fun begins when you get three or more people participating in an all-out slugfest the likes of which you've never seen before. In my estimation, there's a real challenge to playing with large groups of people.To survive (and win), you should probably understand the psychology behind the average group of players.

The group dynamics of a six-player game of *Myth* is really something to behold. Almost without fail the group can be broken down into tidy categories, although not every player fits into the same category in every game. Generally, each player slides comfortably into one of these roles as a game progresses. Sometimes there's no rhyme or reason to why it happens. I will outline each of the roles here. At some point we will all fall into one of these categories, so before you go saying "I'll never do that," just remember you will. This is how it usually breaks down.

The Instigator

These guys can't bear the suspense of a quiet battlefield. They tend to jump right into a fight with all or most of their forces within a minute of the starting gun sounding. They get great pleasure out of hacking away at a nearby enemy as they deal a substantial blow to one of their foes. However, their joy soon turns to sorrow when a third player comes in and wipes the floor with both their forces and the forces they attacked. The Instigator usually ends up dead or running around the map trying to get a win with only two Ghols and a Journeyman. This guy usually learns from this mistake and moves on to another category.

The Chicken

Chickens are the players who are neither fighters nor foxes, instead they're so choked up at the thought of losing any of their units that they hide at the back of the map and run if anyone tries to attack them. The Chickens are usually novice players and shouldn't be confused with the Wimp, who also stays at the back of map but fights when the time is right. The Chickens usually learn that it's no fun *not* fighting and quickly change their ways.

The Wimp

The Wimps are the players who hang back and let everybody else beat the stuffing out of each other, while they sharpen their swords and wait to finish off the wounded troops. Being a Wimp is a great way to win lots of games, but it's also a great way to make everyone hate you. If you wimp out too many times, your opponents will take it upon themselves to kick your butt right back to the chat room. It's okay to be a Wimp once in a while, just don't make a habit of it.

The Hoarder

The Hoarder is, well, just that. These are the players who (when unit trading is available) trade all their high-level units away for as many Thrall and Ghols as they can get. They generally don't use their Archers a whole bunch, but they'll usually have at least four of them at the ready. If your forces are depleted and you only have five or six healthy Warriors on the hill when the Hoarder comes to town, you're toast. The most effective weapon against the Hoarder are Dwarves (and their Satchel Charges).

The Techie

Techies are the opposite of the Hoarders. They trade away all of their low-level units for Warriors and plenty of Archers. These guys are usually experienced players and are confident that they can deal with being outnumbered by a horde of Thrall by using carefully chosen tactics. Techies just about always use their Journeymen to get the Puss Packets from their Wights, and then use their Ghols (with Puss Packets) as first-strike weapons against enemy Archers. If you can take the Techie's Archers out, you're finished.

The Fox

Foxes are very experienced players—the kind that knows *exactly* how far their Archers need to be from the enemy to hit them. They also like to lay Satchel Charges in perfect defensive positions and have their Archers and Dwarves cover their troops so that it's impossible to attack without heavy losses. Foxes are your worst nightmare, but they *can* be had. Look to attack them when they're busy with something (or someone) else.

The Scavenger

Scavengers are the players who trade for lots of Ghols and then send them out scouting. As soon as they see *any* weakness whatsoever, such as three or four unprotected Archers, they'll attack. They essentially use their Ghols to trim the vulnerable parts off of an opponent, without any risk to themselves. It's reminiscent of wolves thinning the herd with surprise attacks. Defeating a Scavenger is extra sweet.

The Homebody

Homebodies are the players who stay at home and fall into a defensive position, especially when they start out on a hill or with a flag. Rather than run away and come back after some of the fighting is over, they dig in and try to hold the position for the whole game. Of course, that's just about impossible if there are more than three players, but the Homebody will still try, game in, game out. Hope springs eternal.

The Bonehead

We are all boneheads the first couple of times we play multiplayer *Myth*. You're even more likely to be a Bonehead if you haven't played much of the single-player version. Boneheads tend to do things that make them lose games very quickly. They have their Dwarves throwing bottles at enemy troops with their own troops nearby. Before they know it, they have blown up their entire army and a few enemies too. Boneheads also tend to lead their army around with their Wight planted firmly in the middle of it. For those who don't know, when the Wight takes three arrows, it creates the largest explosion there is in *Myth*. If a Wight is sitting among your troops and is hit by some enemy Archers from afar—BOOM! Trust me, it's really, really fun to watch—but not if it's your army being blown to bits. Again, most Boneheads learn, so don't despair. Believe me, we've *all* been caught with our Wights, more than once.

BATTLE TACTICS

There are as many opinions and strategies on how to play multiplayer *Myth* as there are people playing it. However, there are a few general tips that will help you stay alive long enough to at least have a chance of winning. Here they are:

1. Generally speaking, you should keep your forces moving on the battlefield as they attack, retreat, flank, and feign. Staying on the move is safer than keeping your units in one location and waiting for the enemy to attack. It can sometimes be difficult to keep track of all your units, so move them together by forming groups with the ALT + number key combinations, and stay alert.

2. Despite their incredible usefulness, explosive units (such as Dwarves with Explosive Bottles and Ghols with Puss Packets) can be as much of a threat to your own forces as they are to the enemy. It's a darn good idea to keep your Wights at a distance from your main forces because a few enemy arrow hits can blow it sky high, along with half your army. Dwarves also need to be maneuvered and managed carefully. They have a tendency to throw their bottles at the enemy, even if your own troops are nearby, so keep a short leash on them.

3. Keep your Archers on the highest ground possible. Archers firing downhill have a distinct advantage over Archers at the bottom of a hill, firing up. It's that darned gravity again!
4. Whenever possible, use fast units like Ghols to attack enemy Archers and Dwarves. This allows your slower units to advance in relative safety. Ghols packing Puss Packets are especially effective for these sorts of attacks.
5. Form a wall of Thrall to protect advancing units. This is a great tactic for safely moving Dwarves forward.
6. Both Thrall and Wights can be hidden under water indefinitely. This can be very handy for surprise attacks or for merely hiding the strength of your forces.
7. Because of their special power, it's best to keep Journeymen near you to heal the wounded. It can be beneficial to place your Journeyman behind a line of Archers to heal them as they take hits. This is a very effective way to win battles dominated by Archers. Also, remember that the Journeymen can instantly kill Undead units like Thrall and Wights using their Mandrake Roots.
8. Try to use your Archers to take out as many important units as possible from a distance. It's always smart to target the enemy's Dwarves with your Archers. If you can take them out before they do any damage to your troops, you'll have a distinct advantage.

UNIT TRADING

The unit trading option can be selected when you start a multiplayer game. When unit trading is active, each player (or Captain you're using teams—see the "Team Play" section later in this chapter) can trade away units in exchange for points. These points can then be used to purchase other units, thus letting you balance your forces as you see fit. It's important to note, however, that trading can only take place *before* you've moved any of your units. If you get anxious and move your Ghols quickly (or for that matter any other unit), then you've lost your chance to trade.

If you want to, get rid of a unit, click on it and press the minus key (-). You'll be awarded a certain number of points based on the unit's strength. The number of points are displayed briefly in a table when you sell your unit (see Table 11.1). To acquire a unit, highlight (click on) the unit you want more of and press the plus key (+). Voilà, your new unit appears. Keep in mind that there are limits to the number of units you can trade, so don't go crazy.

TABLE 11.1: UNIT TRADING VALUES

UNIT	POINTS	UNIT	POINTS
Thrall	1	Spider	1
Warrior	2	Ghol	2
Archer	3	Wight	4
Dwarf	6	Journeyman	6
Trow	20	Berserk	6
Fetch	6	Spider	1
Soulless	3	Myrmidon	2

VETERAN UNITS

During a multiplayer game, units collect experience points for every kill they are responsible for. These kills are represented in the status bar by shields for the living forces, and skulls for the Undead troops. With each additional point (or kill), the unit attacks slightly faster and with greater accuracy and inflicts increased damage on the enemy. Logically then, highly experienced units are the best attackers, and the most important to protect. This is especially true with Archers and Dwarves. When a Dwarf has killed many enemies, it can throw its bottles much more frequently, and with astonishingly greater accuracy. It's worth trying to build up veteran units in multiplayer games.

TEAM PLAY

Team play requires solid coordination between the players on each side. The best game for team play is Capture the Flag on the desert map with six players.

In a team game, one player is chosen as captain of each team. The other team members then select the captain's name in the `Bungie.net` menu of players and click the Join Team button. The players on the same side all share the team color the captain has selected. When the game begins, the captain controls all of the units and is then responsible for dividing them up. To divide them up, they select a group and press the backslash (\) key to detach it. If there's more than one team member, a menu will pop up letting the captain choose to which member the detached units will go.

Ultimate Power

Even after detaching units, the captain still has the power to control all units at all times, which frankly can be very annoying. Make sure you can trust your captain not to take your troops away from you. It is the captain's responsibility to oversee the whole battle, and they have the ability to redirect units if they see them wandering into dangerand to unilaterally change the strategy if there's no time to talk it over with the other team members. Naturally, this can cause some friction, but that's the price of command.

Communication Is King

During a netgame, you can type messages to other players either by Whispering (Y key) to your teammates only or by Yelling (Shift + Y) to all players. After you press the Y key, you then type the message you want to send. Knowing your teammates is important, but not critical. Once in a while, you'll play a few games with someone you've never met before, but you're on the same page (so to speak). Sometimes there's a chemistry between players that allows them to anticipate each other's moves, and they can use this to their advantage and win. It's definitely intangible, and difficult to describe; you can only experience it if you play the team games.

CHALKBOARD

In team games you'll see icons for a pencil and eraser near the Map button. Any team member can use the pencil to mark the map while talking strategy. So instead of simply saying "Send your Archers around the hill and hit the enemy from the rear," you can diagram the movement you're discussing. The eraser clears the map. Clicking the pencil again returns the map to normal. Cool, huh?

THE MULTIPLAYER SCENARIOS

Bungie is famous for the multiplayer scenarios from their highly acclaimed *Marathon* days, but they've really outdone themselves with *Myth*. There's plenty of exciting netgames chock-full of enough variations to make the time fly by and the action seem fresh every time you play the game. The description and goal of each scenario is displayed when you start it up, but it's always handy to have the information in another place, so here it is. I've also included a few tips on how to emerge victorious in every situation.

KING OF THE HILL

King of the Hill begins with a single flag on a hill. The color of the flag matches that of whichever player has a unit within a few feet of it. If more than one player is within that radius, the flag turns gray, and it is considered to be contested. The winner is the one who holds the flag for the longest period of time or who eliminates all of the opposing forces. The game usually lasts 10 minutes (although this can be adjusted), so it's usually hot and heavy from start to finish.

Winning Tips

- If you want to trade units, don't forget to do so *before* you move anything (that is if unit trading is available).
- Move your Ghols quickly to the flag so that you can log some time on it before someone else comes to take it away. Remember, in a 10-minute game with four players, holding the flag for more than 3 minutes is often enough for victory.
- Don't get caught in the melee right away. Save some of your troops for the final battles when everyone else is fairly beat-up.
- Be conservative and don't rush into battle right off the bat. You may end up losing a good portion of your units before you really need to.

CAPTURE THE FLAG

Two or more teams have their own flags in strategic locations. To win you must take possession of all flags. This can be a real bloodbath, especially on the desert map with lots of units throwing themselves at one another.

Winning Tips

- Keep a decent supply of troops at your home base to protect your flag. Don't leave the back door open.
- Depending on the map, try to flank your enemy so that you can attack them from two or three sides at once.
- Hide some of your Undead troops in rivers where they can't be seen, so they can ambush when the time is right. A Wight coming out of the river and taking out a platoon of Archers is a beautiful sight.
- Remember that as you're planning your attack, the enemy could be flanking you.
- Use your resources wisely. In the desert map, it may seem like you have a lot of units, but the enemy does too, so be smart and don't waste them.

STEAL THE BACON

This game revolves around a movable ball, which is the same color as the last player who touched it. The winner is the player who holds the ball at the end of the game's time limit. This game can also go into sudden death, with the players near the ball fighting it out for the victor's crown. Players move their units to dribble the ball back to their side or into hard-to-reach places. The ball can even be shot across the map by explosions. With a unit selected, click on the ball, and they'll dribble it in the direction they're moving.

Winning Tips

- Try to get the ball behind your troops. Protect it with Archers and Dwarves while keeping some Thrall at a distance to slow down advancing enemies.
- Try to stick the ball in the deep part of a body of water, where Living creatures can't get it. Then kill all the enemy's Thrall. Doing so will take away their ability to get at the ball.
- Wait until near the end of the game when everyone else has beaten each other up, and then move your forces in and fight to the death. Remember, you only need one unit left to have control of the ball.

FLAG RALLY

This game is usually more about speed than brawn.There are five flags scattered around the map, and the winner is the first player to get uncontested ownership of all five flags, no matter how briefly.

Winning Tips

- Trade for at least five or six Ghols right away, and then send them after each flag. If you're lucky, you'll reach three or four of the five flags before your enemy.
- Don't divide up your forces too much. Keep an attack force and a defensive force.
- Leave your Archers, a Dwarf, your Journeyman and some Thrall behind at your home flag. These units should be able to protect your flag from enemies, while your attack force captures the flags you need.

CAPTURES

There are a number of balls on the map, and the winner is the one with the most balls at the end of the time limit. This is sort of a hoarding game, where players attempt to stockpile balls behind their troops' lines.

Winning Tips

- Try to grab as many balls as you can right away. Usually, two to four-balls are fairly nearby at the start of the game.
- Use your Ghols to get the balls and bring them back to a central location.
- Another option is to keep the captured balls spread out with relatively small forces guarding them. This may not work, because at least one enemy will attack with a large force, and you'll just end up losing your balls one at a time.

TERRITORIES

There are a number of flags on the map, and the winner is the player who holds the most flags at the end of the time limit. This game can work well with teams, since you'll need to guard flags after they're taken.

Winning Tips

- Trade to bulk up on units that you are the most skilled at using. Ghols are a popular choice in this scenario, and they usually travel in large packs (six or more).
- Be aggressive when capturing the first few flags.
- Don't divide your forces too much.
- Build a strong attack force with units you are skilled at using, and move to capture the majority of flags, plus one. This will give you a safety cushion if one of your flags is taken near the end of the game.
- Keep an eye on the time. Playing too conservatively can leave you with plenty of troops and no time to capture enemy flags near the end of the game.

BALLS ON PARADE

This game is like Capture the Flag, but mobile. Each team has one ball. They must protect it while capturing the enemy ball(s). There is no time limit.

Winning Tips

This eventually comes down to personal preference, but there are a couple strategies that have been known to work in this scenario.

- You can break your forces into two groups, a defensive force (to guard the ball) and a strike force (to go get new balls). The problem with this is that the enemy will often hit your defensive force with everything they've got, thus crushing half your army. If everyone else is following this strategy (or you're playing with newbies), it can work; otherwise, I recommend against it.
- Probably the most solid strategy is to keep most of your troops together and keep your ball with you as you try to take new balls. I often break off a pack of Ghols to search for enemy weak spots or unguarded balls, but other than that an undivided force will suit you the best.

THE MAPS

The choice of map in multiplayer scenarios is very important. It really affects everything from the strategies you use to how you trade your units. It's also important to have a feel for the lay of the land before you enter into battle. Some of the features of these net maps can be used to squeeze a very real advantage out of the game, so be prepared.

I'LL DANCE ON YOUR GRAVE

This is a small map with a central hill. It's used mostly for the classic King of the Hill games. There are five starting locations, and each of five players or teams starts with 22 units.

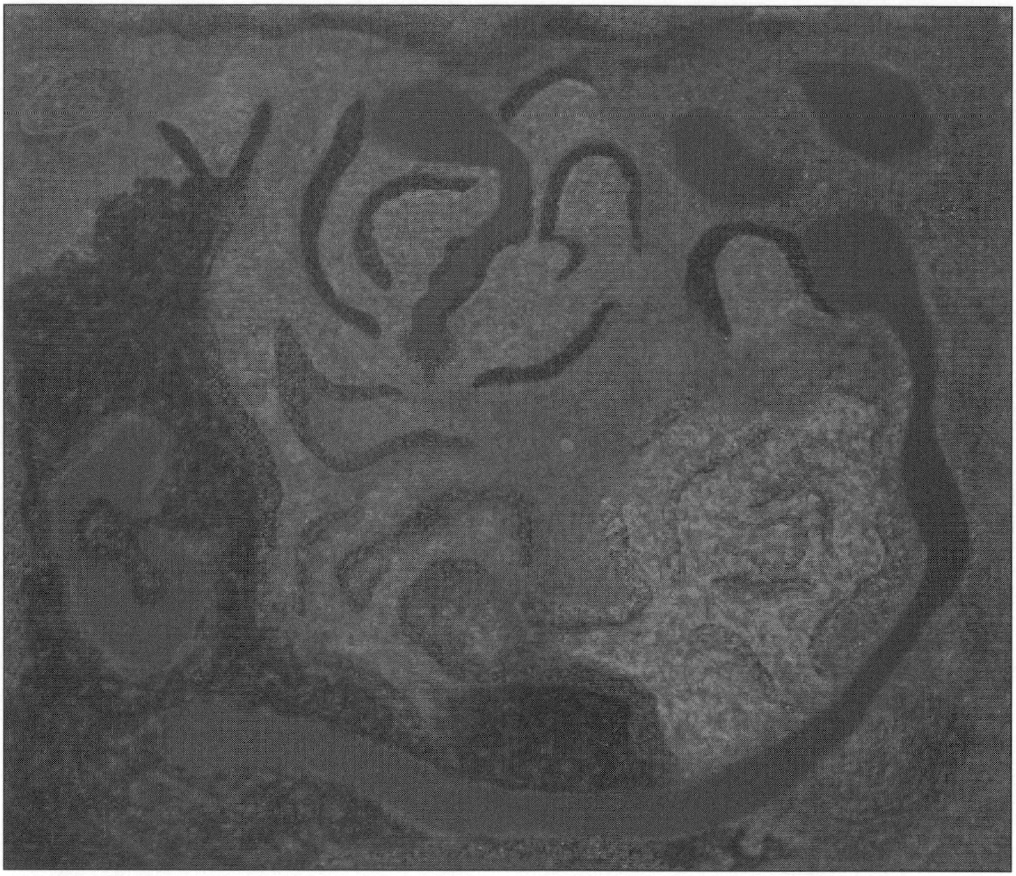

Units Available

- Archer
- Ghol
- Wight
- Journeyman
- Dwarf
- Warrior
- Thrall

THE DESERT BETWEEN YOUR EARS

This is a large map with two hills on either side of a central river and two starting locations. Two players or teams start with 88 units. There are three crossing places—at the top, center, and bottom of the river. Large expanses and rugged topography can hide numerous troops, and the hills are easily defended. This is best played by teams since there are so many units per side.

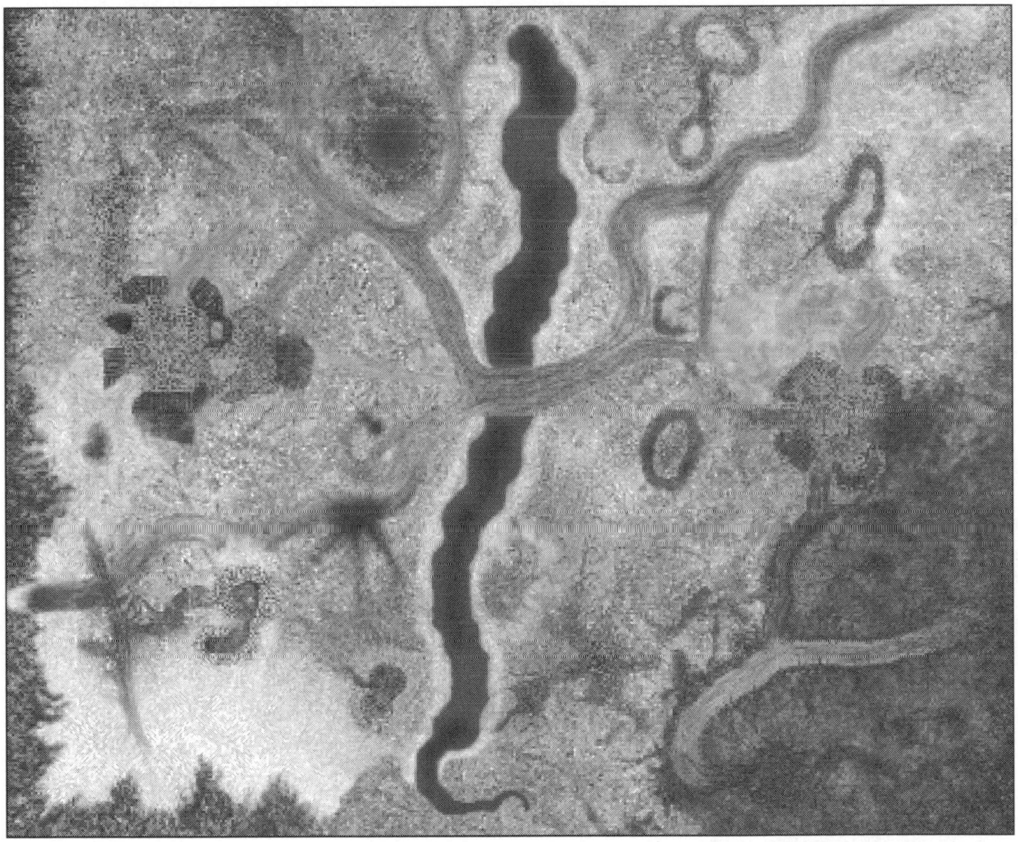

Units Available

- Archer
- Ghol
- Wight
- Journeyman
- Dwarf
- Warrior
- Thrall

MUDPIT MASSACRE

This is a small map with numerous hillocks and a central hill. There are five starting locations, and each of five players or teams starts with 24 units. The rain in Mudpit Massacre can have a major impact on the outcome of the game. Don't count on your Dwarves to save the day—if it's raining, they won't.

Units Available

- Archer
- Ghol
- Wight
- Journeyman
- Dwarf
- Warrior
- Thrall

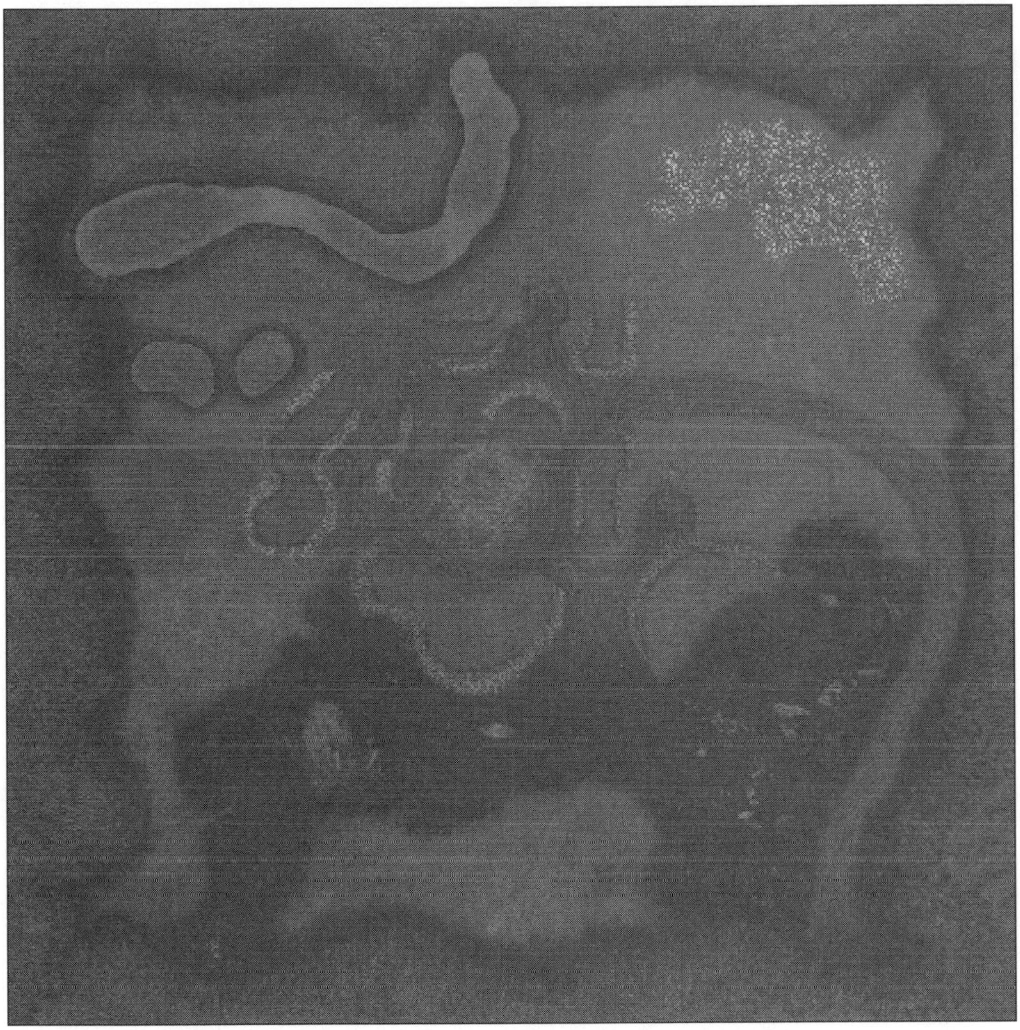

IF I HAD A TROW

This is the Desert Between Your Ears map with some variations in unit configuration. You no longer have Ghols, but instead you've got Trow and Fetches at your disposal!

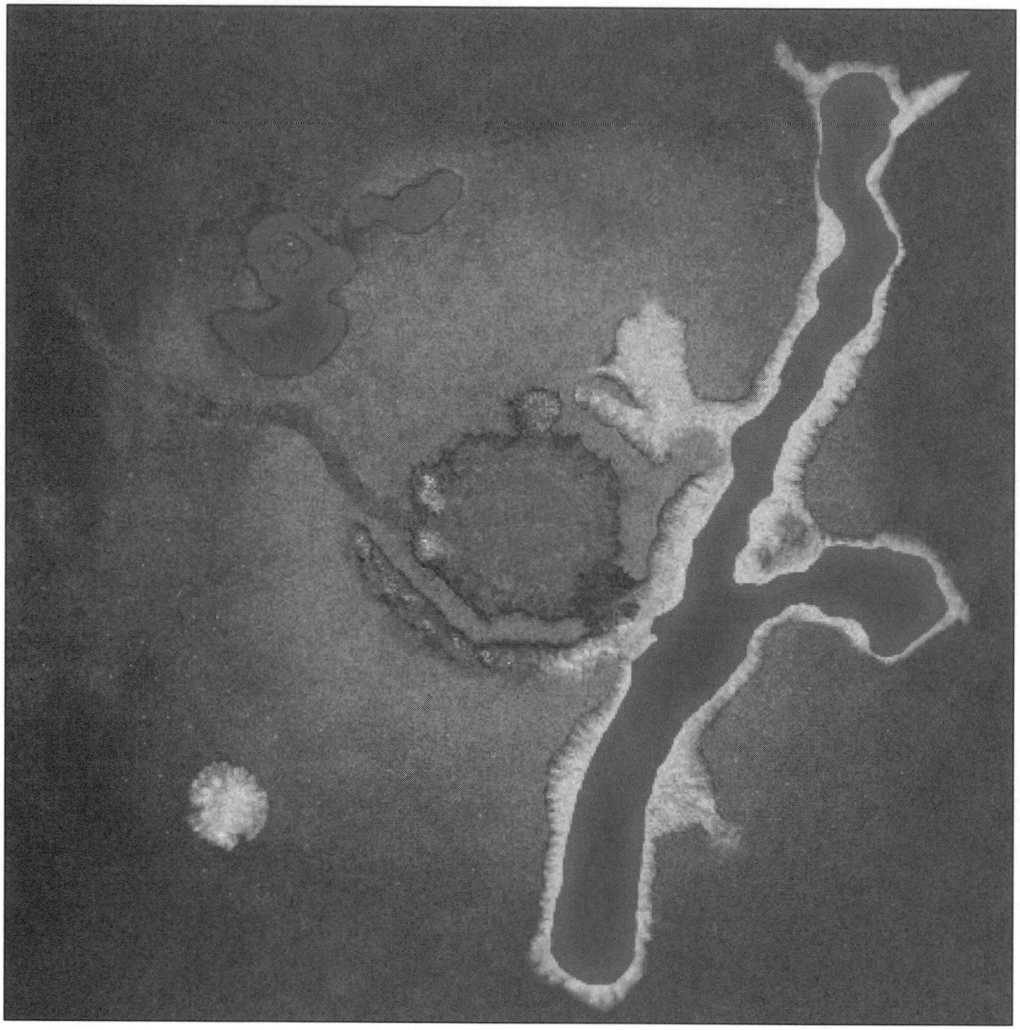

Units Available

-  Fetch
- Trow
- Dwarf
- Soulless

- Myrmidon
- Wight
- Thrall

GROUND ZERO

This map is not unlike Mudpit Massacre. It has the same gloomy overtones, and there is intermittent rain falling throughout the game.

Units Available

- Wight
- Soulless
- Journeyman
- Dwarf
- Thrall
- Berserk

GROUND ZERO (DARK)

This map looks exactly the same as Ground Zero but contains different units.

Units Available

- Warrior
- Berserk
- Fetch
- Trow
- Soulless

I'LL DANCE ON YOUR SPIDERWEB

This is the same map as I'll Dance on Your Grave, but with an alternate set of units. Having different units affects the way a map can be used to your advantage.

Units Available

- Wight
- Berserk
- Soulless
- Spider
- Fetch
- Warrior
- Dwarf

MUDPIT MASSACRE (DARK)

Again, another copy of Mudpit Massacre, but with a different set of units. It makes for an interesting time, especially since you're so used to using Dwarves in the other versions of this map.

Units Available

- Spider
- Trow
- Myrmidon
- Wight
- Thrall
- Fetch
- Soulless

SINGLE-PLAYER MAPS

One of the great things about Myth is that the folks at Bungie decided to let us have access to the single-player maps as well as the special multiplayer maps. There are 25 single-player maps—too many to go into here, but if you are looking for variety, give one of these a try. I should stress, however, that the multiplayer maps were designed with multiplayer strategies in mind, while the single-player maps were designed for the story and single-player action. Therefore, some of these maps might not make a great multiplayer gaming environment, but hey, they're worth a try.

12

THE MAKING OF MYTH

In the last five or six years, computer games have progressively moved from modest developments to huge Hollywood-esque productions with movie stars, sound stages, and million-dollar budgets. Indeed, computer games are no longer created by a couple of teenagers sitting in their parents' basement with a Commodore Amiga and a bag of pork rinds. They are massive endeavors that require teams of professional artists, programmers, and writers. As I was playing *Myth* for the 342nd time (while writing this book), I began to wonder just what went into making *Myth* the incredible game that it is. So I put a call in to the guys at Bungie to try and find out the answers, and guess what they said? "We haven't got time to talk to you, we're too busy making *Myth*. If you want to learn about the game, you're going to have to come here."

Rather than being discouraged by Bungie's busyness, I packed my bags and hopped on the first plane from Calgary to Chicago (well, okay, Calgary to Salt Lake City to Chicago). Upon my arrival, those crazy dudes at Bungie greeted me warmly and gave me a jam-packed, two-day *Myth* cram session. This chapter covers the various areas involved in the creation of *Myth*, including detailed interviews with people intimately involved with *Myth*'s production. So without further ado, here's the inside scoop on the making of *Myth*.

THE GENESIS OF *MYTH*

All games come from some initial idea (usually from the game designer), and in fact many games' genesis stories have become folklore in the gaming community. In *Myth*'s case, the common theory on the genesis of the project is that Jason Jones, the game's designer and lead programmer, was watching the bloody battles in Mel Gibson's *Braveheart* and came up with the idea. However, Jason has a different account. (I still think *Braveheart* influenced the Berserks—just check out those half-painted bodies!)

BART: So, where did the idea of *Myth* come from?

JASON JONES: Well, it's really not all that glamorous. I could probably lie and make up something cool, but I'll tell you the truth instead. We started out doing the natural extension of *Marathon*, which would have turned out to be something along the lines of *Quake*. At that time, the first screenshots of *Quake* were already out, and we sort of knew where they were going, and everybody else did too. We were going to try and do one of those sorts of games, and after about two months of working on it, nobody was really into it at all, and I just had the feeling like we weren't going to be able to pull it off in time.

The whole time we were working on the *Quake*-like game, we had been talking about this other game that nobody thought would work out, and we'd been calling it "The Giant Bloody War Game." We'd sit around talking about the *Quake*-like game, trying to be serious and make some serious decisions about it, and everyone just kept talking about "The Giant Bloody War Game," laughing, having fun, etc. After about two months of that going on, I just showed up at the office one day with the map editor in its most basic form. It could just adjust the heights and stuff and import the color map, and in one day we switched our project from a shooter game that would have had us chasing our competition's tail to what has basically become *Myth*.

GRAPHICS AND ANIMATION

The rolling 3D terrain of *Myth* is nothing short of spectacular, and with a 3DFX graphics accelerator in the mix, it becomes even more incredible. The maps were created by artists using conventional technology, and then they were extruded to give them height and depth. When you look at the detail in the maps, sometimes it's almost as if you're looking at a photograph. The artists were also responsible for the characters in the game. The Undead characters were drawn by Rob Martell, and the Light side's characters were drawn by Mark Bernal. I had a chance to sit down and chat with Mark about the various creative aspects of the game for which he and Rob were responsible.

BART: The characters in *Myth* are sprites and not polygons (which seems to be the way many other games are headed). Obviously you thought that sprites could do the trick for *Myth* (and they did), so what made you make that decision?

MARK: Well, we had done 2D sprites before in *Marathon*, so we already had a sense of what we had to do to make it look good, but the SGI makes it much easier to create 3D-looking sprites.

BART: What did the SGI mean exactly to you as an artist in creating this game?

MARK: It sped up the process of actually creating the views of the characters substantially so that we could get into more interesting things like the lighting

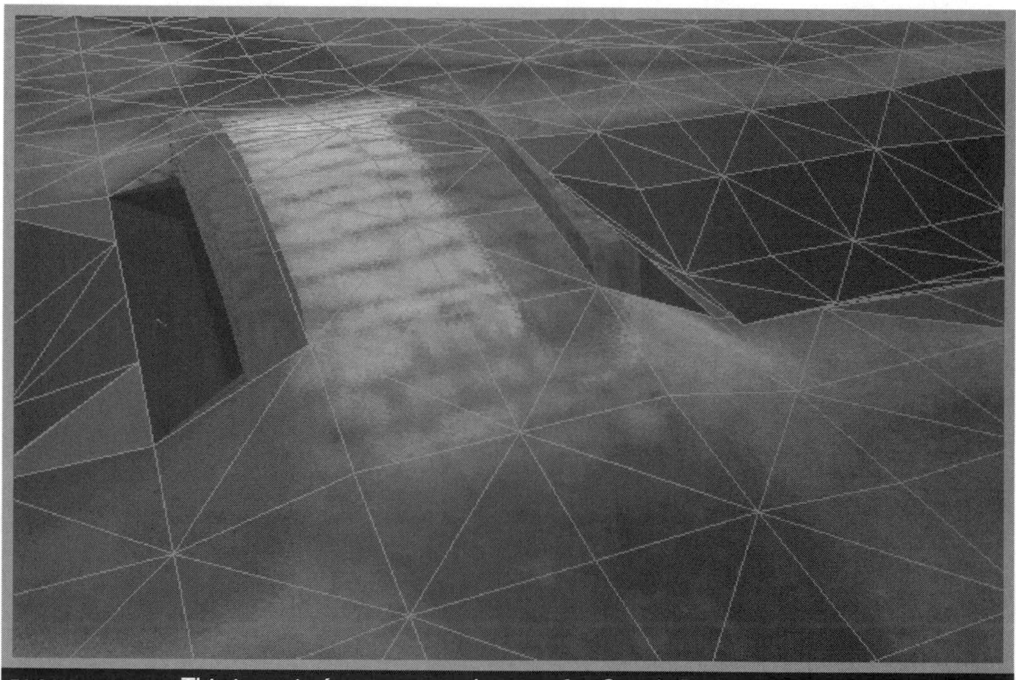

FIGURE 12.1: This is a wireframe set on the map for Crow's Bridge.

effects on the characters and the details. It also made it much quicker to bang out art that we needed quickly, like getting various views of a Satchel Charge or an Exploding Bottle.

BART: You did all the characters on the side of the line; which character(s) are you most proud of?

MARK: Well, I'm surprised by the Dwarf because he was one of the first characters created, but yet he still seems to stand up pretty well [to time] and remains one of the stronger characters in the game [see Figure 12.2].

BART: How did you go about doing the animations for the characters? I've seen the art for the various animations of the Archers, and it's very impressive. Did you get a bow and arrow and start shooting?

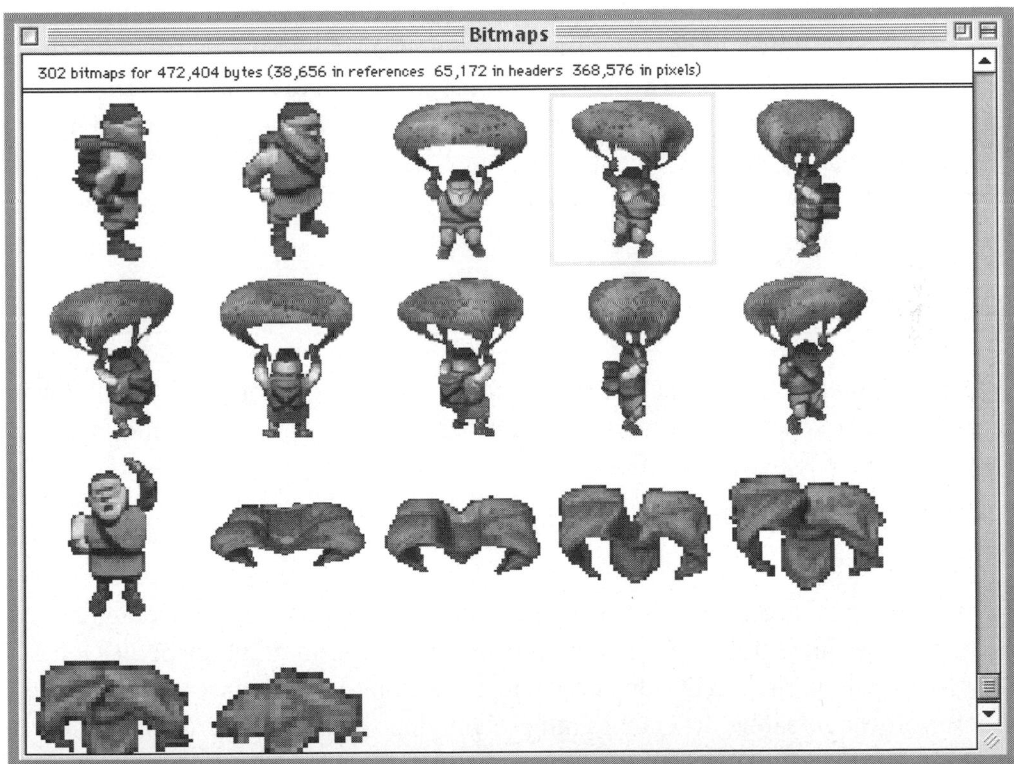

FIGURE 12.2: This is the bitmap art collection for the Dwarf. This particular page contains the art for the parachuting Dwarves.

MARK: Well, it was interesting making the action for the Archer to shoot his arrow. There's a lot of things going on there—like how does he draw the arrow from the quiver, and what's the correct pose for shooting? There are also three angles for shooting to higher elevations. We used reference materials on archery to help get the look just right, but we also used ourselves as examples to ensure that the motions were realistic. This was also true of the other characters, like the Dwarf dropping a Satchel Charge or the Warrior bringing down his sword. It was fun.

BART: The maps are perhaps the most impressive part of the game. They're spectacular to say the least! Tell me about the process of creating a map.

MARK: Once again, the maps had a lot to do with reference. We'd spend time surfing the net, looking at pictures, but we also spent a lot of time looking at things in everyday life. You know, like "Hey, look at that dirt, look at that rock!" Rob would sometimes say something like, "Hey, you guys have got to look at the exit ramp coming to work; it's cool the way you can see the cracks in the cement and the rocks crumbling down." That sort of stuff happened a lot.

Also, *Myth* has the added aspect of seasons, so we had to incorporate snow, rain, deserts, marshes—you name it, we tried to put it in. In the end, I wound up doing over 10 of the maps. By the way, the maps take about 10 days to produce from start to finish, although now I can probably do it faster.

THE PROGRAMMING

What really makes a game like this run is the engine—the guts of the program. I was lucky enough to chat with two of the three programmers—Jason Jones and Jason Regier—about the intricacies of *Myth*.

BART: The physics in *Myth* are really cool. Did any of that evolve from the *Marathon* engine?

JASON JONES: Well, we really liked the way the physics had evolved in *Marathon*. We liked the way grenades arched through the air and how bodies left the ground when hit, and the idea was to just build on that and place it into a game where you were dealing with tactics rather than video game reflexes. That's where it started, but as we went along it got a lot more carried away, like now everyone has their own pieces, and it's a lot more complicated [see Figure 12.3]. I guess that we

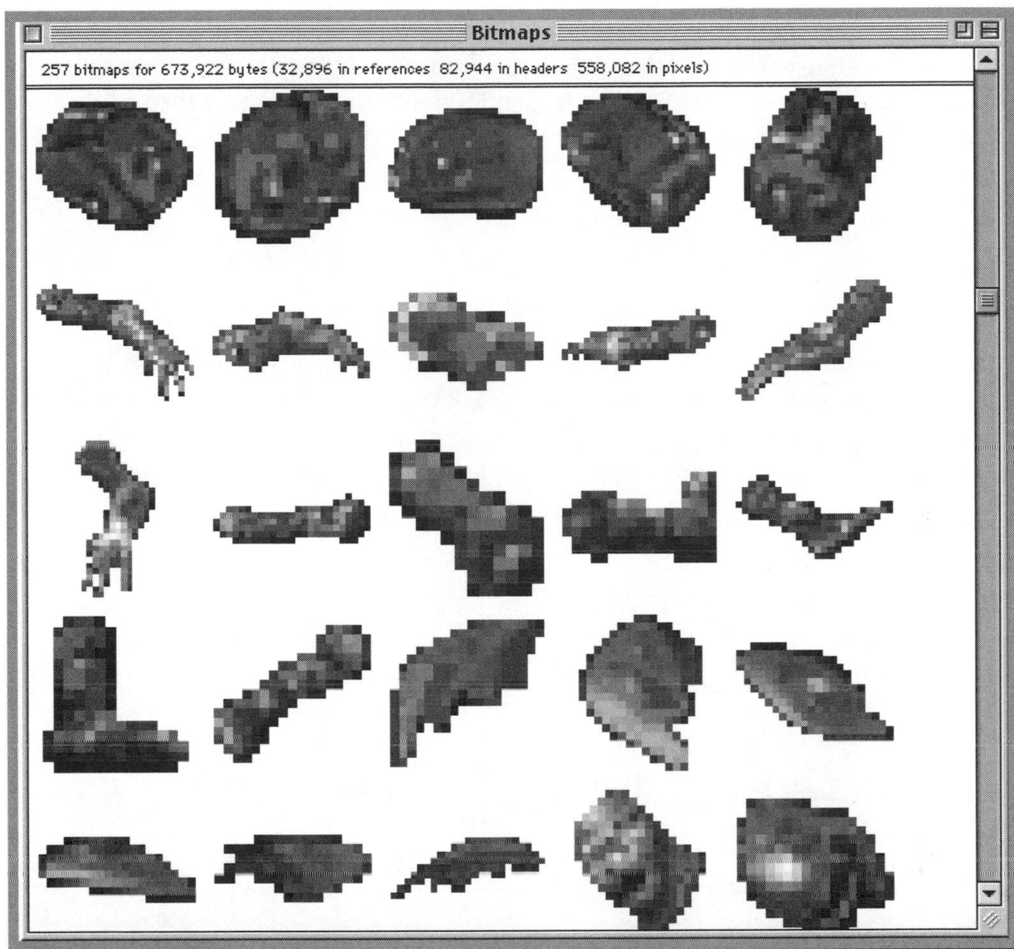

FIGURE 12.3: Each and every character has a complete set of body parts. In this case, these are the pieces you see go flying when a Warrior is blown up.

were trying to take the engine we used in *Marathon* and use it in a game with an entirely different genre.

BART: Everything looks so realistic. Was it a big problem to achieve those effects?

JASON JONES: Yeah, it was. There's a lot of ways to solve a computer equation, and although you know of the "right" way to do it, there's usually another way that may be easier but is just as good. With physics, however, you can't really

do that. For example, if you want to have an Archer hit a target that's at a higher elevation and moving, you have absolutely no alternative but to solve the equation. It's not real, but it's about as real as you get, and if the arrow doesn't fly through the air right, or doesn't bounce off a tree like the gamer is expecting it to, they'll notice. There's just no good way to cheat with the physics, but the end result is very cool.

BART: The tools used for creating *Myth* look very impressive. Did you design those in-house?

JASON REGIER: We have a whole suite of tools for *Myth*, but there are three main tools that we use. One is called the Tag Editor [see Figure 12.4]. *Myth* lies on top of a flexible file system, and every one of those little bits that goes into *Myth* is called a Tag. The Tag Editor lets you edit everything from the physics of the game, to the color of the units, how they move, and how they attack. There's another tool that we use to import graphics called the Extractor, and there's a third tool called

FIGURE 12.4: This is the Tag Editor that enables the Bungie folk to make the units do those things they do. It almost looks like a commercial game editor!

FIGURE 12.5: Bart and Jason Regier are psyched about *Myth*.

Loathing. Loathing is basically the map editor for *Myth*. You import your map into it, you change the heights, and you place your units on the map in Loathing. The fourth tool that complements Loathing is called Fear. Fear takes care of all the models; it is used to import the 3D rendered models into *Myth*.

BART: From my limited experience looking at these tools, they look like they could be included with the game as editors for the public to use. That seems strange to me that a programming tool would look so user-friendly.

JASON REGIER: Well, I helped to write some of the tools. In fact, I wrote the Tag Editor myself, and when I did it, I tried to make it user-friendly for a reason. I can tell you that if a tool is not user-friendly, we (the guys making the scenarios) are not going to spend the same amount of time working on and refining the missions as we do when they are user-friendly.

TAKIN' CARE OF BUSINESS

Alex Seropian is the CEO and cofounder of Bungie Software, and he was nice enough to take some time to discuss the business end of creating an intricate computer game such as *Myth*. In the last five years, several games have been created with budgets of millions of dollars—no kidding! In fact, it was rumored that *Wing Commander IV* was in the 12.5 million-dollar range. Heck, many Hollywood movies don't have budgets that big! So it was with bated breath that I waited to hear how Bungie, with only three programmers and two artists, was able to make one of the most advanced and exciting games ever created for this genre.

BART: I recently interviewed a company that had just made a game that was based on an existing engine, and they used something like nine programmers and six artists over roughly the same length of time it took you to make *Myth*. Bungie is obviously a very small company, so how did you manage to put out such a superior product (from scratch) with only three programmers, two artists, and a partridge in a pear tree?

ALEX: Obviously, we're smarter (laughs). Well, I think we just have a very tight team of very smart and dedicated people working for us here. We think we have cool ideas, and we work very long hours to produce the product you now see. However, I think it's safe to say that we could easily have used more people in the creation of *Myth*, but it's worked out very well nonetheless.

BART: With so much time and money going into one game like *Myth*, the only game you're working on, how important is *Myth* to Bungie?

ALEX: It's huge. This industry is all hit driven, and for a company that's only going to put out one game a year, it's got to be a hit. Otherwise, you can't really make it work for very long. Other companies [the big ones] can support 20 titles a year with a couple of hits and the rest dogs, but that's not the reality for us. As a small developer getting started in the PC market, and with over a million dollars spent to create *Myth*, and a million more to put it out and market it, if the game fails we don't really have another million dollars to do it again. So I think you can see how important it is to get it right the first time.

BART: What's Bungie's motivation?

ALEX: Well, the motivating force behind Bungie isn't actually the do-or-die economic side of it; rather, we're in it purely to make the best game possible.

BART: Where does a million dollars go?

ALEX: A lot of the money goes to the staff; then there's equipment. You know, the SGI alone was over $80,000 (gasp from Bart!). Yeah, and that's just for *one*.

BART: Was it worth getting the SGI?

ALEX: For us, yes. It was exactly the tool we needed, and it worked out well because the artists that used it didn't need it at the same time. And if you look at the graphics in the game that came out of it, we're very happy with the results.

BART: You used animated cutscenes. Were they very expensive? Why did you choose Disney-like animation? Was it cheaper than rendered computer animation?

ALEX: Well, the cutscenes were about $150,000 (for just over three minutes of animation total). And then there's the sound guys; they don't come free either. For the decision on which kind of animation to use, we bid it out and the rendered stuff came back higher.

BART: That's a good thing because I really think the cel animation you have is great, and really adds to the fun of the game. So, what's ahead for Bungie?

ALEX: We've got a new studio out in California, and they're working on an entirely new game engine unlike anything we've ever done before. Otherwise, we don't have our plans set in stone, but we probably want to do a *Myth* scenario pack and a sequel.

QUICK REFERENCE CARD

UNITS	TURNING SPEED	HEALTH	HEALING FRACTION	SPEED	EXPERIENCE VALUE	MP COST
Avatar	200	16.0	0.8	0.016	1	16
Balor	300	30.0	N/A	0.026	2	20
Berserk	200	5.5	0.8	0.02	1	3
Berserk Hero	200	7.5	0.8	0.022	1	6
Dwarf	160	2.188	0.8	0.012	1	6
Dwarf Hero	160	5.0	0.8	0.012	1	5
Dwarf Pathfinder	160	6.0	0.8	0.02	1	5
Fetch	160	2.188	0.8	0.012	1	6
Archer	160	2.188	0.8	0.012	1	3
Archer Hero	160	5.5	0.8	0.011	1	5
Forest Giant	180	30.0	0.8	0.022	2	24
Ghol	200	3.184	0.8	0.019	1	2
Journeyman	200	6.684	0.8	0.013	1	6
Myrmidon	200	5.5	0.8	0.020	1	2
Shade	200	12.0	0.8	0.016	1	16
Soulblighter	300	30.0	N/A	0.040	2	20
Soulless	160	2.395	N/A	0.013	1	3
Spider	180	1.88	0.8	0.020	1	1
Large Spider	180	5.5	0.8	0.020	1	1
Thrall	100	6.5	N/A	0.009	1	1
Trow	180	30.0	0.8	0.022	2	24
Warrior	200	5.5	0.8	0.015	1	2
Wight	100	1.5	N/A	0.009	1	3

LEGEND

- Turning Speed is how fast the unit can turn in degrees per second.
- Health is how much damage your unit can take, in units. It's basically like a hit point system.
- The Healing Fraction is the percentage of a unit's health that can be gained back when healed by a Journeyman. For nearly all the units the value is 80%, although not all units can be healed.
- Speed is just like it sounds: the higher the number, the faster the unit. Even small differences in the numbers can seem like a lot on the field of battle.
- Experience Value is how many experience points you get for killing that unit. Experience adds up and helps your units fire faster, farther, or harder.
- MP Cost is how much a unit will cost you in a multiplayer game.

QUICK REFERENCE CARD

Avatara
Sword Swing Attack—Range: 0.65; Misses: Never; Damage*: 0.699-0.797
Magic Attack—Range: 2-7; Max ammo: 6; Damage: 5-6

Balor
Sword Swing Attack—Range: 0.60; Misses: Never; Damage: 2-2.5
Magic Attack—Range: 0-20; Max ammo: infinite; Damage: 9

Berserk
Sword Swing Attack—Range: 0-0.65; Misses: Never; Damage: 0.547-0.648
Magic Attack—N/A

Berserk Hero
Sword Swing Attack—Range: 0-0.750; Damage: 0.547-0.648
Magic Attack—N/A

Dwarf
Explosive Bottle Attack—Range: 1.5-5.0; Damage: 5-6
Satchel Charge Attack—Range: 0-0; Max ammo: 8; Damage: 5-6

Dwarf Hero
Explosive Bottle Attack—Range: 1.5-5.0; Damage: 5-6
Satchel Charge Attack—Range: 0-0; Max ammo: 8; Damage: 5-6

Dwarf Pathfinder
Explosive Bottle Attack—Range: 2-5.0; Damage: 5-6
Airstrike Attack—Range: 2-5; Max ammo: N/A; Damage: 5-6

Fetch
Lightening Attack—Range: 1.5-5.0; Damage: 3

Archer
Arrow Attack—Range: 1.5-10.0; Damage: 0.5-0.598
Punch Attack—Range: 0-0.45; Max ammo: N/A; Damage: 0.145-0.191

Archer Hero
Arrow Attack—Range: 1.5-10.0; Damage: 0.5-0.598
Punch Attack—Range: 0-0.45; Max ammo: N/A; Damage: 0.145-0.191

Forest Giant
Swat Attack—Range: 0-0.70; Damage: 10-12
Punch Attack—Range: 0-0.70; Max ammo: N/A; Damage: 2.0-2.398

Ghol
Cleaver Attack—Range: 0-0.50; Damage: .5-0.598

Journeyman
Shovel Swing Attack—Range: 0-0.70; Damage: 0.449-0.547

Myrmidon
Blade Slash Attack—Range: 0-0.60; Damage: 0.449-0.547

Shade
Sword Attack—Range: 0-0.650; Damage: 0.699-0.797
Magic Attack—Range: 0-7.0; Damage: 5-6

Soulblighter
Glaive Blow Attack—Range: 0-0.60; Damage: 2-2.5

Soulless
Spear Attack—Range: 1.5-10.0; Damage: 0.5-0.598
Spear Stab Attack—Range: 0.0-0.6; Damage: 0.297-0.395

Spider
Spider Bite Attack—Range: 0-0.60; Damage: 0.594-0.715

Large Spider
Spider Bite Attack (paralyzing)—Range: 0-0.60; Damage: 0.441-0.547

Thrall
Axe Swing Attack—Range: 0-0.60; Damage: 0.699-0.797

Trow
Trow Punch Attack—Range: 0-0.70; Damage: 2.0-2.398
Trow Kick Attack—Range: 0-0.70; Damage: 5-6

Warrior
Sword Swing Attack—Range: 0-0.60; Damage: 20.449-0.547

Wight
Dagger Evisceration Attack—Range: 0-1.0; Damage: 5-6

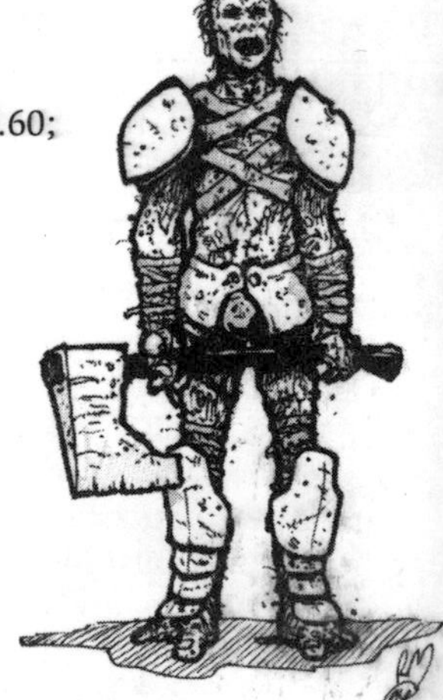

* *The range of damage that each hit is capable of inflicting. The amount of damage you inflict is random.*